Guy Lachapelle, Philippe J. Maarek (Eds.)
Political Parties in the Digital Age

Political Parties in the Digital Age

The Impact of New Technologies in Politics

Edited by
Guy Lachapelle and Philippe J. Maarek

DE GRUYTER
OLDENBOURG

ISBN 978-3-11-040408-1
e-ISBN (PDF) 978-3-11-041381-6
e-ISBN (EPUB) 978-3-11-042373-0

Library of Congress Cataloging-in-Publication Data
A CIP catalog record for this book has been applied for at the Library of Congress.

Bibliographic information published by the Deutsche Nationalbibliothek
The Deutsche Nationalbibliothek lists this publication in the Deutsche Nationalbibliografie;
detailed bibliographic data are available on the Internet at http://dnb.dnb.de.

© 2015 Walter de Gruyter GmbH, Berlin/Boston
Cover illustration: Fakhri-sa/Thinkstock
Printing and binding: CPI books GmbH, Leck
♾ Printed on acid-free paper
Printed in Germany

www.degruyter.com

Table of Contents

Guy Lachapelle and Philippe J. Maarek[1]

New Technologies: Helping Political Parties and the Democratic Processes or Threatening Them?

The evolution of political communication has always been inextricably linked to the evolution of the media, and thereby to the evolution of political systems as a whole. We cannot imagine the rise of the first monarchies without referring to the advent of printed literature, which provided early rulers with a medium for their laws. We cannot imagine the rise of Western Europe without referring to the invention of the printing press. We cannot imagine the emergence of 20th-century totalitarian ideologies without referring to the coming of radio and other instruments of what was then called "propaganda."

The advent of television seemed to mark a milestone in the evolution of political systems by allowing some politicians to bypass, for the first time, the traditional hierarchical pyramid of political parties and make their way into the public arena without party support. Although Eisenhower had certainly been helped by the first political TV spots in 1952, he still owed his presidency just as much to the Republican Party, which had sought him out and accompanied him all the way to the White House. Yet, little by little, in most democracies, male and female politicians were increasingly using their audiovisual charisma to gain pre-eminence independently of party machines. They succeeded with the complicity of TV journalists, who were only too happy to boost their viewership by helping out these "good media customers" rather than party leaders who often looked drab by comparison. In 1960, John F. Kennedy thus became the surprise winner of the Democratic Primaries to the astonishment of his party's higher-ups. Later, he edged out Richard Nixon, undoubtedly through his great performance during the first televised debate between the two men, thus showing once again how things were changing.

This evolution has also been increased by the emergence of political marketing almost everywhere from the 1960s onward, to the point of becoming omnipresent today. Marketing professionals very soon saw how they could capitalize on TV's increased personalization of political communication and thus better reach out to the undecided and abstainers – the "swing voters" who often decide who wins or loses elections. The argument was simple. Since these voters were politically unmotivated and uninterested in politics, they would have to be convinced through expo-

---

1   *Guy Lachapelle*, Professor, Department of Political Science, Concordia University; Secretary General of the International Political Science Association (IPSA/AISP); *Philippe J. Maarek*, Professor, Université Paris Est – UPEC; Director of the Center for Comparative Studies in Political and Public Communication (CECCOPOP).

sure to the candidates' personal qualities – or their opponents' personal liabilities – even to the point for example of asking them to attend to entertainment shows, since these media venues are often the most popular among individuals not interested by politics. This is how Arnold Schwarzenegger managed to become California's governor after running against a political veteran and without hardly ever fielding questions from campaign reporters. He also announced his candidacy on a talk show – a tactic later adopted by a politician as traditional as John McCain. In sum, by speaking directly to voters via television, through the special access gained by their personal charisma, and without bothering with political parties, the main leaders have often bypassed the old structures of party activism which have appeared more and more obsolete. As a result, activism declined considerably in the late 20th century. Activists felt unnecessary and were often disappointed that political communication, which marketing had so "professionalized," had become depoliticized through extreme personalization.

The advent of the Internet and the related emergence of "social" media could have initially been understood as another way for politicians to do without political parties. Howard Dean in 2003–2004 or Ségolène Royal in 2007 have for instance been able to emerge by astutely and innovatively using new, interactive electronic media, the so-called "Web 2.0." The influence of the new media, however, cannot be so unequivocally reduced to politicians having one more tool in their hands. At the same time, thanks to the Web 2.0 simple citizens have now been able to upload videos right away from their smart phones to "YouTube" or "Dailymotion" or they can "tweet" their feelings and get an immediate echo from all kinds of people. These new possibilities for communication seem to have rekindled a spirit of individual activism that political parties can once more try to channel. In addition, electronic media like the Internet are accentuating the trend toward "glocalization" of the public and political sphere that had earlier begun with the advent of television, while pushing this trend into new areas. In a world where each of us is directly linked to the whole world through media globalization, our relations with intermediate structures, including States, are increasingly tenuous, as Habermas pointed out in "The Postnational Constellation." On the other hand, across normal interaction, each of us still enjoys relations of communication with the "local" sphere, i.e., other individuals with whom we have close relationships, whether centred on our workplace, our business, our friends, or our family. The Internet has completed this glocalization by enabling any individual to become in turn a source of both vertical and horizontal communication, thus breaking the monopoly that politicians had back in the television age – which has turned out to have been just a temporary phase.

As a result, political parties are again becoming indispensable to the recreation of social and political relationships. They are the only ones present on both sides of the new political and public sphere. They remain in the centre, through their means of communication, and their ability to master the new ways of digitalization and computerized information (so called "Big Data"). They are present on the periphery, through their networks of locally based activists. This explains the success of the grassroots campaigns that so greatly helped Barack Obama's two election victories. It also explains François Hollande's 2012 victory in France, after tirelessly canvassing the country and going from one schoolyard to another. Meanwhile, Nicolas Sarkozy seemed stuck in the Élysée presidential palace and much farther removed from the grassroots.

So have we come full circle? Has the digitization of modern political communication paradoxically brought back to the forefront those who are still the best instruments of traditional political communication – political parties? This is the question that the contributors to this volume will be asking.

To start off, *Kenneth Janda* will retrace the history of the introduction of electronic means of political communication to the United States, from the first punched card calculators to today's digital social networks. He astutely points out that back in 1960 John F. Kennedy's victorious presidential campaign was preceded and structured by an effort to simulate the upcoming vote electronically. He clearly shows that beginning in 2004, with Howard Dean's presidential campaign, the Internet gained the upper hand, greatly changing the political parties both in themselves and in their relations with public opinion – the electorate. On the other side of the Atlantic, integration of technological innovations into the practices of German parties and citizens is described by *Reimar Zeh and Christina Holtz-Bacha*, who show how much the Internet became key to the 2013 legislative election campaign while not really undermining the "traditional" media's importance in that election. They provide new insights by also arguing that social media use seems to have encouraged voting for "independent" parties rather than for the ones that have traditionally held power in that country for the past half-century.

The new technologies are having major impacts on activism, as exposed especially by *Eric Montigny and Isabelle Gusse* in their respective chapters. For *Eric Montigny*, both in Québec and in the rest of Canada, the new technologies may very likely deviate from their original purpose because of their impersonal mode of communication, which excludes direct, face-to-face contact with voters. He also points to the frequently almost tautological nature of political communication via social media like Twitter, where an ultimately rather small group of citizens leads to one talking to another via a closed circuit. The arguments of one or another thus circulate in a loop and feed only into the personal convictions of a few people. In this, he sees an ongoing decline of political activism, with the remaining generations of old-style activists steadily dying off. The evolution of partisan commitment, in Québec's case, is studied within a related line of thought by Isabelle Gusse, who recalls that the earlier modes of family-based or local political socialization have become largely obsolete, and that would-be activists are now being asked to become experts in understanding and knowing how to use digital tools for political communication before they can start working. For her, both trends undoubtedly explain why activists have demobilized and lost interest, the digital age having widened the tacit distance between the decision-making bodies of political parties and the "field." Again, a gap is emerging between the major parties and the others, the latter seeming to benefit more from modern digital communication – with the "youth" factor also mattering a great deal in this differentiation.

Social media, and their relative importance, are of particular interest to *Ashley Murchison*, on the one hand, and to *Karine Prémont and Charles-Antoine Millette*, on the other. Using the case of New Zealand, Ashley Murchison explains that while implementing the most modern means of "2.0" digital political communication, the country's political parties ultimately misuse them by operating them rather as an instrument for "traditional" top-down communication from the party to the voters. The parties either do not know how or do not want to take advantage of other ways of using them for communication and are doing little to exploit the interactivity that social media make possible. For instance, Green Party activists do not allow public comments on their Web pages. On the other hand, despite much greater use of the potentialities of social media in the United States, *Karine Prémont and Charles-Antoine Millette* argue that the main failing of that country's political communication – "attack ads" or negative campaigning, which have already long been amplified by television – has worsened with the advent of social media because of their characteristic lack of regulation. There has thus been a rise in personal attacks – which are so hard to refute and even harder to erase from the Net – and in the anecdotization of campaigns. Social networks amplify the slightest gaffe or slipup, thus creating an avalanche of phoney news items that are often unreliable, politically insignificant, and not without influence on the public. Karine Prémont and Charles-Antoine Millette therefore see the insertion of social media in political communication as providing only illusory participation. For them, the flow of communication created by social media often results in a bundle of anecdotal news items that harms candidate communication and candidate image more than it helps political processes – hence the worry over the growing expansion of digital communication around the world. In Great Britain, however, David Deacon and Dominic Wring stress the important role of "traditional" print media in the rise of nationalist political currents and in particular of the UKIP. This resilience of the press in that country is noteworthy.

The advent of digital communication has affected and helped change political "leadership" phenomena that are discussed successively by *Guy Lachapelle and Philippe J. Maarek*. Guy Lachapelle uses the example of the Parti Québécois to show that the much-talked-about arrival of digital political communication in the United States during the 2004 presidential campaign greatly affected that country. Nonetheless, the introduction of the Internet still looks like a half-baked intrusion that does more to fog up than clear up political communication. Digital political communication still seems to be poorly controlled by political parties and their leaders. Finally, Philippe J. Maarek shows that in France the intrusion of electronic media has undeniably made political communication more personalized. This personalization has been further accentuated by the 2000 amendment of the French Constitution. By shortening the French President's term of office to 5 years and by making the legislative elections follow his own, this reform has greatly strengthened the President's pre-eminence over legislators who, in a sense, "owe" him their electoral success. Although electronic media have thus aided this personalization, easy access to such media has also exposed politicians to a higher level of risk, beginning with the leaders... and the President himself, as Nicolas Sarkozy and then François Hollande have learned at their expense.

It thus clearly appears to the great majority of contributors to this volume that the impact of new digital technologies on political parties and processes has been and remains undeniable. Certainly, political parties that have wanted it have known how to use them. They have even been able sometimes to capitalize on digital communication, thereby often reversing the previous trend toward a decline of political activism. But this integration into political communication seems to be incompletely mastered by political parties and even a source of danger. As we enter the digital age, more and more individuals can speak up and make themselves heard, and this is often seen as a danger by the parties, which often prudently prefer to limit use of new technologies to the one top-down direction to which they have grown accustomed – sometimes justifiably so. Indeed, the new media, in particular social media, and more so than television, are helping politicians to emerge outside traditional political channels, are tending to strengthen personalization and also, through a boomerang effect, are trivializing political communication and endangering politicians by placing them under a sword of Damocles: immediate repercussions may follow their least slipup or poor choice of words, instantly caught by the increasingly watchful eye of any one's smartphone connected to the Internet. Modern political marketing and political parties do not seem to have completely mastered digital political communication – to the extent that such a thing is fully possible. Digital political communication seems to be making a rather ambiguous contribution that is very promising and yet very threatening to political parties and also to democratic processes.

The editors take this opportunity to gratefully acknowledge the assistance of Claude Berlinguette in bringing about this book, notably by doing all the copy editing of the manuscript.

Part I: The Integration of Technological Innovations in the Practices of Parties and Citizens

Kenneth Janda[1]

Innovations in Information Technology in American Party Politics Since 1960[2]

By definition, the English word, "innovation," means change – a new way of doing something. It also connotes improvement – that the change is beneficial. The term "technology" by itself connotes "improvement to something already existing."[3] Hence, the English phrase, "innovations in information technology in party politics," implies that the changes result in progress. Progress is customarily defined as a positive advance toward some higher goal or standard. Deciding whether technological innovations in party politics results in progress, however, depends on the values of the observer.

Most political observers in the United States have concluded that innovations in information technology constitute progress, almost unqualified progress, toward democracy and good government. Consider computer communications over the Internet. Political scientist Matthew Hindman's 2009 book, *The Myth of Digital Democracy,* reviewed the prevailing optimistic arguments:[4]

> Those arguing that the Internet is transforming politics come from the upper echelons of politics, journalism, public policy, and law. [The 2004 Democratic presidential hopeful] Howard Dean campaign manager Joe Trippi effuses that "the Internet is the most democratizing innovation we've ever seen, more so even than the printing press."[5] The Internet's increasing importance may be the only thing that Trippi and [President George W.] Bush-Cheney campaign manager Ken Mehlman agree on. The key lesson of the 2004 campaign, according to Mehlman, is that "technology has broken the monopoly of three [television] networks, "and instead of having one place where everyone gets information, there are thousands of places."[6]

Hindman cited similar comments over two more pages before concluding, "It may be comforting to believe that the Internet is making U.S. politics more democratic. In

---

1 Professor, Department of Political Science, Northwestern University, United States.

2 A nearly identical paper in Russian was prepared for the conference, "Political Engineering in the Area of Social Communication," Russian State University for the Humanities (RSUH), Moscow, October 31–November 1, 2013.

3 See the definition at http://encyclopedia2.thefreedictionary.com/Technological+innovation and also at http://en.wikipedia.org/wiki/Technology.

4 Matthew Hindman, The Myth of Digital Democracy (Princeton, NJ: Princeton University, Press, 2009), p. 2.

5 Joe Trippi, The Revolution Will Not Be Televised: Democracy, the Internet, and the Overthrow of Everything. (New York: Regan Books, 2005), p. 235.

6 Quoted in R. Crowe, "Bush, Kerry Aides Reflect on '04 Campaign," *Houston Chronicle* (January 27, 2005), p. A11.

a few important ways, though, beliefs that the Internet is democratizing politics are simply wrong."[7]

Writing in 1997, over a decade before Hindman's book, physicist-turned-political scientist Gene Rochlin voiced similar concerns in *Trapped in the Net: Unanticipated Consequences of Computerization.*[8] According to Rochlin, "The enduring myth is that extensive computerization and networking will distribute power as well as information and technical capacity more evenly through industry, offices, bureaus, and the society at large."[9] More generally, Rochlin reminds us that unanticipated and undesirable consequences lurk among the promises of technological innovations.

In contrast to Hindman's concern with the Internet's impact on democracy and Rochlin's with computerization's effects on society, my essay is decidedly limited. It chronicles the evolution of technological innovations in party politics in the United States. What were the noteworthy innovations in how information is collected, analyzed, and utilized? How have the American political parties, founded more than 150 years ago, adapted to these innovations since the use of mainframe computers in the 1960 campaign for president? While not an exhaustive report on the evolution of technology in American party politics since, this paper – in its trip through time – provides a fairly comprehensive survey of developments over the last half-century.

Technological innovations alter relationships among individuals and groups in all societies. The development of automobiles took jobs away from blacksmiths and carriage makers. Television ended what was called the "golden age" of radio in the United States. U.S. newspaper sales fell with the rise of the Internet. Thus too, technological innovations in politics have altered the relationships between party organizations and candidates. Initially, American national party organizations gained power because they could afford expensive computer facilities while candidates could not. As the cost and complexity of computing lessened, however, candidates surged past party organizations in applying the technology to their election campaigns. In recent years, as politicos realized the importance of high-quality political data and the difficulty in obtaining such data, central party organizations recovered some of their power. At least our national party organizations have become more important concerning presidential campaigns in general elections. Concerning primary election campaigns – which are largely peculiar to the United States, aspiring candidates still campaign independently of party organizations.

The essay concludes by judging in broad terms the effects on party politics of innovations in information technology. Note its focus on party politics rather than

---

7 *Ibid*, p. 3.
8 Gene I Rochlin, *Trapped in the Net: Unanticipated Consequences of Computerization* (Princeton, NJ: Princeton University Press, 1997).
9 *Ibid.*, p. xiii.

on election campaigns. As the historical review will demonstrate, most innovations originated not within the parties but outside of them. They came from candidates operating independently of the party organization. At least in the American political system, new techniques for collecting and processing information have served to underscore – if not to accentuate – the long-standing decentralization of power in American party organizations. But new demands for more comprehensive and more accurate data on voters have produced centralizing tendencies.

In places, this survey draws heavily from my other writings on computer technology and from personal experiences dealing with both parties.[10] I footnote text extracted from sources for which I own the copyright. I do not set that text off as quoted material, but I do show quotation marks when the material comes from copyrighted sources held by others. Although focusing on information technology in American party politics, this survey begins by describing how today's information technology first appeared in American government. The technology appeared much earlier than many people think.

1 Data Processing Before the Dawn of Computers

In the late 19th century, long before electronic computers came along, information technology exploited electro-mechanical manipulation of holes punched in paper forms called punchcards. In 1885 the U.S. Census Bureau was still compiling data collected in the Census of 1880. "It was obvious," writes Herbert Hyman, "that if the country's rate of growth continued, the time would not be far off before a new census would have to be undertaken before the previous one had been published."[11] The punchcard was invented by Dr. Herman Hollerith of the U.S. Census Bureau to cope with anticipated problems of compiling information on large numbers of cases for the 1890 census.[12]

In Hollerith's invention, metal brushes made electronic contact with metal rollers through holes punched into paper cards. As the cards – which acted as insulators – passed between the brushes and the rollers, electronic impulses tripped electro-magnetic counters, converting holes into numbers depending on the timing of

---

10 The primary sources are Kenneth Janda, *Data Processing: Applications to Political Research*, 2nd *ed.* (Evanston, IL: Northwestern University Press, 1969; Kenneth Janda, *Information Retrieval: Applications to Political Science* (Indianapolis: Bobb-Merrill Company, 1968); Kenneth Janda, Jeffrey Berry, and Jerry Goldman, *The Challenge of Democracy*, 1st *through* 9th *editions* (Boston: Houghton Mifflin, 1987–2008); and Kenneth Janda, Jeffrey Berry, and Jerry Goldman, *The Challenge of Democracy*, 10th *through* 12th *editions* (Boston: Wadsworth, 2009–2014).
11 Herbert Hyman, *Survey Design and Analysis* (Glencoe, Ill.: The Free Press, 1955), p. 19.
12 Janda, 1969, p. 8.

the impulses when contact was made.[13] The cards could also be sorted into piles according to specific holes punched in specific locations. Hollerith built the card readers for the 1890 U.S. Census, and in 1896 founded the Tabulating Machine Company. It merged with others in 1911 to form the Computing Tabulating Recording Company (CRT) – whose name changed in 1924 to the International Business Machines Corporation, inspired by the name of CRT's Canadian operation.[14]

In addition to the company that became IBM, various firms (e.g., Remington Rand) developed equipment to count and sort punchcards. As these devices appeared at American colleges and universities in the 1930s, students of politics employed the technology.[15] As early as 1931, Charles Samenow began recording information on punchcards in a study that eventually involved more than 35,000 court cases.[16] Not long afterwards, Charles Hyneman published his classic comparative studies of 7,500 legislators serving in thirteen states during all legislative sessions from 1922 to 1935.[17] In the late 1930s, IBM introduced a sorting machine that, with some modifications, was widely used over the next five decades to the end of the punchcard era.[18] So scholars employed mechanical forms of information technology prior to the advent of computers.

More importantly for the history of technology in party politics, counting-sorters were the mainstay of the new industry of public opinion research. In the 1930s, George Gallup, Elmo Roper, and other polling pioneers began taking national surveys of public opinion using sample surveys involving a thousand respondents. Interview responses were coded into numbers, recorded on punchcards, and tabulated by running the cards through a counting-sorter. Polling companies often stored their punchcards to keep as historical records and to re-analyze them if needed. In 1947, Elmo Roper founded the Roper Center for Public Opinion Research to

13 For further explanation, see Janda, 1969, pp. 15–19.
14 This is the account in http://en.wikipedia.org/wiki/History_of_IBM#1880s.E2.80.931924:_The_origin_of_IBM.
15 Curiously, the literature of the 1930's reveals more on data processing methodology than the contemporary literature. For example, see Mona Fletcher, "The Use of Mechanical Equipment in Legislative Research," *The Annals of the American Academy of Political and Social Science,* 195 (January, 1938), 1–8; and "Bicameralism as Illustrated by the Ninetieth General Assembly of Ohio: A Technique for Studying the Legislative Process," *American Political Science Review,* 32 (February, 1938), 80–85. See also, Charles S. Hyneman, "Tenure and Turnover of Legislative Personnel," *American Academy of Political and Social Science Annals,* 195 (January, 1938), 21–31. A variety of punchcard applications to social science research in general is reviewed in G.\V. Baehne (ed.), *Practical Applications of the Punched Card Method in Colleges and Universities* (New York: Columbia, 1935).
16 Charles U. Samenow, "Judicial Statistics in General," in Baehne, *op. cit.,* pp. 319–26.
17 Charles S. Hyneman, *lococit.* and "Who Makes Our Laws?" in John C. Wahlke and Heinz Eulau (eds.), *Legislative Behavior* (Glencoe, Ill.: The Free Press, 1959), pp. 254–65. Reprinted from *Political Science Quarterly,* 55 (1940), 556–81.
18 For explanation of how a counting-sorter worked, see Janda, 1969, pp. 53–57.

collect, archive, and redistribute punchcard collections of opinion survey data from various survey organizations.[19] Polls stored at the Roper Center were used in the first major use of computing technology in political campaigns.

Early versions of computers were built in Britain in 1948 at the University of Manchester and the next year at Cambridge University.[20] Soviet scientists also built the BESM (БЭСМ) series in the early 1950s.[21] In the United States, the first commercial computer, UNIVAC I, was marketed in 1951. The next year, IBM built its first commercial "high-speed" computer, the 701. The University of Illinois appears to have been the first university in the United States to make a computer (ILLIAC I) available for general research purposes.[22] The IBM 650 – said to be the first mass-produced computer – was marketed in 1953 and soon appeared on university campuses. Indiana University had its 650 (about the size of an SUV) in the basement of the astronomy building when I began graduate study in 1957 as a research assistant to Charles Hyneman, who told me to learn how to use it. The 650 generated punchcard output from punchcard input, had very limited memory (2k), and had few programs suitable for political research, but it was a thrill to turn it on, sit at the controls, and operate it alone in the basement.

2 The 1960s: The First Light of Dawn

The U.S. Democratic Party was the beneficiary of an ambitious, pioneering application of computer technology to electioneering in the 1960 presidential election. Technologically out-flanked in that election, the Republican Party recovered and surged ahead of the Democrats for the 1964 election.

Democratic Party

Although it may not have been the first application of computer technology to party politics, the attempt to simulate the outcome of the 1960 presidential election was the most fascinating. The story of the Simulmatics Project is told in *Candidates, Issues, and Strategies: A Computer Simulation of the 1960 Presidential Election*, by Ithiel de Sola Pool, Robert P. Abelson, and Samuel L. Popkin, its creators.[23] Their

---

19 For history of the Roper Center, see http://www.ropercenter.uconn.edu/center/roper_history.html.
20 For a brief review of computer history, see http://en.wikipedia.org/wiki/Computer.
21 The abbreviation stands for "Bolshaya Elektronno-Schyotnaya Mashina" ("Большая Электронно-Счётная Машина"), literally "Large Electronic Computing Machine." Soviet computing equipment is reviewed at http://en.wikipedia.org/wiki/History_of_computer_hardware_in_Soviet_Bloc_countries.
22 Janda, 1969, p. 95.
23 Ithiel de Sola Pool, Robert P. Abelson, and Samuel L. Popkin, *Candidates, Issues, and Strategies: A Computer Simulation of the 1960 Presidential Election*, (Cambridge, MA: The M.I.T. Press, 1964).

idea to simulate the 1960 election was hatched in early 1959 and proposed in May to leaders of the Democratic Party, including Paul Butler, Chairman of the National Committee.[24] It envisioned analyzing 50 polls prior to the 1952, 1954, 1956, and 1958 elections on 100,000 respondents that were stored on punchcards in the Roper Public Opinion Research Center.[25] (Another 15 polls prior to the 1960 election representing 30,000 citizens were added later.) A group at the Democratic National Committee (DNC) agreed to support the effort, pending further review.

The principals organized themselves as The Simulmatics Corporation and began to prepare the data for analysis. As described by Pool, Abelson, and Popkin:

> In essence, the data available to us were reduced to a 480 × 52 matrix. The number 480 represented types of voters, each one being defined by socioeconomic characteristics. One voter-type might by "Eastern, Metropolitan, loser-income, white, Catholic, female Democrats." Another might be "Southern, rural, upper-income, white Protestant, male Independents." Certain types with small numbers of respondents were reconsolidated, yielding the total of 480 types actually used.
>
> The number 52 represented what we called in our private jargon "issue-clusters." Most of these were political issues, such as foreign aid, attitudes toward the United Nations, and McCarthyism [...].
>
> One can picture the 480 × 52 matrix as containing four numbers in each cell. The first number stated the total number of persons within a voter-type who had been interrogated on that particular item of information. The other three numbers trichotomized those respondents into the percentages pro, anti, and undecided or confused on the issue.[26]

The 480 voter types inspired the political scientist and successful novelist, Eugene Burdick, to write a fictional book, *The 480,* about a computer simulation of the 1964 campaign.[27] In his Preface, Burdick acknowledged having access to reports from the Simulmatics Corporation but said that his novel "is entirely a projection by the author."[28]

From the beginning, The Simulmatics Corporation decided not to try to predict the outcome of the 1960 election – described as "the number one question at the Democratic National Committee." Its goal instead was to estimate "the relative gain or loss to be obtained from adopting one strategic alternative or another."[29] In June

24 *Ibid.,* pp. 15–16.
25 At that time, the Roper Center's archive of punchcard poll data was located at Williams College in Williamstown, Massachusetts. The Roper Center has since moved to the University of Connecticut at Storrs.
26 *Ibid.,* pp. 24–25.
27 Eugene Burdick, *The 480* (New York: McGraw-Hill, 1964). Burdick also authored *The Ugly American* (1958) and *Fail-Safe* (1962).
28 Burdick, *The 480,* p. x.
29 Pool, Abelson, and Popkin, *Candidates, Issues, and Strategies* p. 43–44.

1960, Simulmatics delivered "a report on the Negro vote in the North" based on the data collection.[30]

After the Democratic National Convention nominated John F. Kennedy for president in July, 1960, Kennedy's campaign committee (not the DNC) asked Simulmatics for three more reports: "on the image of Kennedy, the image of Nixon, and foreign policy as a campaign issue."[31] The reports were requested on August 11 and delivered on August 25. However, the most pressing issue for the Kennedy campaign that August was how to handle the religious issue of Kennedy's Catholicism. Simulmatics addressed the specific question, "What would happen if it became the dominant issue of the campaign, which it easily could if prejudice continued to rise, as indeed it seemed to be doing, and if the candidate also responded in the open forum?"[32]

Candidates, Issues, and Strategies devotes 19 pages describing the formulas and statistical analysis employed in simulating public opinion concerning Kennedy's stance on the religious question. The authors concede that their simulation was deterministic, not stochastic. It did not produce different outcomes after each run, to reflecting the effects of chance factors in the mode. It was more like "running the numbers" in a complex spreadsheet using different assumptions. Simulmatics' report to the Democratic National Committee was limited to 32 Northern states ranked from where Kennedy would do best to where worst.[33] The researchers recommended "frankness and directness rather than avoidance" in confronting the religious issue, advice that coincided with what Kennedy got from contemporary polling. "But certainly when Kennedy decided to confront the bigots head on, he himself could not say what part in his decision was played by any one piece of evidence."[34]

The 1960 Simulmatics simulation of the presidential election not only sparked a popular novel, it drew considerable attention within the social science community. A Google Scholar search of "Simulmatics" in April 2013 turned up 280 references, about one-third appearing in the 1960s. Although the company demonstrated that computer technology could play a positive role in the 1960 presidential election, the DNC failed to embrace computer technology in preparing for the 1964 election. The Simulmatics team did simulate the 1964 election, but they undertook the project "for scientific purposes" without sponsorship of the DNC, saying "the Democratic Party had virtually no systematic research program in 1964."[35]

Perhaps the DNC abandoned computer technology in 1964 because President Kennedy was assassinated in 1963 and because the new president, Democratic

---

30 *Ibid.*, p. 17.
31 *Ibid.*, p. 18.
32 *Ibid.*, p. 45.
33 *Ibid.*, pp. 56–57.
34 *Ibid.*, p. 22.
35 Ithiel de Sola Pool, Robert P. Abelson and Samuel L. Popkin, "A Postscript on the 1964 Election," *American Behavioral Scientist*, 8 (May, 1965), pp. 39–44 at p. 43.

Lyndon Johnson, was expected to thump Republican challenger Barry Goldwater – as occurred. However, the reason was probably more deeply rooted in the relationship between the Democratic Party and its presidents. According to Daniel J. Galvin's book, *Presidential Party Building*, Democratic presidents from Kennedy to Clinton "were not out to build a new majority but to make use of the one that they had."[36] They tended to exploit, not build the national party organization. Regrettably, the Simulmatics project's pioneering efforts to introduce computing technology into American party politics soon faded from memory. A comprehensive 1980 study of technology in party politics that began with the origin of the party system failed to mention the 1960 simulation of the presidential election.[37]

Republican Party

In *Presidential Party Building*, Galvin studied the relationships between presidents and their parties' national organizations from Dwight Eisenhower in 1952 to George W. Bush in 2008. In contrast to Democratic presidents, Galvin credited Republicans for working "persistently to build their party into a strong and more durable political organization."[38] In 1950, the Republican Party – which had lost the previous five presidential elections – compensated by developing its organization, and the emphasis on organization continued for decades afterward. David Karpf describes this response as "the outparty motivational incentive."[39] Ben Cotton, General Counsel to the Republican National Committee (RNC) in 1981, stressed this point in a personal letter:

> Republicans have historically, at the National Committee level, been far ahead of the Democrat [sic] National Committee in the technical aspects of training and campaigning. This derived more out of necessity than anything else. The Democrat Party [sic] has historically been able to rely upon the tremendous resources of the labor movement. The Republicans, on the other hand, had to create a grass roots effort.[40]

A study of the sizes of the paid staff of both national committees from 1952 to 1977 found that the RNC averaged 204 employees to the DNC's 132.[41] Moreover, the RNC research division was also more active, publishing detailed analyses of election

---

36 Daniel J. Galvin, *Presidential Party Building: Dwight D. Eisenhower to George W. Bush* (Princeton, NJ: Princeton University Press, 2010), pp. ix–x.
37 Stephen E. Frantzich, *Political Parties in the Techological Age* (New York: Longman, 1980).
38 Galvin, Presidential Party Building, p. ix.
39 David Karpf, The MoveOn Effect: The Unexpected Transformation of American Political Advocacy (New York: Oxford University Press, 2012), pp. 126–127.
40 Ben Cotton's letter to me dated February 6, 1981, written on RNC letterhead.
41 Cornelius P. Cotter and John F. Bibby, "Institutional Development of Parties and the Thesis of Party Decline." *Political Science Quarterly*, 95 (Spring, 1980), pp. 1–27.

results since at least 1960.[42] In the late 1960s, the Republican Party (and the Nixon white House) commissioned numerous public opinion surveys, many under the direction of political scientist David R. Derge. (Disclosure: David Derge supervised my 1961 PhD thesis at Indiana University.) Just the descriptive summary of the Derge Collection in the Richard Nixon Library, contains 50 references to computer printouts or statistics in its holdings.[43]

The The New York Times reported it on January 28, 1964:

> The electronic device, manufactured by the Eastman Kodak Company, is being used in a political campaign for the first time. It is capable of finding in seconds microfilmed records of most of what Mr. Goldwater has said on most subjects for several years. The machine then flashes his words on a small screen and can be made to photocopy any page quickly.[44]

The Republican's Rair system (Recordak automated information retrieval) did not prevent Barry Goldwater from losing the presidential election that year in spectacular fashion to Lyndon Johnson. Nevertheless, the RNC persevered and upgraded its information retrieval technology to Eastman Kodak's MIRAcode (Microfilm Information Retrieval Access code) system in 1967 for the 1968 presidential election.

Whereas Rair used punchcard data to locate microfilmed images of text, the MIRAcode system stored three-digit codes in binary format directly on microfilm cassettes containing about 1,000 pages each.[45] Codes tagged to individual pages could be searched (using Boolean logic) at the rate of 100 pages per second. As stated in *A Manual for the Information Retrieval System at the Republican National Committee*:

> The input process begins with the Republican National Committee's Clipping Bureau which reads and clips an average of 65 newspapers (including major dailies and a representative sampling of out-of-town sources) as well as a number of magazines. Each day a folder of approximately 200–250 clips is sent to the Research Division where it is sorted into our prime areas of concern: Democratic Administration – Executive Officers including the President, Vice-President, Cabinet and White Horne officials as well as examples of government mismanagement, waste, etc. (until January, 1969); Democratic Opposition (the Democratic Party, the Democratic National Committee, key Democratic legislators and office holders); George Wallace; the war in Vietnam; and Ray C. Bliss. (In addition to the newsclips, numerous articles from periodicals, the CONGRESSIONAL RECORD, Congressional hearings and TV transcripts are routed to Research and either filmed in their entirety or reference-coded for Miracode.)[46]

---

42 Republican National Committee. *The 1960 Elections: A Summary Report with Supporting Tables.* (Washington, DC: Republican National Committee, 1961).

43 See http://nixon.archives.gov/forresearchers/find/textual/findingaids/findingaid_derge.pdf.

44 "Goldwater Inspects Device That Recalls All He's Ever Said," *New York Times* (January 28, 1964), p. 16.

45 Kenneth Janda, "Political Research with MIRAcode: A 16mm. Information Retrieval System," *Social Science Information*, 6 (April-June, 1967), 169–181.

46 Research Division, *A Manual for the Information Retrieval System at the Republican National Committee* (Washington, DC: Republican National Committee, February, 1969), p. 5.

Having purchased the MIRAcode system with NSF funds in 1967 for my cross-national study of political parties,[47] I was invited to inspect the RNC's operation in 1970 at its new building, the Eisenhower Republican Center. There, scores of staff members in business attire worked professionally in offices with printed titles outside their doors. The RNC also had a separate library, staffed by a librarian. During the same trip to Washington, I also visited the Democratic National Committee, which occupied a floor of the Airline Pilots' Association. The DNC's research center consisted of a large room whose walls were flanked by mismatched filing cabinets surrounding a large central table seating a few college-age interns in dungarees, shuffling through documents and newspaper clippings. Whereas the NRC's operation looked like a business firm, the DNC's looked like an academic department. The RNC used the latest information technology; the DNC did not. David Karpf attributes the RNC's acceptance of business equipment as the "ideological congruence" factor.[48]

3 The 1970s: The Mainframe Computer Era

Using state-of-the art computers in the 1970s meant working with large, expensive equipment that demanded a crew of trained technicians, occupied a good deal of space, drew a lot of electricity, generated considerable heat, and required massive cooling capacity. Hence, computing was done in special areas (often separate buildings) called computing centers. Mainframe computers typically employed "time-sharing" systems that allowed multiple users to run programs concurrently. The users needed to have "accounts" on the system against which the cost of their runs could be charged to compensate for the millions of dollars required to operate the computing center. Universities across the United States supported computing in teaching using institutional funds, while individual researchers were expected to ask for thousands of dollars in computing funds when making grant requests.

At the start of the decade, most data were entered into the computer by punchcards, but data were increasingly entered via keyboards at cathode ray terminals located in the computing center but occasionally over telephone lines from remote locations. The point is that computing in the 1970s was an expensive, highly centralized operation. The RNC acquired its own computer in 1977 and upgraded to a newer one in 1979, but the DNC did not get its own mainframe until the early 1980s. If they used computers at all, candidates and even most state political parties contracted for services from commercial computing centers. Computer applications

---

47 My project was sponsored by the National Science Foundation, Grant GS-1418 in 1966 and GS-2533 in 1969.
48 Karpf, *The MoveOn Effect*, pp. 126–127.

in party politics were mainly for analyzing polling data and for maintaining mailing lists of sympathetic voters and likely contributors.

Nevertheless, our current international computing environment originated with mainframes. What we today call the Internet began in 1969 when, with support from the U.S. Defense Department's Advanced Research Projects Agency, mainframe computers at four universities were linked to form ARPANET, which connected thirty-seven universities by 1972.[49] Following the growth of other distinct computer networks (such as BITNET, designed for IBM mainframes), new communications standards worked out in 1983 allowed these networks to be interlinked, creating the Internet.[50]

4 The 1980s: Mainframes Yield to Mini and then Microcomputers

For most of the 1980s, the RNC and DNC relied on mainframe technology for their computing applications. The RNC had already been using its own computer in its own building. The DNC did not construct its own building in 1984,[51] but it began using computers for similar types of purposes earlier. A 1984 report in the *National Journal* stated:

> Only recently, the DNC instituted computerized media mailing lists. Reporters, columnists, broadcasters and other media people are coded according to criteria that allows the DNC to pull out "tailored" lists from its computer for media mailings.

DNC participants described the effort as "an effort to catch up technologically with the Republicans." Indeed, the same article said:

> The RNC is far ahead of its Democratic counterpart in computer technology. The committee has had a sophisticated computer operation in force for several years. Thomas B. Hofeller, the committee's director of computer services, reported that the RNC uses a time-sharing system that can perform more than 80 jobs at one time. "Basically, the computer operation has four functions," he said. "It keeps our books, our accounts payable and our Federal Election Commission reports; it maintains various lists of names, including political contacts, media members and financial donors; it keeps us in contact with our large number of field operatives, who carry microprocessors and communicate back and forth with the RNC through computerized mail; and it contains lots of data entries, which helps in our demographic research."

---

49 Material in the next two paragraphs was extracted from Chapter 6 of *The Challenge of Democracy, 5ᵗʰ ed.*

50 See http://smithsonian.yahoo.com/Internethistory.html.

51 David John Menefee-Libey, *The Politics of National Party Organization: The Democrats from 1968 to 1986* (Unpublished PhD dissertation, University of Chicago, December 1989), Chapter 7, p. 270.

Hofeller noted that using computers in campaigns requires a skilled technical staff. "It's important also to have the wherewithal to maintain and expand the operation," he added. His division is allotted a net budget of slightly more than $1 million, less the fees he charges party affiliates for using the RNC's computer facilities. The state Republican parties, GOP candidates, the Reagan-Bush '84 Committee, the Republican National Convention officials and other divisions within the RNC all have access to his division's computers.[52]

In her doctoral thesis, "The Presidential Campaign Organization of the 1970s and the 1980s: How It Has Adjusted to Political and Technological Changes," Teresa Smith singled out the CATI system (Computer Assisted Telephone Interviews), saying:

> CATI is expensive, costing about one half a million to install, and currently, its use for political polling has been rather restricted. In the 1984 elections, the Republicans used the CATI system, but the Democrats used it only in a limited way in the nominating period and none of the major Democratic polling firms have been able to justify installing it for their phone bank operations because of its costs to date.[53]

Teresa Smith also reported this telling quotation from David Broder, the distinguished political columnist for the *Washington Post*:

> I was struck once more by the enormous gap between the resources the Republicans and Democrats bring to the presidential campaigns. It's not just money – although the GOP's advantage in that commodity is significant enough. At least as important is the inequality of political research, polling and political planning. Time after time, Republicans were stunned to hear from the Democratic operatives that questions they assumed had been matters of major discussion and careful polling by their opponents had been decided in the dark as it were.
> [...]
> There is something in the Democrats that makes them resistant to the systematic application of survey research and the discipline of developing detailed strategic plans for targeting and winning the necessary 270 electoral votes. Deep-down they are more inclined to rely on their instincts – for better or worse.[54]

As Mr. Hofeller made clear: running a mainframe in the RNC's computer center was an expensive operation. But in the mid-1980s, mainframes offered the only practical way to employ computers in party politics.

---

52 "Strides in Technology Are Changing The Face of Political Campaining [sic]," *National Journal*, (April 7, 1984).

53 Teresa V. Smith, "The Presidential Campaign Organization of the 1970s and the 1980s: How It Has Adjusted to Political and Technological Changes," (Washington, DC: Georgetown University, Unpublished PhD Dissertation, 1986), p. 264.

54 *Ibid.*, p. 269.

The terms – mainframe computers, minicomputers, and microcomputers – are not technologically precise.[55] Generally speaking, minicomputers rivaled mainframes in their computing capacity but – thanks to advances in electronics – were physically much smaller, cheaper, cooler, and easier to operate and maintain. Although the Digital Equipment Corporation (DEC) introduced its first VAX minicomputer in 1977, the popular line of VAX minicomputers did not seriously challenge mainframe computers until the 1980s.[56] At universities across the nation, professors in the physical and medical sciences opted out of central computing, concluding that it was cheaper to request funds to install their own minicomputers in their own labs.

The rise of microcomputers accelerated the trend away from centralized computing. Although three microcomputers were commercially available the U.S. in 1977 – the Apple 2, the Radio Shack TRS-80, and the Commodore PET 2001 – the industry did not take off until IBM introduced its "Personal Computer" in 1981.[57] Soon other companies were making IBM-compatible PCs. In 1982, the Kaypro Corporation marketed a portable computer, the Kaypro II, which ran an operating system that was incompatible with IBM. In 1984, Apple launched its own non-compatible personal computer, the Macintosh.

The history of centralized computing at Northwestern University, my university, exemplifies its history at other American universities. Vogelback Computing Center, which opened in 1965, was a new building specifically designed to house a large mainframe computer. During its first 15 years, students streamed through it round-the-clock, feeding data into a large Control Data Corporation Cyber computer and picking up their output, which was typically spread over multiple 11″ by 14″ pages. When I served briefly as Vogelback's Acting Director in 1984, IBM, Kaypro, and Macintosh computers competed with the Cyber within the very walls of the computing center. Meanwhile, computing labs with microcomputers spread across campus. Vogelback itself was razed in 1999, about the time that university computing centers closed across the country.

People favored microcomputers because they could enter data and programs directly into equipment that they personally operated. As users purchased their own computers, even the need for computing labs decreased. As coaxial cable replaced telephone lines, users exploited online connections to the Internet. Widespread use of microcomputers expanded its use in business, scholarly research, and party politics. Microcomputers not only distributed computing away from brick-and-mortar computing centers, they also distributed computing away from the national party organizations to party candidates.

---

55 For a discussion of the classification, see http://www.komecomputers.com/classification-of-computers.html.

56 See the brief history of VAX computers at http://en.wikipedia.org/wiki/VAX#History.

57 For a concise history of microcomputers see http://microcomputerhistorymuseum.com.

5 The 1990s: The Early Years of the Internet

In its early years, the Internet was used mainly to transmit messages, known as electronic mail or "e-mail," among researchers. In 1991, a group of European physicists devised a standardized system for encoding and transmitting a wide range of materials, including graphics and photographs, over the Internet, and the World Wide Web (WWW) was born. In January 1993 there were only fifty websites in existence.[58] In early 2013, over 2 billion Web users could read text, view images, and download data from over 600 million sites websites worldwide.[59]

The Internet debuted in statewide U.S. election campaigns in 1992, when Democratic senatorial candidate Jerry Brown, former governor of California, sent e-mail messages to supporters.[60] Later in 1992, some Reform Party members voted for their presidential candidate over the Internet. On August 18, the party convened at Valley Forge, Virginia, where Ross Perot was declared the winner with 65 % of the primary vote to Dick Lamm's 35 %. Most of the 49,266 votes were cast by mail (88 %), with relatively few phoned to an 800 number or submitted over the Internet (8 and 4 % respectively).[61]

The first official White House web site was launched on October 20, 1994, during President Bill Clinton's administration.[62] The first major candidate web site appears to be that of Democratic senator Dianne Feinstein running for reelection from California in 1994. The same year, the nonpartisan Minnesota E-Democracy held the first online U.S. Senate and gubernatorial candidate debates. In 1995, the Democratic National Committee created the first web site for a major party. By 1995, there was enough material to fill a 375-page book, *Politics on the Net*.[63] It classified the political information on the Internet as real news reported by professionals, opinions and debates expressed by and involving citizens, publications by governments at all levels, and statements from political parties and other political organizations.

By 1996, the Internet was the hottest new media in political campaigning. Not only did both major parties and some minor parties put up their own home pages, so did presidential candidates – including several seeking the Republican nomination.

---

58 John December, Neil Randall, and Wes Tatters, *Discover the World Wide Web with Your Sportster* (Indianapolis, IN: Sams.net Publishing, 1995), pp. 11–12.
59 "January 2013 Web Server Survey," http://news.netcraft.com/archives/2013/01/07/january-2013-web-server-survey-2.html.
60 The information on early campaign web sites comes from Jill Zuckerman, "Candidates Spin Web of Support on Cybertrail," *Chicago Tribune*, 3 December 2003, p.º13.
61 Rogers Worthington, "Reform Party Selects Perot in Low Turnout," *Chicago Tribune*, 18 August 1996, p. 14.
62 The date for the first White House web site and some other "firsts" in this paragraph came from http://techpresident.com/news/23313/politics-and-internet-timeline-updates.
63 Bill Mann, *Politics on the Net* (Indianapolis, IN: Que Corporation, 1995).

There were "official" sites (endorsed by the candidates) and "unofficial" ones, sometimes created by supporters-and sometimes by opponents. Parody pages early in the nomination campaign, for example, targeted both [Republicans] Pat Buchanan and Bob Dole.[64] During the drafting of the 1996 Republican platform on abortion, the pro-life forces mounted an e-mail campaign to hang tough going into the convention.[65] On August 12–15 during their convention, the Republicans created a website for online "chats" with party supporters and such officials as Senator Bob Dole and House Speaker Newt Gingrich.[66]

Inevitably, the Internet was proposed as a systematic means for registering citizens' opinions or votes. However, only 21 % of respondents in a 1996 national survey said that they "ever" used a computer "at work, school, or home" to connect with other computers on the Internet, and only 3 % ever obtained information on the presidential campaign.[67] At the start of the 1998 election year, the number of Americans connected to online information sources was estimated to be 50 million (28 % of the population).[68] Some experts felt that the Internet could have a major impact on the congressional elections and that it might be "used by people as the primary source of information about political campaigns."[69] Ted Mondale, Democratic candidate for governor of Minnesota, bought the first online banner ad. In 1998, two other major Democratic candidates made Internet firsts: Ed Garvey, running for governor of Wisconsin, posted his contributor information online; and Senator Barbara Boxer, running for reelection in California, sold campaign items online.

Also in 1998, a reporter wrote an article titled "Wired for Votes: Is the Internet finally Fulfilling Its Campaign Promise?" Appropriately distributed via email, it stated:

> While 1998 may be remembered as the election year in which the Internet finally became a force in American politics, this year's cybercampaigns are also revealing many of the rough edges associated with more traditional methods of campaigning – including dirty tricks, shameless profiteering, and jousting between office-seekers.
> [...]

---

64 Edmund 1. Andrews, "The '96 Race on the Internet: Surfer Beware," *New York Times*, 23 October 1995, p. 1.
65 James Coates, "Internet Is the Latest Player in Campaign Politics," *Chicago Tribune*, 18 August 1996, Section 4, p. 5.
66 Cited in http://techpresident.com/news/23313/politics-and-internet-timeline-updates.
67 Pew Research Center for The People & The Press, "TV News Viewership Declines," News Release, 13 May 1996. National survey of 1,751 adults during April 19–25, 1996.
68 Pew Research Center, "Campaign '96 Gets Lower Grades from Voters," *News Release*, 15 November 1996, p. 32.
69 Rachel Van Dongen,"Wired for Votes: Is the Internet Finally Fulfilling Its Campaign Promise?" *Roll Call Online,* posted on the Campaigns and Elections list server (CAMPEL-L), 12 February 1998.

With an estimated 50 million Americans now online, the Internet has the potential to have a major impact on an election cycle for the first time, according to the growing number of cyberpoliticos and campaign consultants.[70]

Despite the flurry of Internet activity in 1998 congressional races, campaign consultants were mainly experimenting with the medium in preparation for full-scale usage in the 2000 presidential campaign.[71] In 1999, former Senator Bill Bradley, who sought the Democratic nomination for president, petitioned the Federal Election Commission to approve matching funds for Internet credit card contributions and then raised over a million dollars during the last half of the year.[72]

6 2000: Internet "Firsts" in Party Politics

The Internet became even hotter in the 2000 election cycle.[73] The major and minor parties and presidential candidates seeking their party's nomination all had home pages. There were "official" sites (endorsed by the candidates) and "unofficial" ones, sometimes created by supporters-and sometimes by opponents. There were so many more false sites for candidates that Yahoo! created its own Web page listing candidate "parody pages".[74] Regardless of the political fun people had on the Internet, only 11 % of the public said that they got most of their campaign news from that source-even when respondents were allowed two answers for "most." The public ranked the Internet far below television as their major source of campaign news (70 %), below newspapers (39 %), and even below radio (15 %).[75] Concerning the 2000 election campaign, the Internet did not qualify as a medium for reaching the masses, but it was a superb medium for communicating among politically active groups.

Candidates liked the Internet because it was fast, easy to use, and free – saving mailing costs and phone calls. Apart from candidates, party organizations also used the Internet to establish identity and cultivate supporters. Blessed with substantial

---

70 The article by Rachel Van Dongen, "Wired for Votes: Is the Internet Finally Fulfilling Its Campaign Promise?" appeared February 12, 1998 on the SErtelt@aol.com listserve, CAMPEL-L: Campaign 98 on the Web.
71 David L. Haase, "Candidates (maybe) and friends stake out their domain for the 2000 campaign," *Chicago Tribune*, 23 February 1998, Section 4, p. 7.
72 Bill Bradley's Internet fund raising is outlined at http://techpresident.com/news/23313/politics-and-internet-timeline-updates.
73 The next two paragraphs came mostly from Chapter 9 of *The Challenge of Democracy*, 7th Ed. (2002).
74 The URL on 15 January 2001 was <dir.yahoo.com/Government/U_S__Government/Politics/Humor/1996_Presidential_Election/Candidate_Parodies/>
75 Pew Research Center, "Despite Uncertain Outcome, Campaign 2000 Highly Rated," *News Release*, November 16, 2000, p. 18.

financial resources, the two major parties maintained the most stable and resource-ful websites.[76] Ever since the advent of computers in the 1950s, the national Repub-lican Party led the Democratic Party in adoption of new information technology. That may be due to Republicans' link with business, or to its greater money – prob-ably both. In 2000, the Republican National Committee had fifteen people working with Internet technology compared with only three at the Democratic National Committee.[77] Despite some impressive applications in the 2000 campaign, politi-cians were only learning how to use the Internet, and Internet buffs were only learn-ing how to approach politics. Internet coverage of the Republican and Democratic nominating conventions, for example, fell short of expectations, and visits to politi-cal websites covering the conventions actually fell during the coverage.[78]

The Internet allowed campaigns to communicate continually with activists on substantive issues, campaign appearances, requests for help, and requests for mon-ey. In 2000, Senator McCain conducted the first Republican presidential campaign fundraiser entirely on the Internet, collecting more than $1 million within forty-eight hours.[79] Also in 2000, the Arizona Democratic Party held the first binding online primary election; and the Republican Party scored its own Internet first: reg-istering 1 million activists online. Two years later, Claude "Buddy" Leach via the first live Internet broadcast announced candidacy to be governor of Louisiana. De-spite these Internet "firsts" in party politics, the new technology did not have that much impact on the 2000 presidential campaign between Republican George W. Bush and Democrat Al Gore – who was the first candidate to send a video campaign message by e-mail.[80]

While politicians' early use of the Internet brought them publicity, it did not of-ten produce winning results. Jerry Brown was not elected to the Senate from Cali-fornia in 1992 despite his pioneering use of e-mail. Ted Mondale did not win the Minnesota Senate seat in 1998 despite his first online banner ad, nor did Ed Garvey become governor of Wisconsin after posting his contributor information online. Being the first candidate to raise a million dollars online, Bill Bradley failed to win the Democratic nomination in 2000. Senator McCain did not capture the Republican presidential nomination; "Buddy" Leach did not become governor of Louisiana; and Al Gore did not win the presidency (although he did win the popular vote). The ef-

---

76 Bob Kolasky, "Both Parties Use the Net to Revive Their Relevance," *Inter@active Week*, 3 July 2000, pp. 34–36.

77 Neil Munro, "The New Wired Politics," *National Journal*, 22 April 2000, p. 1260–1263.

78 LeslieWayne, "Online Coverage Fell Short of the Hype," *New York Times*,19 August 2000, p. A10.

79 Frank James, "E-Campaigns Grow Up," *Chicago Tribune*, 11 February 2000, p. 3. See also Tina Kelley, "Candidate on the Stump Is Surely on the Web," *New York Times*, 19 October 1999, p. 1.

80 For a list of twelve Internet firsts in politics, see page 14 at http://www.docstoc.com/docs/38521469/ElectionMall-Technologies-Inc.

fects of the Internet were more significant in the 2004 campaign, when ten Democratic hopefuls sought to succeed President Bush.

7 2004: Internet Usage Affects Party Politics

In 2004, the first prominent Democrat to declare his candidacy for president was Howard Dean.[81] As former governor of a small state (New Hampshire) and with little national visibility, Dean was favored by only 3 % of respondents in a January 2003 poll.[82] Quickly building his campaign around the Internet, Dean raised over $1 million online by spring 2003, eclipsing Bill Bradley's fund-raising rate for his 2000 presidential campaign.[83] By the end of the year, Dean had raised almost $14 million, said to be a one-year record for Democratic presidential fundraising.[84] The same poll that placed Dean at 3 % in January had him at upwards of 25 % in December and leading all Democratic aspirants.

Although Dean lost the Iowa caucuses and failed to win the Democratic presidential nomination, he demonstrated the power of the Internet, not just for raising unprecedented amounts of funds but also for mobilizing his supporters. The architect of Dean's Internet campaign, Joe Trippi, also backed the creation of the first presidential campaign "web log" or *blog*, a frequently updated site for posting campaign developments and comments, and even short essays, on election politics.[85] Blogs proved effective in involving potential supporters, and by the midst of the 2004 primary season, virtually every presidential web site was connected to a blog.[86] Beginning with the 2004 election, presidential and congressional candidates relied heavily on the Internet to raise campaign funds and mobilize supporters.[87]

The Internet's most demonstrable affect on party politics was to hasten the breakdown of the national legislation to limit spending in presidential campaigns

---

81 Information in this paragraph and the next was extracted from Chapter 9, *The Challenge of Democracy, 8ᵗʰ Ed.* (2005).
82 NBC News/*Wall Street Journal*, January, 2003.
83 Robert J. Kloz, *The Politics of Internet Communication* (Lanham, MD: Rowman & Littlefield, 2004), pp. 77–78.
84 Glen Justice, "Dean Raises $14 million and Sets Reord, Aides Say," *New York Times*, December 30, 2003, p. A17.
85 Jeanne Cummings, "Behind Dean Surge: A Gang of Bloggers and Webmasters," *Wall Street Journal*, 14 October 2003, pp. A1, A14.
86 Lee Gomes, "Blogs Have Become Part of Media Machine That Shapes Politics," *Wall Street Journal*, 23 February 2004, p. B1; Christopher Conkey, "Checking Out Candidates' Sites," *Wall Street Journal*, 16 March 2004, p. D3.
87 Adam Nagourney, "Internet Injects Sweeping Change into U.S. Politics," *New York Times*, 2 April 2006, pp. 1 and 17.

by inducing candidates to accept public funding.[88] The 1971 Federal Election Campaign Act was amended in 1974 to provide $10 million in matching funds to presidential aspirants during the primary season and $20 outright to major party nominees for the general election. Both sums were indexed for inflation so the amounts grew over time. All major candidates for president from 1976 through 1992 accepted public funding of their primary election campaigns and thus adhered to the limitations on raising and spending campaign funds. But in 1996, wealthy publisher Steve Forbes declined public funds in the primary season, and did so again in 2000 accompanied by Texas governor George Bush. Competing for the Republican nomination, both candidates raised and spent much more than otherwise possible. For the most part, Forbes and Bush raised their funds from people via traditional methods and did not rely on the Internet.

Like Forbes and Bush in 2000, Democrats Howard Dean and John Kerry, and President Bush (who had no meaningful opposition), in 2004 declined public funds in the primaries so that they could spend more than the $37.3 million (adjusted for inflation) allowed by accepting public funds. Dean's decision in particular was based on knowing that he could raise millions over the Internet. In keeping with his "ideological congruence" explanation that had supported Republicans' use of mainframes, David Karpf implies that Democrats (like Dean) changed their view of information technology as it shifted from mainframes to microcomputers linked to the Internet. Karpf said, "According to this perspective, the Internet's "bottom-up" nature is simply better suited to anti-hierarchical progressive ideology."[89]

Despite opposition from some Democratic leaders, Howard Dean was elected Chairman of the Democratic National Committee in 2005 over several other candidates. Observers expected him to utilize information technology in fundraising and campaigning, and they were not disappointed. Daniel Kreiss details Dean's technological innovations in *Taking Our Country Back: The Crafting of Networked Politics from Howard Dean to Barack Obama*.[90] Kreiss says that Dean hired two staff members from his 2004 campaign – Ben Self and Joe Rospers – who helped create the firm, Blue State Digital (BSD). They were to assess the state of technology and to improve it. Kreiss describes the sad picture at the DNC in 2005:

> Rospars and Self's findings made it clear that the national party's voter file was in complete disarray. The data was of extremely low quality and; despite the considerable investment of former chairman Terry McAuliffe in a national Voter database, the party's basic technology was

---

88 The information in this paragraph was extractd from Chapter 9, *the Challenge of Democracy, 8th Ed.* (2005).

89 Karpf, *The MoveOn Effect*, pp. 126–127.

90 Daniel Kreiss, Taking Our Country Back: The Crafting of Networked Politics from Howard Dean to Barack Obama (New York: Oxford University Press, 2012).

lacking. The national party had few means of compiling and storing data on the electorate or even its supporters.[91]

[...]

Candidates often repeat the aphorism that "all politics is local." For much of the twentieth century and well into the first decade of the twenty-first, the saying was true for the Democratic Party's voter data. Unlike the Republican Party, which had a strong centralized party organization and corresponding national voter file that grew out of pioneering direct mail efforts, the Democratic Party had a more decentralized structure, with strong state party organizations. The Voter files of the state parties reflected this. Each state maintained its own record of its electorate, chose the information it collected and the systems it used to house data, set its own "rules of access, arid determined the data's format. Across states, there was little in the way of standard categories of information collected or practices for updating voter records. The Iowa Democratic Party, for instance, kept detailed caucus records dating back over a decade, while other states lacked anything more than a list of registered voters.[92]

Self and Rospers began their work.

As the technology director for the party, Self led the effort to create a national voter file. This proved to be a deeply challenging undertaking that involved both rebuilding the technical infrastructure of the party and negotiating data-sharing agreements with all the state parties. Building this national voter file was a priority for Dean, given widespread failures in state voter files and database technologies during the 2004 general election. Looking ahead to 2008, Dean and Self worked out a deal in which the national party assumed the costs of improving and maintaining the state voter files and building a new database to house them in exchange for permission to aggregate and access them. Self commissioned the firm Voters Activation Network (VAN) to customize its online interface so that party and campaign staffers could continually access and update the voter file database. The system that resulted is called "VoteBuilder," which the national party provides free of charge to the states. "VoteBuilder" refers to the Democratic Party's data (the state voter files as well as commercial data) and the VAN interface system around it. As a key piece of infrastructure for Democratic campaigning, VoteBuilder extended the ability of the party and its candidates to contest elections and to target the electorate. It enabled Democratic candidates for offices from staff senate to president to share data across campaigns and election cycles while ensuring that the voter file was continuously uploaded with quality data. All of the major Democratic presidential candidates' field campaigns used VoteBuilder in 2008.

As Self worked on the voter file project, Rospers, as the head-of a newly reconstituted Internet Department, implemented Blue State Digital's campaign platform for the party.[93]

Ironically, the DNC's technological ascension was fed not by acquiring innovative hardware or writing innovative software but by accumulating lots of good quality data. That old-fashioned practice recalled the 1960 Simulmatics project, which analyzed hundreds of thousands of interviews with voters in previous elections to simulate voters' responses to John Kennedy's Catholicism. Those data were carefully

---

91 *Ibid.*, p. 99.
92 *Ibid.*, pp. 99–100.
93 *Ibid.*, p. 16.

collected over time, cataloged, and archived at the Roper Center, a central organization founded in 1947.

Data collection, cleaning, and processing for computer analysis is a time-consuming effort best entrusted to a professional staff of permanent employees. Kreiss alludes to the technological and political nature of the process of incorporating the state data into an integrated database for analysis:

> As such, the national party offered to clean and supplement the data of the state parties, as well as provide the databases to house and fund an online interface to access this data. This came to be an approximately $6 million undertaking, requiring both technological development and hiring staff and outside vendors. The national party proposed funding all of this in exchange for the state parties sharing their data. While state parties would still retain formal ownership, they had to provide their data to the national party. The state parties, meanwhile, would set their own rules to determine which candidates could use the voter files and what functionality and types of data they would have access to. States would also be able to charge campaigns for access to their voter files, provided that it was a fixed price. These voter files, meanwhile, would be continually updated through canvassing conducted by campaigns during election cycles.[94]
>
> [...]
>
> The Party also engaged in a massive data-cleaning effort to make its information on the electorate as accurate as possible, hiring firms to provide such things as correct phone numbers. Staffers also hired vendors to provide better data on voters, particularly in states that the national party and presidential candidates had long ignored but that were newly relevant under Dean's 50-state approach.[95]

In building a new national database from state files in preparation for the 2008 presidential election, the DNC was finally developing what the RNC had created years earlier. In a sense, the DNC's product leapfrogged over the RNC's. Like an underdeveloped country that creates a telephone system using cell phones instead of land lines, the DNC developed a better database by building by acquiring more accurate data and using newer technology. Kreiss said, "The Republicans had nationalized their voter file much earlier and had built modifications to their database system on an older technology base."

> Given that [Republicans] had superior, voter files, databases, and turnout operations, in addition to enjoying the presidency for much of the 2000s, there was little incentive to develop new systems. As a result, the Republican Party had fallen behind the Democrats in its knowledge of the electorate by the 2008 presidential campaign.[96]

Neither national party organization, however, plays any significant role in presidential campaigns until party conventions choose the nominee at their summer conven-

---

94 *Ibid.*, p. 108.
95 *Ibid.*, p. 109.
96 *Ibid.*, p. 101.

tions prior to the general election in November. At the crucial state of winning the party nomination, presidential hopefuls must operate on their own, relying on their own campaign staff and organization to win the nomination.

8 2008: Internet Usage Changes Party Politics

According to adjustments for inflation under 1974 Federal Finance Campaign Act, presidential primary candidates in 2008 could qualify for $21 million in public matching funds, allowing them to spend $42 million during the primary campaign season if they accepted public funding. Of the leading candidates, only John Edwards accepted public funds, meaning he could spend no more than $42 million. All other leading candidates in both parties financed their primary campaigns from private sources. In just January 2008, the month Barack Obama won contests in Iowa and South Carolina, he raised $32 million from 170,000 new contributors, mostly online.[97] By July 2008, Obama had raised over $400 million.[98]

Candidates need not win stunning victories to raise large sums on the Internet. Republican Ron Paul, who trailed in the polls, raised $4 million online in a single day.[99] Nor was a specific candidate required at all. A Democratic political action committee, (www.ActBlue.com), set up web pages for all Democrats who filed for elections. It promised to raise $100 million for them in the 2007–2008 election cycle.[100] Nor did one have to be in the United States to contribute. Through the first six months of 2007 and mostly through the Internet, candidates raised over $500,000 from American citizens living abroad.[101]

Buoyed by his success in raising funds over the Internet for his primary campaign, Obama made the unprecedented decision to forego public funding for the 2008 general election. Previously, from 1976 to 2004, every major party nominee for president had accepted public funds (and spending limits) for the general election. John McCain, his Republican opponent and coauthor of a law limiting campaign finance, agreed to accept public funds and limit his spending for the general elec-

---

97 Leslie Wayne and Jeff Zeleny, "Enlisting New Donors, Obama Reaped $32 Million in January," *New York Times*, 1 February 2008, pp. A1 and A14.

98 Obama's fund-raising in 2008 comes from http://www.cnn.com/ELECTION/2008/money/index.html.

99 Katharine Q. Seelye and Leslie Wayne, "The Web Finds Its Man, and Takes Him for a Ride," *New York Times*, 11 November 2007, p. 22.

100 Leslie Wayne, "A Fund_Raising Rainmaker Arises Online," *New York Times*, 29 November 2008, p. A22.

101 Russ Buettner and Marc Santora, "In '08, Campaign, Money Chase Circles the Globe," *New York Times*, 22 September 2007, pp. 1 and 12.

tion to the inflation-adjusted $84.1 million. Unencumbered by the law, Obama raised and spent more than twice as much during that period.[102]

Also in 2008, presidential candidates (mainly Democrats) advertised on political blogs and were also into social-networking sites – both commercial (Facebook, MySpace) and their own (for example, Obama's MyBO and McCain's McCainSpace). Samuel Popkin, a co-author of the book on the 1960 Simulmatics project, described the Obama campaign's use of the new media.[103] Popkin wrote that David Plouffe and David Axelrod, Obama's campaign gurus, "changed the organization of the campaign to take advantage of the Internet to use peer-to-peer communication for persuasion, Get out the Vote (GOTV), and fund raising."

Still, the Internet was not very productive, for relatively few people went online for political information or activity. A national survey in late December 2007 asked respondents to name two sources for "most of" their news about the presidential campaign. Most people (71 %) named television, nearly one-third (30 %) cited newspapers, and one-quarter (26 %) said the Internet.[103] When asked about specific ways in which they "regularly" learn about the presidential campaign, Young people of ages 18–29 were far more likely to name the Internet (42 %) while those over 50 cited the nightly network news.

Using data from national surveys in 2004, 2006, and 2008, Thad Hall and Betsy Sinclair profiled "The American Internet Voter."[104] They wrote:

> We find that Internet users are not divided by a partisan difference; Democrats are not more likely than Republicans (or other party registrants) to be active Web users or to use the Internet for Political purpose. We see no systematic evidence that the Internet users in 2008 are substantially different than the Internet users in 2004, although we highlight a few small differences in our empirical analysis. We do see indications that individuals who use the Internet to confirm their existing political preferences are increasingly likely to participate and additionally that users with access to the Internet are increasingly likely to donate to political campaigns.[105]

In addition, they found "that older individuals use the Internet significantly less, that better-educated individuals access the Internet more, and that individuals who are employed access the Internet more."[106] They note that these findings, which

---

102 It is difficult to pin down the general election expenditures for Obama and McCain, for one account, see http://www.opensecrets.org/pres08/
103 Samuel L Popkin, *The Candidae* (New York: Oxford University Press, 2012), pp. 95–97.
103 Pew Research Center for the People and the Press, "Internet's Broader role in Campaign 2008," News Release, 11 January 2008.
104 Thad E. Hall and Betsy Sinclair, "The American Internet Voter," in Costas Panagopoulos (ed.), *Strategy, Money and Technology in the 2008 Presidential Election* (London: Routledge, 2012), pp. 151–172.
105 *Ibid.*, pp. 152–153.
106 *Ibid.*, pp. 163–164.

confirm the presence of a "digital divide" noted by other authors,[107] contradict the "democratizing" effect claimed for the Internet.

Despite the increased reliance on the Internet by citizens for information and by candidates for fund-raising, Internet advertising got only "small slice of campaign spending in 2008," according to a company that tracks advertising. Because Internet users seek out what they want to view, the best way to reach average voters was still through local broadcast television.[108] And campaign funds raised via the Internet were usually siphoned off by television advertising.

9 2012: Mobile Devices Open Avenues to the Internet

A wireless handheld device (the Blackberry) was introduced in 1999, but it did not sell millions of units until the mid-2000s, reaching 14 million subscribers in 2008.[109] In addition to making telephone calls, a BlackBerry could provide online functions such as web browsing and emailing and could take photos and play music. BlackBerrys were popular communication devices among politicians, and Barack Obama relied on his during his 2008 presidential campaign. Marketed as a "smart" phone, the first Apple iPhone appeared in 2007 and by 2008 had sold about 13 million units – similar to BlackBerry then.[110] The first Android smart phone was not marketed until 2008, but Android phones sold quickly and often. By 2011, Android sales had surpassed sales of iPhones, with BlackBerry far below.[111] In 2012, over 1 billion people worldwide used some type of smart phone, including 35 % of people in the United States.[112]

The family of mobile devices was augmented by the announcement of Apple's iPad in January 2010. Within a year, Apple had sold 14 million iPads, and over 80 million were sold prior to the 2012 presidential election.[113] Using their smart

107 See, for example, Pippa Norris, Digital Divide: Civic Engagement, Information Poverty, and the Internet Worldwide (New York: Cambridge, 2001).

108 Emily Steel, "Why Web Campaign Spending Trails TV," *Wall Street Journal*, 14 December 2008, p. B4.

109 BlackBerry sales figures come from http://mobilemoo.com/blackberry/blackberry-guides/the-history-of-the-blackberry/.

110 Early Apple sales figures come from http://www.zdnet.com/blog/hardware/iphone-and-ipod-sales-to-date/2819.

111 Comparative smart phone sales data come from http://www.zanura.com/blog/reviews/iphone-review/android-versus-iphone-market-share-2/.

112 Smartphone usage comes from http://ansonalex.com/infographics/smartphone-usage-statistics-2012-infographic/.

113 Apple iPad sales come from http://ipod.about.com/od/ipadmodelsandterms/f/ipad-sales-to-date.htm.

phones and their iPads or other tablet devices, millions of potential voters could access – and respond to – political messages online without sitting before a desktop computer or even toting a laptop. One unanticipated consequence of this technological innovation was to end existing limits on presidential campaign spending. Loads of money could be made so easily over the Internet, that candidates simply refused to accept the piddling millions offered by public funding under the 1974 legislation and thus be bound by spending limits.

Having refused public funds for the primary season in 2008 in preference to raising and spending far more than he otherwise would have been allowed, President Barack Obama again refused public funds during the 2012 primary season en route to his renomination. So did all major Republican presidential hopefuls in 2012. Only Libertarian presidential candidate Gary Johnson, Green Party candidate Jill Stein, and Buddy Roemer – who sought the nomination of the online organization, Americans Elect – had applied for and qualified for public matching funds.[114] Neither Obama nor his Republican opponent, Mitt Romney, accepted the $91.2 million in public funds that were available for the general election in 2012. Unencumbered by spending limits in either the primary or general election periods, Obama spend over $700 million and Romney almost $450 million.[115] Thanks in part to the ease of raising huge amounts of political money over the Internet, Congress failed in its 1974 attempt to limit presidential campaign spending by offering modest amounts of public funds.

The 2012 presidential campaign developed a relatively new attempt at using the Internet: "microtargeting" voters, sending specific messages to computer screens of selected viewers.[116] As in online marketing, visits to campaign websites generate information for providers who slip digital markers or "cookies" into the users' computers.[117] That information is matched with other user information – e.g., make of car – stored in a huge database. Campaign consultants then match those data with voting records, turnout, and party registration (but not voting choice, which is protected). Then they can frame ads targeted at visitors to conservative (or liberal) websites who shop for expensive Lexus (or cheaper Ford) cars, who are registered Republicans (or Democrats), and who are frequent voters. Consultants can produce targeted Internet ads cheaply, transmit them with little expense, and – very importantly – send them quickly in reaction to breaking news.

---

114 See the FEC website at http://www.fec.gov/press/bkgnd/fund.shtml.
115 Presidential campaign spending for 2012 came from http://www.opensecrets.org/pres12/.
116. Tanzina Vega, "Online Data Helping Campaigns Customize Ads," *New York Times*, 21 February 2012, pp. 1–13.
117 Information in this paragraph is extracted from *The Challenge of Democracy, 12th Ed.* (2014).

Wayne Steger provides an extensive account of marketing and candidate messaging in the 2012 presidential election.[118] He credits President Obama's campaign for out-performing the campaign of his Republican challenger Mitt Romney:

> The Romney campaign's research appears to have had critical flaws in assessing voter preferences and turnout. The Romney campaign failed to integrate its databases with its "get out the vote"(GOTV) operations and experienced systemic failures and delays on election day.[119]
> [...]
> In contrast to the highly accurate information used to guide Obama's campaign strategy, messaging, and communications, the Romney campaign operated with less extensive and sometimes inaccurate information about the electorate...Romney's database operation began later than the Obama campaign's operation, was not as well funded, and did not catch up, particularly with respect to attitudinal data gained through polling, mining of online data, and feedback from field staff.[120]

Steger notes that it was more difficult to document the Romney campaign's usage of technology, "because most of this work was contracted to consulting and marketing firms. These firms maintain proprietary rights on their activities and have been less than forthcoming about what they did during the campaign."[121]

Concerning the campaigns' use of social media, Stephen E. Frantzich surveyed the usage in 2012.[122] Both Obama and Romney, of course, had the inevitable candidate web sites, and both required visitors to register with e-mail addresses and zip codes "allowing the campaigns to capture e-mail addresses for future communication."[123] Both also used Facebook (an online social networking service) and Twitter (another online networking service limited to 140 characters). Although relatively "old" in computer technology (Facebook was founded in 2004 and Twitter in 2006), 2012 marked their first extensive use in a presidential campaign.[124] Frantzich reports data showing that "Obama won hands down in terms of the number of Facebook

---

118 Wayne P. Steger, "A Transformational Political Campaign: Marketing and Candidate Messaging in the 2012 Election," in William J. Crotty (ed.), *Winning the Presidency 2012* (Boulder, CO: Paradigm Publisher, 2013), pp. 74–89.

119 *Ibid.*, p. 75.

120 *Ibid.*, p. 77.

121 *Ibid.*, p. 89.

122 Stephen E. Frantzich, "'Are We Halfway There Yet?' New Technology and the 2012 Election," in William J. Crotty (ed.), *Winning the Presidency 2012* (Boulder, CO: Paradigm Publisher, 2013), pp. 90102.

123 *Ibid.*, p. 91.

124 For the use of Facebook in the 2010 congressional campaign, see Alan Steinberg, "Facebook and the Midterm Elections: Cyber-participation and Turnout," Paper Prepared for the 2013 Midwest Political Science Association Annual Meeting. For the use of Twitter in the 2011 Gubernatorial Elections, see Marija Anna Bekafigo and Allan McBride, "Who Tweets about Politics? Political Participation of Twitter Users during the 2011 Gubernatorial Elections," Paper Prepared for the 2013 Midwest Political Science Association Annual Meeting.

friends and Twitter followers."[125] However, as he notes, "Twitter and Facebook are still relatively limited sources of campaign news, with only about 12 % of the online public turning to Facebook to follow the campaign and 4 % relying on Twitter."[126]

10 Some Caveats about Information Technology and American Party Politics

Despite politicians' demonstrated success in using the Internet to raise money, their efforts to produce votes are harder to establish. Even in 2012, relatively few people got campaign news via the Internet. Surveyed early in the 2012 primary season, 72 % of respondents reported hearing or seeing campaign television commercials, whereas only 16 % received e-mails, 15 % visited a candidate's website, and only 6 % followed the candidate on Twitter or Facebook. Two months after the election, a national survey in January 2012 asked respondents whether they "learned something" about the presidential campaign or candidates from various news sources. Most people named some form of television (cable news, 36 %; local TV news, 32 %; network news, 26 %), and only 25 % named the Internet.[127]

However, evidence suggests that those who do rely on electronic technology are politically astute and involved. Scholars estimated that as many as half of American voters in 2004 sought political information online during the presidential election campaign.[128] Moreover, they found these "Online Political Citizens" to be disproportionately "politically influential":

> They are seven times more likely than the general public to have attended a political rally, speech or protest in the last two to three months. They are nearly five times more likely to have contacted a politician, three times more likely to have written a letter to the editor, and three times more likely to belong to groups trying to influence public policy.[129]

When compared with influentials in the general public, however, online influentials have weaker ties to their local community and to long-term obligations, perhaps

125 *Ibid.*, p. 92.
126 *Ibid.*, p. 94.
127. "Cable Leads the Pack as Campaign News Source," The Pew Research Center for the People and the Press, 7 February 2012, at http://www.people-press.org/files/legacy-pdf/2012%20Communicating%20 Release.pdf.
128 Joseph Graf, *Political Influentials Online in the 2004 Presidential Campaign* (Washington, D.C.: Institute for Politics, Democracy and the Internet, George Washington University, 5 February 2004), p.º34.
129 Ibid., p.º15.

reflecting the relative youth of online enthusiasts.[130] Online participants also tend to associate with like-minded partisans – except when they encounter occasional "trolls" of opposite persuasion who seek to disrupt a candidate's blog. Some observers see a dark side to the pattern of intense online debate among like-minded people, called "cyberbalkanization."[131] As one asked, "If Political Fragmentation Is the Problem, Is the Internet the Solution?"[132]

Finally, one must note the inaccuracy of the phrase, "information technology and American party politics," as applied to scholarly literature. Most authors really write about how *candidates* use the technology, not *parties*. The indexes to books on information technology prior to 2012 seldom cite either the Democratic Party or the Republican Party. For example, the index to the informative collection of studies, *Politicking online: The Transformation of Election Campaign Communications*, contains no entry for political parties, no entry for the Democratic Party, no entry for the Republican Party, but a sole entry for the Republican National Convention.[133] With the exception noted in the next paragraph, all of the other sixteen chapters mention parties but usually as an attribute of a candidate or as an entity that does not require much discussion. For example, the study on candidate web sites states that links to a political party are risky "because the campaign has no control over the information presented there and it may not be entirely consistent with the candidate's message."[134]

The exception was a study of the 2005 German Bundestag Election, which found almost as many party organization bloggers (76) as candidates (83).[135] Studies of online election campaigns in Australia and other countries by Rachel Gibson and others suggest that "well-resourced parties ran better designed multi-functional sites that delivered more information and greater opportunities for participation and fi-

---

130 Ibid., p.º34.

131 Amy Harmon, "Politics of the Web: Meet, Greet, Segregate, Meet Again," *New York Times*, 25 January 2004, Sec. 4, p.º16.

132 William A. Galston, "If Political Fragmentation Is the Problem, Is the Internet the Solution?" in *The Civic Web: Online Politics and Democratic Values*, ed. David M. Anderson and Michael Cornfield (Lanham, Md.: Rowman & Littlefield, 2003), pp.º35–44.

133 Costas Panagopoulos (ed.), *Politicking online: The Transformation of Election Campaign Communications*. (New Brunswick, NJ: Rutgers University Press, 2009).

134 James N. Druckman, Martin J Kifer, and Michael Parkin, "The Technological Development of Candidate Web Sites: How and Why Candidaes Use Web Innovations," in Costas Panagopoulos (ed.), *Politicking online: The Transformation of Election Campaign Communications*. (New Brunswick, NJ: Rutgers University Press, 2009), pp. 21–47 at p. 25.

135 Stffen Albrechet, Maren L. Übcke, and Rasco-Hartig-Perschke, "Under Construction": Weblog Campaigning in the German Bundestag Election 2005," in Costas Panagopoulos (ed.), *Politicking online: The Transformation of Election Campaign Communications*. (New Brunswick, NJ: Rutgers University Press, 2009), pp. 179–199, at p. 186.

nancial donations.[136] Parties in other countries, which have a more central role in government, may be more directly engaged in information technology than parties in the United States. Scholars have long described American parties as being highly institutionalized but also exceptionally decentralized. Their nature is in keeping with our decentralization of government and – importantly – our system of choosing party candidates for office through primary elections generally open to all voters.

11 Summary and Conclusions

At the risk of slighting important signposts along the evolutionary time-trail, I offer five summary observations about innovations in information technology in party politics since the 1960s.

1. From the 1960s through the 1980s, the national committees of the two major parties played a more important role in applying information technology to electoral campaigns than they did during the next two decades, certainly during the period from 1990 to 2004.

In 1960, the DNC supported a computer simulation of the 1960 presidential election, and in 1964 and 1968 the RNC developed a system to store and retrieve the speeches of presidential candidates. The national committees had to assume these roles – if they were to be assumed at all – because the equipment was expensive and very few people had the skills to operate the equipment.

2. From the 1960s through the 1980s, the RNC devoted more resources to information technology than the DNC, and achieved more impressive results, especially in raising funds from small contributors.

Although the DNC supported the pioneering simulation of the 1960 election, it neglected to support the follow-up simulation of the 1964 election, which it regarded as "in the bag." Two factors favored the RNC's persistence: (1) Staffed by business-types, the RNC was more accustomed to handling and processing information with "IBM" machines than the Democrats, staffed by academic-types; and (2) Having fewer self-identified party members, Republicans felt the need to overcome their numerical disadvantage with technological superiority.

---

136 See Rachel K. Gibson, "Normalizing or Equalizing Party Competition? Assessing the Impact of the Web on Election Campaigning," *Political Studies*, forthcoming; Rachel K. Gibson and Ian McAllister (2011): Do Online Election Campaigns Win Votes? The 2007 Australian "YouTube" Election, *Political Communication*, 28 (No. 2), 227–244.

3. During the decade and a half from 1990 to 2004, party candidates –not party organizations – led in introducing technological innovations in electoral campaigns.

With the emergence of the Internet, the manufacture of increasingly powerful microcomputers, and the spread of computing skills across the population, individuals (and young ones at that) applied information technology creatively to election campaigns. More often than not, this technological creativity failed to result in election victories, for two reasons: (1) underdogs, more often than top dogs, experimented with the new technology; and (2) relatively few voters were using the Internet during that period.

4. Beginning with the 2004 presidential election, computer-based technological innovations significantly affected party politics.

When Howard Dean raised millions in campaign funds online, politicians across the country realized that the Internet was no longer a novelty of marginal value but an essential component of electoral campaigns. The prospects of raising millions of dollars online induced all the leading presidential candidates in 2008 to decline accepting public funds for their primary campaigns, which freed them from spending limits. Candidate Barack Obama also declined public funding for his campaign in the 2008 general election. In 2012, all major candidates in both parties declined public funds for the primary season, and both major party candidates – Democrat President Obama and his Republican challenger Mitt Romney – declined public funding for their general election campaigns. So one unanticipated consequence of online politics was to help nullify the congressional attempt to limit campaign spending in presidential elections under the 1974 Federal Election Campaign Act.

5. Three factors in the evolution of information technology – declining costs, increased capabilities, and swift pace of innovation – have favored party candidates over party organizations in applying information technology to electoral politics.

Today, virtually everyone planning to run for public office can afford a computer that can fit in a brief case. The computer will operate faster, draw less electricity, and have more storage capacity than computers housed in the national party committees in the 1960s through the 1980s. Tomorrow, computers will be even smaller, faster, cooler, and have more capacity. Tomorrow, people will develop computer applications to electoral campaigns that are unknown today. Those people will be young people. They will not be employed in regular jobs by party organizations but by candidates operating outside the party organization. Generally speaking, innovations in information technology favor candidates over parties.

6. However, one critical factor for successful application of information technology in election campaigns favors party organizations – the collection of useful data on populous electorates.

Data on millions of citizens is costly to collect, costly to render useful, and costly to maintain over time. For these critical tasks, organizations have advantages over individuals. In recent elections, both the RNC and the DNC – particularly the DNC – toiled to collect such data. Consequently, the national party organizations have recently reasserted their roles in applying information technology to party politics, at least in the general election campaigns for U.S. president. Decentralization still reigns during the season of American presidential primaries, when candidates fight among themselves outside of the national party organization to win their party's nomination.

7. Although the trajectory of technological innovations in party politics in the United States may have parallels in other countries, my observations apply strictly to the American party system.

Nevertheless, the "Americanization" of electoral campaigns abroad suggests that the American experience will be reflected in some extent in other countries. In her study of party communications across nations, Pippa Norris contends that structural contrasts elsewhere will preclude "following a single 'American' model."[137] Although new technologies have changed campaigning for election, they did so "mainly by supplementing rather than replacing older channels." However, she also noted, "with new technologies, central campaign headquarters can now much more tightly control local activity.[138] One can expect local party leaders to oppose the centralization of power that comes from innovations in information technology.

To illustrate how local party leaders can frustrate technological innovation, I relate my own failed story of trying to computerize the Democratic Party in Cook County, Illinois. From 1955 to 1976, the City of Chicago – contained within Cook County – was second only to New York in population. Richard J. Daley served as mayor of the city and chairman of the Democratic Party throughout that time, until his death in 1976. His Cook County Democratic Party was regarded as the most powerful party organization in the nation, and stories abounded of how precisely Daley could predict, and then deliver, the Democratic vote in general elections.

---

137 Pippa Norris, "Developments in Party Communications," in *Pollitical Parties and Democracy in Theoretical and Practical Perspectives* (Washington, DC: National Democratic Institute for International Affairs, 2005), p. 21
138 *Ibid.*

On Daley's death, different people filled the positions of city major and county chairman. In 1982, the sitting mayor, Jane Byrne, helped elect a controversial alderman, Edward Vrdolyak, to be chairman of the 80-member Cook County Democratic Party Committee. The same year, my Northwestern colleague, Michael Bakalis invited me to meet with Chairman Vrdolyak to talk about computerizing the committee's files. (Bakalis had been elected to statewide offices in the 1970s as a Democrat and enjoyed close connections with the Party.)

In 1982, I met with Chairman Vrdolyak and some committeemen on several occasions, discussing what would required to adapt the central committee's files to computer processing. It soon became clear that there was almost *no* paper information at the party headquarters in the Bismarck Hotel. (If Chairman Daley really knew precisely how country citizens would vote in elections, he did not draw his information from information in party files.) The 50 city committee members and the 30 township committee members outside the city *did* have information on voters, but these 80 committeemen were not willing to provide the Chairman Vrdolyak with that information to be put in a central database. My written proposal to develop a database for the Cook County Democratic Party never got to a vote, as far as I can tell. The committeemen were not ready for innovative information technology, if it meant surrendering their control of information.

This essay began by quoting from the opening pages of Matthew Hindman's, *The Myth of Digital Democracy*. In his conclusion, Hindman reviews the state of American democracy and the abilities of online politics to improve its politics:

> The central criticisms have been remarkably consistent over the past half century – namely, that U.S. democracy fails to provide adequate representation across lines of race and class, and that it fails to bridge the gap between polity elites and the mass public.
> [...]
> In the areas where the evidence is the clearest, the Internet seems like the answer to a problem that U.S. politics did not have.[139]
> [...]
> Ultimately, then, the Internet seems to be both good news and bad news for the political voice of the average citizen. The Internet has made campaigning financing more inclusive, and allowed broad, diffuse interests to organize more easily. For motivated citizens, vast quantities of political information are only click away. Internet politics is not just politics as usual; online interests are hardly a perfect reflection of the on-line political landscape.[140]

Concerning party organizations, the impact of information technology has changed over time. When computers were large, expensive, and difficult to operate, only well-funded party organizations could afford them, so technology had a centralizing effect on party politics. As computers became small, inexpensive, and easy to use,

---

139 Hindman, The Myth of Digital Democracy, p. 141.
140 *Ibid.*, p. 142.

candidates used them to run their campaigns independently of party organizations, so technological innovations had a decentralizing effect. As the quality of the information being processed becomes increasingly important, institutional size and organizational resources matter once again. Only well-funded party institutions with professional staffs will be able to acquire, prepared, and maintain the data that lead to victories in general elections in populous countries. Does this amount to progress? It depends on the values of the observer.

Reimar Zeh and Christina Holtz-Bacha[1]

Internet, Social Media Use and Political Participation in the 2013 Parliamentary Election in Germany

Expectations were running high when the internet became available for political communication. Terms like e-democracy, e-government, e-campaigning and e-voting stand for the hopes that were associated with the new possibilities of online communication and its interactive capacities. Politicians have long embraced the internet for their communication activities by establishing their own homepages and as a platform for their advertising. The proliferation of web 2.0 and the prospect of directly linking up with citizens raised further optimism as to the political engagement of voters.

In a democracy, participation of citizens is regarded as a crucial basis for the legitimation of the representatives by the represented. Political actors are expected to inform citizens about their decisions and activities, citizens give their feedback at least by taking part in elections or by engaging in more active forms of political participation.

Studies on the use of the internet and social networking sites for political communication and particularly their role in motivating or hindering political participation have only been presented during the last 10 to 15 years. Their findings are mixed and only few studies are based on a design that allows for clear statements about causality in the case of correlations.

1 Previous Research

In a meta-analysis of research on the effects of internet use on political engagement, Boulianne (2009) identified 38 studies, which were conducted in the U.S. and were based on American respondents. Political engagement was defined in a wide sense and encompassed political and civic forms of political activity but was restricted to behaviors relating to political institutions. In general, Boulianne's findings speak for a positive relationship between internet use and political engagement; only few studies established significant negative correlations. The likelihood of positive correlations increases when the internet use measure refers to news, public affairs or campaign information. Most studies, however, do not allow for the assessment of causal direction. The differing claims about causality and the few studies that tested

1 Professors, Department of Communications, Friedrich-Alexander-Universität Erlangen-Nürnberg, Germany.

both directions lead Boulianne (2009) to suggest a reciprocal relationship where internet use motivates political engagement and vice versa.

The meta-analysis was restricted to studies using a definition of political and civic engagement that excluded political knowledge, political interest and attitudinal variables. In addition to this particular scope, the study also revealed the heterogeneity of the research, which limits the comparability, and the possibility of general conclusions. Some of the studies were done in a campaign context, others independent of electoral communication. The studies used different measures for use of the internet and for political behavior, also often lumped together in indexes and as intervening variables and were based on different samples. Finally, the studies were done at different times and thus in different stages of the development of the internet which, as Boulianne (2009) showed, can have an influence on how internet use affects political engagement.

Boulianne's (2009) meta-analysis also attributed an important role to political interest in the relationship because some studies reported that the effect of the use of the internet lost significance once political interested was entered in the analysis. In order to clarify the influence of political interest in the relationship between internet use and political activity, Boulianne (2011) used panel data from the American National Election Study (2008–2009) to examine reciprocal effects between the use of different kinds of news media (print, TV, internet) and political interest. The analysis established different patterns for the use of television news on the one side and use of print or online news on the other. In this study, respondents who were interested in politics and talked about politics with family or friends were more likely to watch the news on television, which in turn stimulated further talk about politics whereas watching TV-news did not have a direct effect on political interest. In contrast, the use of print or online news generates interest in politics that then leads to an increase in political talk. Therefore, Boulianne (2011) concludes that the use of online news stimulates political interest and increases political activity to a greater extent than it serves an instrumental function for those who are already interested in politics. Similarly, in a study that was based on data from the 2004 American National Election Study, Xenos and Moy (2007) found direct effects of internet use on basic information acquisition and thus supported the instrumental perspective. At the same time, their study revealed that results for civic and political participation and talking about politics with family and friends were contingent on levels of political interest and rather supported the psychological approach.

In her meta-analysis of previous research, Boulianne (2009) decided to concentrate on research done in the US and, besides the amount of studies, argued that the geographic focus allowed for control for exogenous variables which could have an impact on the relationship between use of the internet and political engagement: "For example, international studies would introduce differences in political culture, political institutions, and political processes related to key political behavior (e.g., voter registration process, predetermined election dates)." (Boulianne, 2009, p. 195).

That raises the question whether findings from one country can be generalized for other countries or whether there might be cultural factors intervening that prevent generalization. However, strictly comparative research that would allow for assessing the influence of (political) culture is missing. Therefore, it must be left open whether findings from the U.S. where most of the research on the relationship between internet use and political engagement was done can be translated to other countries.

In that respect, research in Germany is scarce. Whereas the development of online communication has been regularly documented thanks to the online study organized by the public broadcasting corporations ARD and ZDF (first in 1997), there is a lack of further analyses of differentiated forms of media use and how they affect political knowledge, attitudes and behavior. One exception is a longitudinal study on the consequences of the internet on political communication (Emmer, Vowe & Wolling, 2011; Emmer, Wolling & Vowe 2012; Vowe, 2014).

Based on an eight-wave panel design spanning eight years from 2002 until 2010 they examined how political communication patterns changed over time. Their analyses revealed that online communication was used much less for political purposes than the traditional news media. However, differences are decreasing over time. The study also showed that online communication for political purposes did not replace traditional political communication but rather plays a role as an addition to existing forms of political engagement. Activation effects were mostly assessed within either the online or the offline sphere whereas activities in the two spheres were mostly unrelated and only few effects occurred across the offline and the online world (Emmer, Wolling & Vowe, 2012). According to different patterns of political communication, the study identified five types of users with the 'Silent Majority' accounting for about one half of the German population and the 'Digital Citizens' who make up for about 15 %. Whereas the Silent Majority is in no way interested in politics, the Digital Citizens are characterized by above-average political interest and use of the online media for their political communication activities (Vowe, 2014, pp. 40–41).

A 2012 study on political communication of young people (22 to 35 years) came to the conclusion that, just as offline, only a minority shows political engagement online. Only 14 % ever wrote political posts, about 9 % contacted a politician but 34 % signed an online petition (Ritzi, Schaal & Kaufmann, no year). The findings also show that political engagement – online as well as offline – if at all, remains an activity of the better-educated social groups and the internet has not (yet) been effective in closing the political participation gap the high and low status groups.

Concentrating on the 2009 parliamentary election campaign, which was supposed to be the first digital campaign in Germany, Römmele and Einwiller (2012, p. 108) found that 15 % of the voting age population got into contact with the campaign through social media, four per cent posted information about the ongoing campaign in a social network. Party identification and age proved to be influential factors for actively engaging in the campaign though the social networks.

2 Online communication in Germany 2013

As in other countries, the use of the internet has increased tremendously in Germany during the last years. In 2012, more than 53 million Germans (14 years+) were online providing for a penetration rate of almost 76 %, which places Germany in the upper midrange, worldwide (Eimeren & Frees, 2013). The increase in the last years was mainly due to users in the 50+ age group making the internet a communication channel for all age groups. The two most important applications on the internet are the use of search engines (83 %) and writing and receiving e-mails (79 %). Ranking third is the targeted search for specific information (61 %) (Eimeren & Frees, 2013, p. 369). In 2012, 59 % of the online users looked for news online "frequently" or "occasionally" which represents a 13 point increase compared to 2004 (Eimeren & Frees, 2013, p. 370). While this development seems to speak for a gradual replacement of the traditional news media, data show that people preferably turn to the traditional media's websites for news delivery and only a very small population seeks news exclusively online (e.g., Hölig & Hasebrink, 2013, p. 525–526). Thus, when it comes to news, they are just changing the channel but not the source.

Whereas the internet is more and more reaching all age groups, this is not yet true for the social networking sites (SNS) which still remain attractive mostly for the younger age groups. In 2013, 46 % of the German online users (14+) also used SNS. With 87 % who use SNS at least occasionally, the age group from 14 to 19 is the most active, followed by the 80 % users in the age group from 20 to 29 while only 16 % of the oldest age group (50+) is active on SNS (Busemann, 2013). SNS, however, are overwhelmingly used for personal contacts and staying in contact with friends and families. Among SNS users, 43 % send personal mails or write posts on a daily basis, and 33 % say they follow daily what happens in their network. SNS, however, are not a channel for political engagement. Only 6 % of the SNS users look for news every day (Busemann, 2013, p. 394).

At the beginning of the 2013 election campaign there was little doubt that the party of Chancellor Merkel would end up as strongest party which would put them in the position to form the new government. The most discussed issue of the campaign therefore was, in which coalition Merkel would continue her chancellorship. With this lack of suspense, the campaign received comparably little attention of traditional media (see Leidecker & Wilke, 2014; Zeh & Schulz, 2014). Yet, the parties integrated the full scale of online media into their communication strategies. First party-websites appeared in the 1998 election, social media accounts emerged in anticipation of the European election in 2009 (Schweitzer, 2011). While party websites provided ample information on the electoral manifesto, social media and especially party tweets mostly accompanied campaign activities and signaled traditional media appearances to their followers (Dusch et al., 2014; Stärk, 2014).

Against the background of a growing importance of the Internet for campaign activities and the hope that social media in particular would enhance interest and participation, this study explores the role that online media played during the German parliamentary election campaign in 2013. It first sets out to compare the use of traditional campaign channels and the "new media" by different types of voters. In the second step, it analyses the influence of the use of different campaign channels on political participation.

To address our research questions we use data from two surveys conducted in the frame of the German Longitudinal Election Studies (GLES). GLES is a long-term project funded by the DFG (Deutsche Forschungsgemeinschaft = German Research Foundation) "to track the German electoral process over an extended period of time and at an unprecedented level of detail" (GLES, 2014). It is laid out to study voters, media and candidates for the national elections of 2009, 2014 and 2017. Both surveys that cover the weeks leading up to Election Day contain several media use indicators. The seven wave panel (ZA5704) especially looks at the contact to campaign information provided by the parties whereas the rolling-cross-sectional survey (ZA5703) provides various indicators of traditional and new media use by the voters.

3 Findings

According to the demographics of media users, we would expect the biggest impact of political internet activities among the young and the better educated. Adding to that, political interest is an important factor explaining the voters' exposition to the election campaign. First, we will look at the most important channels of campaign communication and focus on the non-mediated forms (Paletz & Vinson, 1994) as TV ads, posters, direct mailing, party websites and the partys' social media accounts. Figure 1 tracks the importance of these channels during the 2013 campaign. Clearly, the traditional forms of political advertising still have a substantial reach, compared to online media, especially during the hot phase of the campaign – the last four weeks. Cumulating the panel data, posters reach 80 % of all voters, followed by television ads. Furthermore, direct mailing, either through traditional mail, email or text messages, produces more contacts than the party websites or their social media presence. However, about one third of the electorate has visited at least one party website during the campaign. Yet, the online contacts require a certain degree of activity from the voter whereas posters, TV ads and mail come more or less unsolicited.

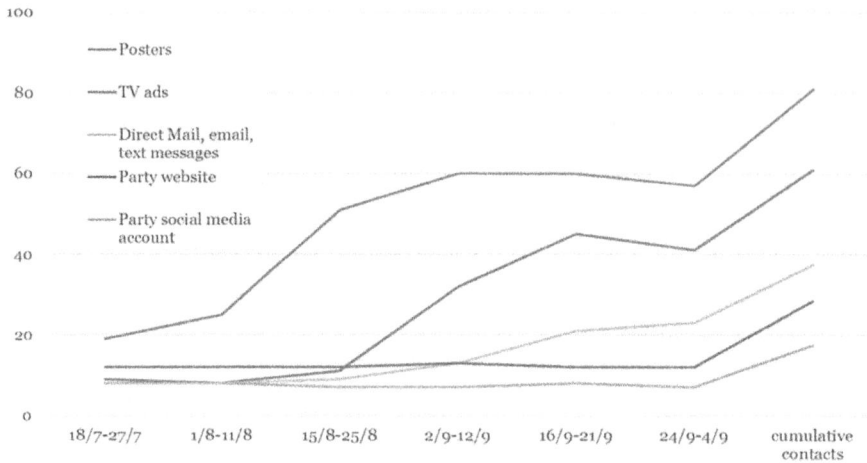

Figure 1: Contact with the election campaign
[Source: ZA5704 wave 2–7]

Certainly, the reach of these channels varies with age, education, political interest and partisanship. These factors provide for different degrees of mobilization and subsequent in different patterns of media use. Dalton's mobilization typology provides a useful tool summarizing these factors (Dalton, 1984). Schmitt-Beck and Schrott (1994) as well as Schulz (1997) demonstrated that this typology connects to different patterns in media exposure during election campaigns.[2] We therefore believe that they also connect to different patterns of online behavior. The cognitive mobilized apartisans should experience a high need for keeping up to date, which might stimulate their interest in all sources of political information. The cognitive partisans, however, should experience a lower but still substantial need for information, which may be limited to their own party. The apolitical and ritual partisans need little information, since they have already made up their mind in one way or another. Adding to that, young voters should generally prefer online information.

Table 1 summarizes the attention that the different subgroups devote to campaign information coming directly from the parties. The results for the age groups are in line with our expectations. While there are only few differences in the attention for traditional channels, information provided through the internet reaches young voters more effectively. Remarkably, there is only a small difference between the reach of party web sites and the parties' social media accounts indicating the overall importance of online media among the younger voters. Yet, the traditional channels of electoral advertising still enjoy higher penetration rates with all age

---

2 The operationalization of the typology here was adopted from Schmitt-Beck and Schrott (1994, p. 551).

groups which can be attributed to the fact that they are harder to evade than online information.

Contrary to our expectations, cognitive partisans pay more attention to campaign information disseminated by the parties than the other mobilization types. If the cognitive mobilized apartisans look for political information, they do not turn to the parties more frequently than the other groups. Therefore, party identification seems to be an important reason to turn to online information and, in addition, it increases the attention paid to classical political advertising.

Table 1: Channels of party information
[Source: ZA5704 wave 2–7]

In %	Age		Dalton's mobilization types				Total
	18–29 years	30 years and more	Apolitical	Ritual Partisan	Apartisan	Cognitive Partisan	
Posters	2	81	59	81	84	92	81
TV ads	56	62	42	66	60	72	61
Direct Mail, email, text messages	34	38	19	39	37	48	37
Party website	32	28	11	28	25	42	28
Party social media account	27	16	7	14	15	26	17
N	494	3,187	756	415	1,213	1,262	3,681

Summing up, there is little evidence that online information provided by the parties reaches voters on a large scale. Party websites and, to a lesser extent, the parties' social media accounts are preferably used by those who are already aligned to the party. Similar patterns emerge for the traditional campaign channels. Partisans pay more attention to or retain more information from political ads than non-partisans. On the other hand, especially the apartisans, the mobile and well-informed voters, also look for information cues offside party channels. In this respect, another dataset from the GLES-Survey provides more detailed information on media use during the last weeks before Election Day.

The rolling-cross-sectional survey comprises a daily sample of about 100 respondents. Media consumption is measured on a days-per-week scale. Thus, the measures are not directly comparable with the results from the GLES election panel

but the relations between the different channels and types of voters can nevertheless be compared.

As expected, young voters use the internet nearly on a daily basis (see Table 2).
Since this measure encompasses all only activities from online shopping, chatting,
gaming to writing emails, it only partially grasps the importance of the internet as a
source of political information. Here traditional news media still dominate even
among the young voters. In comparison with the older age group, they show a
slightly higher exposure to newspapers and television news from ARD, which is
Germany's oldest public service channel. Their use of other news media shows no
difference to the population average. On top of that, the young do not talk about
politics less frequently than the rest of the electorate. Again, the cognitive partisans
show a slightly higher interest in political information from offline and online
sources and they are slightly more expressive since they talk more about politics
than the apartisans.

Independent of their partisanship, voters with a low cognitive mobilization
show higher interest in news delivered by the commercial television channels and
from Germany's leading tabloid newspaper BILD. They do not talk much about politics and show little interest in online media.

Table 2: General media consumption
[Source: ZA5703]

Days per week	Age		Dalton's mobilization types				Total
	18–29 years	30 years and more	Apolitical	Ritual Partisan	Apartisan	Cognitive Partisan	
Tabloid (BILD)	0.5	0.5	0.7	0.8	0.5	0.5	0.5
Broadsheets	2.4	4.0	3.1	3.9	3.9	4.3	3.9
ARD	3.1	4.8	4.3	4.9	4.7	4.9	4.6
ZDF	0.6	2.3	1.5	2.3	2.1	2.4	2.1
RTL	0.8	0.8	1.1	1.2	0.7	0.7	0.8
SAT.1	0.2	0.3	0.4	0.4	0.2	0.2	0.2
General internet use	6.5	4.3	3.0	2.7	5.0	5.0	4.5
Internet as new source	2.2	1.7	0.6	1.0	1.8	2.1	1.7
Social media use	1.2	0.3	0.3	0.2	0.4	0.4	0.4
Conversation about politics	1.6	1.6	0.7	1.2	1.7	1.9	1.6
N	794	6,907	1,106	586	2,926	2,584	7,701

Regardless of the quantitative dominance of traditional news, online information is an integral part of campaign communication. Although a lot of news coming from the internet in general and from SNS in particular originates from traditional media outlets – often disseminated through their websites, effects of online communication on political participation cannot be ruled out. The survey data provide two indicators of political participation: the frequency of talking about politics with friends, relatives and colleagues as reported here in Table 2 and, of course, the intention to cast a vote measured on a five-point probability scale.

The impact of media exposure on participation is assessed by two regression models. Socio-demographics are introduced as control variables as well as the number of days until Election Day. The two participation measures that are used as dependent variables are related with each other and are therefore also entered as independents in the model for the respective other variable. The set of daily media exposure measures represent the third set of independent variables. Political interest is not used here as a regressor variable for technical reasons. Already media use and political participation show a high level of multicollinearity that can still be limited by standardizing the variables. Political interest, however, is highly correlated with all other measures and therefore pushes the degree of multicollinearity above tolerable boundaries. Yet, since we assume that the interplay between interest in politics and internet use has an additional effect on our measures for participation, we introduce the interaction effects between political interest and the exposure to online communication in the second step of the regression models.

Results are shown in Table 3. Overall, talking about politics with others is better explained by the independent variables than voting intention. A significant but yet low impact of media exposure emerges for both participation measures. As was expected, age and education influence the dependent variables positively whereas gender has no noteworthy impact. Even running the regressions separately for women and men reveals no noteworthy different patterns (models not reported here).

The closer the election comes, the more people talk about politics. This is of course an effect of the rising visibility of the campaign and increasing media events like debates and special programs on television as Election Day approaches. According to the standardized regression weights, the proximity of the election is the most influential factor on the disposition to talk about politics with others, whereas the impact on the voting intention is comparatively small. The participation variables also exert a minor but still significant positive influence on each other, which disappears though as soon as the interaction effects are entered into the model. All media indicators except for tabloid readership and viewing commercial news have a positive influence on the frequency of political conversation. Interestingly, the use of online news is the strongest media predictor followed by newspaper reading. Adding to that, the impact of television news is relatively small. Those who tend to talk about politics with others get their information preferably online or from newspapers. Newspaper reading also appears to be an important factor in raising the inclination to vote as well as watching the news on the public TV channel ARD. People's motivation to cast their vote on Election Day is affected neither by general internet consumption nor by social media activity.

Notably watching the news on the commercial channel SAT.1 reduces the intention to vote. It is, however, open for discussion whether it is the content of the news show that is to be blamed for the decrease of political participation or rather lack of political interest that stands behind the correlation. Yet again, entering political interest into the regression model would wipe out all effects due to the enhancement of multicollinearity.

Table 3: OLS regressions on political participation
[Source: ZA5703]

	Dependent: Conversation about politics Standardized beta weights		Dependent: Probability to cast a vote Standardized beta weights	
Controls	1. Step	2. Step	1. Step	2. Step
Days to election day	0.22 ***	0.22 ***	0.06 ***	0.07 ***
Age	0.07 ***	0.06 **	0.05 **	0.04 *
Gender (female=1)	0.03	0.03 *	0.01	0.02
Education	0.07 ***	0.07 ***	0.09 ***	0.08 ***
Political Participation				
Probability to cast a vote	0.03 *	0.02	n.a.	n.a.
Conversation about politics	n.a.	n.a.	0.03 *	0.02

	Dependent: Conversation about politics Standardized beta weights		Dependent: Probability to cast a vote Standardized beta weights	
Media Consumption				
Tabloid use	0.01	0.01	0.02	0.02
Broadsheet use	0.14 ***	0.14 ***	0.09 ***	0.08 ***
ARD TV news	0.05 **	0.05 **	0.07 ***	0.06 **
ZDF TV news	0.09 ***	0.09 ***	0.02	0.02
RTL TV news	0.02	0.02	-0.02	-0.02
SAT.1 TV news	0.00	0.00	-0.05 **	-0.05 **
General internet use	0.04 **	0.04 **	0.01	0.01
Social media use	0.09 ***	0.10 ***	-0.01	-0.03
News from the internet	0.15 ***	0.16 ***	0.04 *	0.09 ***
Interaction effects				
General internet use X political interest		0.08 ***		0.07 ***
Social media use X political interest		0.01		-0.04 *
News from the internet X political interest		-0.04 **		-0.13 ***
N	4,586		4,586	
F	72.59 ***	61.96 ***	18.64 ***	16.66 ***
R²	0.18	0.18	0.05	0.06
Durbin-Watson		2.03		2.00
Max VIF	1.55	1.66	1.55	1.68

* p < 0.05; ** p < 0.01; *** p < 0.001

Does information behavior interact with political interest? It can be assumed that the positive impact of news consumption is stronger among those with a high degree of political interest or, put the other way round, no matter how much news is consumed by the political disinterested, it would not promote political participation. In order to test these assumptions interaction terms of political interest with the three online media use variables were introduced into the regression models. The interaction terms have virtually no impact on the explanatory power for the frequency of talking about politics with others, but still two of the three effects show statistically significant regression weights. Furthermore, they partially contradict our expectations. One the one hand and as was expected, the positive impact of general internet exposure is amplified by a rise in political interest. On the other hand, the interaction term for internet news consumption is negative which indicates a decrease of the impact on the dependent variable (political conversation) through growing political interest. A similar pattern is found in the regression model for the likeliness to vote: The interaction effect for general internet use is positive whereas the interaction terms for internet news and social media activity are negative. Overall, the interaction effects for voting intention are stronger and therefore improve the model considerably. In addition, the negative interaction effect for internet news and political interest proves to be the strongest regressor in the equation.

The interpretation of the findings comes with two caveats. First, technically speaking, the introduction of interaction terms requires the inclusion of the involved variables, which in this case is not possible for political interest as was explained above. Secondly, we do not know precisely how the interaction effects are constituted. As well as reducing political participation among the highly political interested, a negative interaction effect could also mean an increase political participation through media exposure among the political disinterested. There is some evidence, that getting news form the internet increases the probability to vote among the disinterested, while the effect among the interested shows no linear pattern.

Since online media are far more integrated into the everyday life of the younger generation, we assume that the mobilizing effects of media differ from those among the older voters. Using age as a control variable would not reveal these different patterns, two separate models were calculated for the two age groups with the first group encompassing voters from 18–29 years, the second 30 years and older (Table 4). Remarkably, the use of television has no mobilizing effects on younger voters and the significant effects of online media are generally stronger for the young age group than for the older voters. To a certain extent this reflects the dramatic decline in television consumption which is no longer the medium of the young generation. Despite the overall decrease in newspaper readership, reading broadsheets still has a mobilizing effect. In general, the two models display a better fit for the younger age group, indicating more residual, habitualised mobilization among older voters. That means that political participation is less influenced by external factors that are variable in the short run – like political communication through old and new media.

Among the young social media uses seems to stimulate political conversation. The way in which political conversations are measured leaves additional room for interpretation, since it does not differentiate between online and offline conversations. In this line of thinking, conversations about politics can be a part of social media activity – technically rendering the relationship between the two variables tautological.

Table 4: OLS regressions on political participation split by age groups
[Source: ZA5703]

	Dependent: Conversation about politics Standardized beta weights		Dependent: Probability to cast a vote Standardized beta weights	
Controls	18–29 years	30 years and over	18–29 years	30 years and over
Days to election day	0.26 ***	0.22 ***	0.02	0.07 ***
Age	-0.10 ***	0.09 ***	0.11 **	0.02
Gender (female=1)	0.03	0.04 *	0.10 *	0.01
Education	-0.05	0.07 ***	0.13 **	0.07 ***
Political Participation				
Probability to cast a vote	0.06	0.02	n.a.	n.a.
Conversation about politics	n.a.	n.a.	0.07	0.02
Media Consumption				
Tabloid use	-0.02	0.01	-0.02	0.02
Broadsheet use	0.18 ***	0.12 ***	0.09 *	-0.08 ***
ARD TV news	0.04	0.04 *	0.02	-0.06 **
ZDF TV news	0.00	0.09 ***	0.02	-0.02
RTL TV news	0.05	0.02	-0.06	-0.02
SAT.1 TV news	-0.06	0.01	-0.07	-0.05 **
General internet use	0.02	0.04 **	0.07	0.01
Social media use	0.15 ***	0.08 ***	-0.01	-0.03
News from the internet	0.13 ***	0.16 ***	0.07	0.08 ***
Interaction effects				
General internet use X political interest	0.13 *	0.07 ***	0.23 ***	0.05 **
Social media use X political interest	0.06	-0.03	0.03	0.03
News from the internet X political interest	-0.05	-0.04 *	-0.16 *	-0.12 ***
N	489	4,096	489	4,096
F	11.70 ***	51.13 ***	6.55 ***	14.09 ***
R²	0.27	0.18	0.16	0.05
Durbin-Watson	1.93	2.01	2.05	1.99
Max VIF	1.82	1.72	1.55	1.68

* p < 0.05; ** p < 0.01; *** p < 0.001

4 Conclusion

Parties and their candidates are well represented in the online world. Maintaining a website and feeding social media accounts with current information became an integral part of election campaigning. Whether it remains a channel of communication outside elections campaigns is another question. On top of that political actors (like most corporations and enterprises as well) use social media, like they used web pages and like they use traditional media – to disseminate (campaign) information. The interactive, discursive potential of the social media remains largely unused.

Our analysis shows – once again – that traditional media still matter. Among the communication channels that parties employ to address their voters directly, posters and spots dominate. Even among young voters there are no signs (yet) that online media are more successful in terms of reach. Taken into account that German parties are granted free access to airtime for their spots on public television and that the production costs especially for audiovisual material are similar for traditional and online media, online media are also less effective in economic terms.

Hopes that parties could increasingly bypass journalistic gatekeepers through websites or social media accounts to reach for new strata of voters are not fulfilled: The few who make use of online media are chiefly partisans. Adding to that, even though the internet is increasingly an important news source – among the young the most important news source – the traditional gatekeepers are not losing power. People turn to the well-established media brands also in the online world when looking for news. Thus technically the internet so far as not much more than an additional line of dissemination for the same information.

The second research question addressed the participatory gain of online and social media. Although traditional media still matter here as well, our analyses show that online information and to a certain extent social media activity foster political talk and the willingness to vote independently. Again, the argument that traditional and online media are quite the same concerning the content applies, but the respondents see a difference between them as the regression models suggest. We can therefore only speculate that reading or watching the news online might be more engaging then reading it on paper or watching on a proper television set.

References

Boulianne, S. (2009). Does Internet use affect engagement? A meta-analysis of research. *Political Communication, 26*(2), 193–211. doi: 10.1080/10584600902854363

Boulianne, S. (2011). Stimulating or reinforcing political interest: Using panel data to examine reciprocal effects between news media and political interest. *Political Communication, 28*(2), 147–162. doi: 10.1080/10584609.2010.540305

Busemann, K. (2013). Wer nutzt was im Social Web? Ergebnisse der ARD/ZDF-Onlinestudie 2013. *Media Perspektiven*, 391–399.

Dusch, A., Gerbig, S., Lake, M., Lorenz, S., Pfaffenberger, F. & Schulze, U. (2014, in print). Post, reply retweet – Einsatz und Resonanz von Twitter im Bundestagswahlkampf. In C. Holtz-Bacha (Ed.), *Massenmedien und Wahlen. Die Bundestagswahl 2013*. Wiesbaden: Springer VS.

Eimeren, B. v. & Frees, B. (2013). Rasanter Anstieg des Internetkonsums – Onliner fast drei Stunden täglich im Netz. *Media Perspektiven, 7–8*, 358–372.

Emmer, M., Vowe, G. & Wolling, J. (2011). *Bürger Online. Die Entwicklung der politischen Online-Kommunikation in Deutschland*. Konstanz: UVK.

Emmer, M., Wolling, J. & Vowe, G. (2012). Changing political communication in Germany: Findings from a longitudinal study on the influence of the internet on political information, discussion and the participation of citizens. *Communications: The European Journal of Communication Research, 37(3)*, 233–252. doi: 10.1515/commun-2012-0013

Hölig, S. & Hasebrink, U. (2013). Nachrichtennutzung in konvergierenden Medienumgebungen. International vergleichende Befunde auf Basis des Reuters Institute Digital News Survey 2013. *Media Perspektiven, (11)*, 522–536.

Leidecker, M. & Wilke, J. (2014, in print). Langweilig? Wieso langweilig? Die Presseberichterstattung zur Bundestagswahl 2013 im Langzeitvergleich. In C. Holtz-Bacha (Ed.), *Massenmedien und Wahlen. Die Bundestagswahl 2013*. Wiesbaden: Springer VS.

Paletz, D. L. & Vinson, C. D. (1994). Mediatisierung von Wahlkampagnen. Zur Rolle der amerikanischen Medien bei Wahlen. *Media Perspektiven, (7)*, 362–368.

Ritzi, C., Schaal, G. S. & Kaufmann, V. (no year). *Zwischen Ernst und Unterhaltung – Eine empirische Analyse der Motive politischer Aktivität junger Erwachsener im Internet*. Hamburg: Helmut-Schmidt-Universität/Universität der Bundeswehr.

Römmele, A. & Einwiller, S. (2012). Soziale Medien in der Bundestagswahl 2009. *Zeitschrift für Parlamentsfragen, 43*, 103–113.

Schmitt-Beck, R. & Schrott, P. R. (1994). Dealignment durch Massenmedien? In H.-D. Klingemann & M. Kaase (Eds.), *Wahlen und Wähler. Analysen aus Anlaß der Bundestagswahl 1990* (pp. 543–572). Opladen: Westdeutscher Verlag.

Schulz, W. (1998). Wahlkampf unter Vielkanalbedingungen. Kampagnenmanagement, Informationsnutzung und Wählerverhalten. *Media Perspektiven, 2*, 378–391.

Schweitzer, E.J. (2011). Mediatisierung im Online-Wahlkampf: Befunde einer vergleichenden Inhaltsanalyse deutscher Partei-Websites zu den Wahljahren 2002–2009. In E. J. Schweitzer & S. Albrecht (Eds.), *Das Internet im Wahlkampf*, Wiesbaden: VS Verlag für Sozialwissenschaften.

Stärk, M.-T. (2014, in print). Der Wahlkampf im Internet. Eine Analyse deutscher Parteiwebsites zur Bundestagswahl 2013. In C. Holtz-Bacha (Ed.), *Massenmedien und Wahlen. Die Bundestagswahl 2013*. Wiesbaden: Springer VS.

Vowe, G. (2014). Digital Citizens und Schweigende Mehrheit: Wie verändert sich die politische Beteiligung der Bürger durch das Internet? Ergebnisse einer kommunikationswissenschaftlichen Langzeitstudie. In K. Voss (Ed.), *Internet und Partizipation. Bottom-up oder Top-down? Politische Beteiligungsmöglichkeiten im Internet*. Wiesbaden: Springer VS.

Xenos, M. & Moy, P. (2007). Direct and differential effects of the Internet on political and civic engagement. *Journal of Communication, 57*, 704–718.

Zeh, R. & Schulz, W. (2014, in print). TV-Nachrichten über Kanzlerkandidaten. Die Trends seit 1990. In C. Holtz-Bacha (Ed.), *Massenmedien und Wahlen. Die Bundestagswahl 2013*. Wiesbaden: Springer VS.

Part II: **The Consequences of New Technologies on Activism**

Eric Montigny[1]

The Decline of Activism in Political Parties: Adaptation Strategies and New Technologies

Political parties continue to fulfil the functions of selecting political leaders, formulating policies and mobilizing voters and thus remain key actors in the democratic process. They have been the subject of a great many critiques, though. Some observers have discussed the prospect of their disappearing as parties of activists (Katz & Mair, 1995) (Bardi et al., 2014) (van Biezen & Poguntke, 2014). Others have seen the political party becoming just one of several vehicles for representing interests as democracy undergoes a profound transformation. (Diamond & Gunther, 2001). Parties would still, however, retain the essential democratic functions of selecting leaders, structuring electoral alternatives and organizing the government. Clearly, though, changes are taking place within parties that affect not only their internal democracy but the role and place accorded to activism, as well.

Neither Canadian federal nor Quebec provincial parties have been immune to these trends. For many years now, they have been undergoing significant internal change as activism has declined and new technologies have emerged to offset this shift. These changes have had a major impact, particularly on the parties' internal democratic life, on the way they are financed and on the way they organize election campaigns. In light of these developments, one might well ask whether the traditional political activist is an endangered species.

The decline in activism is due to a number of factors. First, there is a natural tendency to centralization within parties. Second, parties must contend with a prevailing climate of distrust towards the political class and partisan activity. Third, parties have to deal with new competition from other types of engagement; many people prefer to advance their convictions through different organizations that better reflect their ideals, such as interest groups promoting specific issues or social movements. While the species is thus in decline, transformations are taking place in the role activists play within parties and in the factors that motivate them.

Our objective here is not so much to explain the precise causes of this decline as to outline its consequences for the way parties operate. The change tends to favour greater centralization of power in the hands of the leadership, but it also presents parties with a number of organizational challenges: How are they to achieve the same partisan ends with fewer activists? How are they to mobilize voters with fewer volunteers? What are the effects on relations between the party leadership and the activists?

---

1 Professor, Department of Political Science, Université Laval, Canada.

To answer these questions, we shall start by describing the different forms party activism currently takes and the decline that has been observed. With this contextual information, we shall draw up an inventory of the adaptation strategies that parties have adopted to court the electorate, mobilize sympathizers, obtain financing, and maintain or develop their organization.

As political staffs have become professionalized, new technologies have become crucially important adaptation strategies for parties. We shall accordingly attempt to identify the new technological means parties use to mobilize voters, communicate with their sympathizers and raise funds. We shall conclude with a brief discussion of the strengths and limitations of these tools.

1 The decline of activism and the shift to new forms of engagement

For some years now, numerous studies have sought to explain the decline in voter participation (Gélineau & Teyssier, 2012). Far less research has been conducted on the decline in traditional activism in political parties. Yet, it seems logical to connect the two phenomena. In Canada, investigators have noted a decline in party identification (Crête & Blais, 2013). Clearly, there should be association between the downward trend in participation and a major drop in the propensity of voters to belong to a political family. Logically, if the pool of voters shrinks and the number of people identifying with a party falls, a smaller pool of voters will be available – and interested enough in political life – to get actively involved in or join a party. Given that young people vote less than their elders, the problem of recruiting a new generation of activists becomes critical, too.

Is this phenomenon a reflection of a crisis of confidence in political institutions? In a 2012 Quebec poll[2], more than half the respondents felt that political parties are all alike and there is really nothing to choose among them. Another study found that trust in political parties has also fallen (Pelletier & Couture, 2012). Federally, it dropped from 34.3 % in 2005 to 26.1% in 2010. In Quebec, the change was even more marked with a decline of 43.1 % to 28.6 %. Political parties have tried to adapt to this growing cynicism, notably by more specifically targeting their potential voters and using negative advertising more.

Researchers have sought to determine the profile of political activists who join a Canadian federal party. It turns out that few people actually do join. A few years ago, 16 % of Canadians said they had already worked actively for a federal party,

---

2 CROP poll conducted for the *Indice citoyen des institutions* of Université Laval's Chaire de recherche sur la démocratie et les institutions parlementaires.

but fewer than 2 % said they had joined one (Howe & Northrup, 2002). The vast majority thus tend not to be active within the political party they support. Nor are activists representative of the population as a whole. According to Cross and Young (2004), the standard profile is as follows: male, older, university educated, and Canadian born. Very few young people are thus involved. All in all, people devote little time to activism, and new members devote even less. In addition, most members do not think their engagement has a decisive impact on party policies (Cross & Young, 2004). In this light, party renewal and the future of traditional party activism face challenges of great complexity and significance.

Quéniart and Jacques (2001) found traditional party activism to be changing into a sort of "multi-activism." The data they gathered from young, politically active women in Quebec point to new forms of engagement. Their activism tends focus on supporting a particular cause rather than the full range of ideas espoused by a political party. The implication, then, is that party loyalty is much more tenuous and based primarily on a specific issue. Moreover, involvement is thus not limited to a party but extends as well to interest groups and movements concerned with the issue.

In Quebec, chang es in the Parti Québécois (PQ) illustrate the same trend. The PQ, which was originally seen as a party of ideas, has gradually changed into a party concerned with power. This transformation was reflected in the evolving motivations of PQ activists (Montigny, 2011). By 2003, more than two out of three were working primarily to have their party form the government. Barely 16 % were involved because of their ideas. Similarly, in the British Labour Party, "[w]hilst in the past experienced activists were keen to attend conference to participate in negotiations about composites and then debates on an activist-driven agenda, places were increasingly taken by those members happy to play a more passive role" (Russell, 2005: 204).

It should be noted that political parties are generally reluctant to provide a full description of their activist base. It is therefore hard to come to an accurate assessment of the decline they have experienced. In Quebec, though, two indicators in the data provided by the Chief Electoral Officer (*Directeur général des elections*) can be used to track changes in activism over time: number of donations and income from membership dues[3]. Thus, from 1994 to 2012, the number of donations received by the Parti Québécois, a party with a well-known tradition of broad-based fundraising, fell markedly from 83,000 to 23,000. Contributions to the Parti Libéral du Québec also fell, but not as sharply.

---

3 Except for the CAQ which charges no membership dues.

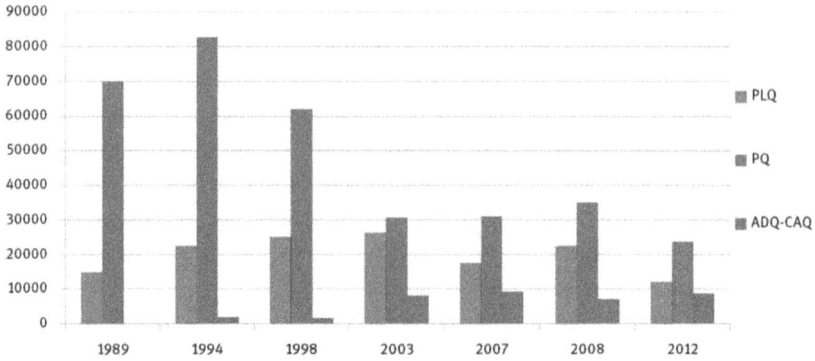

Figure 1: Changes in number of donations – PLQ, PQ & ADQ-CAQ
[Source: Annual reports of the DGEQ]

Membership dues have also fallen, though less steeply. The PQ peaked in 1981 with $1.4 million, and the PLQ topped out in 1985 at close to $1 million. In 2012, the PQ collected $326,000 and the PLQ $473,000.

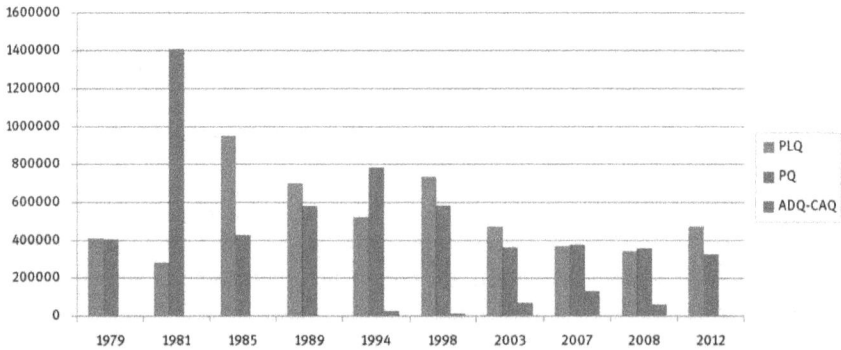

Figure 2: Changes in income from membership dues – PLQ, PQ and ADQ-CAQ
[Source: Annual reports of the DGEQ]

The decline in activism has been accompanied by a change in the very nature of political engagement. The motivations driving activism in the established parties have been becoming rather more pragmatic than ideological. The duties assigned to activists are changing, too, and assuming new forms. These changes have had somewhat paradoxical results internally for the parties. All the federal and Quebec provincial parties have changed their statutes to provide for the leader to be selected by the members, thus giving activists greater prominence. This trend towards open leadership selection is by no means insignificant. Selection procedures, once the preserve of party elites and then of convention delegates, are evolving into a system of primaries. While votes have generally been closed and restricted to members, the Liberal Party of Canada opened up the process more in 2013, when Justin Trudeau was chosen, by allowing sympathizers who were not members to take part. The Liberals thus opened the door wider to eventually holding American-style primaries.

Several indicators thus point to a decline in traditional party activism and a shift towards new forms of engagement. Meanwhile, parties are trying to develop new ways of operating to mask this decline, particularly with respect to the selection of the leader. When all is said and done, though, parties have been left with fewer members, fewer activists and fewer donors. The members they do have are also older and so, in the final analysis, less available to carry out tasks that used to be performed by volunteers; it is simply harder for older people to go canvassing door to door or to hang posters.

2 Adaptation strategies

Political parties are trying to adapt to this new reality. There is even discussion of them as "franchise systems," on the model of commercial enterprises, with the centre offering local organizations the tools and services they need to conduct campaigns (Carty, 2004). To win elections, parties and candidates require several different types of resources that in the past were essentially provided by volunteers. The three principal ones are: 1) financing, 2) advertising and 3) identifying potential voters for election day. Changes have occurred on all three of these fronts.

Paradoxically, while the number of donors has declined, election campaigns have become increasingly professionalized and, consequently, increasingly costly. Professionalization involves both a greater role for communications specialists and intensive use of survey and research data. These changes, taken together with a background discourse about the need to fight corruption, can result in increased state funding. Thus in Quebec, the passage of Bill 2 in 2012 reduced the maximum allowable contribution by a voter to a party to $100. To compensate for this decrease, the legislation substantially raised state funding based on the number of votes a party receives. Federally, though, the Conservative Party in power has traditionally been able to raise more funds from donors than its main opponents. It therefore sees a comparative advantage in reducing state funding for political parties and in 2011 accordingly passed a law to provide for its gradual abolition.

Changes have taken place with regard to election advertising as well. The larger parties now employ professional firms to put up election posters, a task previously performed by volunteers. They have also centralized the supply of advertising. Depending on their budgets, candidates, like franchisees, can select from publicity options provided by head office. They can access a range of advertising products and adapt them to their means. This practice has existed since the 1970s and so is hardly new. Over time, it has helped centralize campaigns and promote a unified message. In this regard, social media constitute a new space affording activists a measure of freedom of action.

Meanwhile, the identification of potential voters remains a crucial element in political parties' election efforts, especially in a context of falling voter participation. Indeed, the need to canvass and identify supporters and to get out the vote on election day can only be greater since each vote weighs more and can make a real difference in the final outcome. However, political parties no longer have the human resources they used to have to accomplish this work.

When party identification was stronger, local organizations could rely on back-of-the-envelope calculations by their canvassers, especially in rural areas. Village and neighbourhood organizers knew the local population and could be asked how they thought people would vote. Twenty years ago, when there were enough volunteers to accomplish the task, parties favoured systematic door-to-door canvassing. Such an exercise depends on having a large number of volunteers criss-crossing a constituency to contact the voters in person in their home. This approach is considered to be most effective because it allows canvassers to gauge voters' nonverbal reactions. About ten years ago, ageing memberships led parties to start turning to telephone canvassing with volunteers calling each voter on the electoral list to find out whom he or she supports. This strategy has the advantage of requiring fewer workers than going door-to-door while enabling older people to participate. The constant decline in the number of activists has meant that even this task has become harder to carry out, though, leading parties to adopt automated tools to perform it.

In short, in terms of human resources, parties are trying to make do without activists but achieve the same results. Unable to raise enough money from donors, they have turned to the state. For visibility, publicity and communication, they have turned to professionals. To canvass voters, they have turned to automated tools. Parties are increasingly trying to make up for the decline in traditional activism by the targeted use of new technologies. These changes have had an impact, particularly on the internal life of political organizations.

3 The effects of new technologies

The decline of traditional activism has changed the way parties operate on both the organizational and communications levels. New technologies have been enlisted to make up in part for the lack of volunteers. However, the technologies can in turn substantially change the internal dynamics of parties, the role reserved to activists and, consequently, what motivates people to become activist members. More specifically, we can discern four processes at work in relation to the new technologies: 1) the growth of Web strategies, 2) the use of databases (big data) in more targeted political operations, 3) the redefinition of the concept of the member, and 4) the changing role of local organizations.

Web strategies. With every election, parties further refine their Web strategies and increasingly incorporate social media into their national strategies. The range of Web strategies is still rather limited in Canada, though, and parties use them primarily for information, recruitment and fundraising purposes (Giasson et al, 2013). Originally, Canadian and Quebec political parties saw the Web as a tool for making information accessible to voters. This more passive approach left it to voters to take the first step and visit a website or make a donation online if they wished. For a number of years now, parties have been utilizing the Web in a much more proactive fashion: for example, by using social media for political positioning and connecting with supporters.

There are several advantages to using social media such as Facebook and Twitter for political purposes. Messages can be disseminated unfiltered by traditional media, undistorted by any intermediary. Large numbers of voters can be contacted at less cost than through traditional advertising campaigns. In addition, messages can be targeted to specific categories of voters, for example, with original content that may go viral on the Internet. Lastly, social media allow parties to create a true virtual community of supporters; they may ultimately even become a true instrument for mobilization. Still, social networks suffer from certain limitations and pose certain risks. To begin with, it is important not to confuse the virtual world with the real world. Few voters are comfortable with social media, and the ones who are are not representative of society as a whole. One sometimes has the impression that a social network is a sort of bubble, an enclosed world all its own in which party supporters engage in discussions with each other, and no one's opinion is changed. In addition, and paradoxically, while parties are increasing their efforts to centralize and control the message, the advent of social media has heightened the risk that gaffes will occur. Indeed, a single click can drastically change the dynamics of a day on the campaign. Moreover, social media accelerate political debate and the pace of attacks. They also increase the number of actors involved: candidates, activists and members of the political staff. In Quebec, the advent of more intensive Web strategies has substantively affected parties in three ways.

First, parties tend to use social networks to frame issues in order to define both themselves and their opponents. Although this strategy has limited reach among voters, it connects parties with opinion leaders, especially journalists. The exercise is even more effective when party leaders engage in it directly; it helps shape their image while they hammer home the core themes of their political message. The hope is, of course, that the traditional media will pass the message on.

Secondly, since the costs are low, the use of the Web makes it easier for parties to engage in more negative advertising. At the federal level, since the middle of the last decade, the Conservative Party has employed negative advertising on the Internet to attack its rivals without having to incur high costs. The Conservatives use the Web aggressively, particularly in English, to ascribe negative traits to leaders of other parties. In the 2012 Quebec elections, the PLQ notably adopted this strategy against the PQ leader, portraying her as a street demonstrator and thus in no way a head a government. Because it costs so little and because, when properly executed, it is so effective in defining an adversary, negative advertising is liable to become an increasingly prominent feature of the Canadian political landscape.

Thirdly, the use of the Web raises the issue of party activists on social media. Social networks provide activists with a much larger arena for discussing issues than formal party structures do. The following question then arises: Does tweeting constitute activism? There is as yet no obvious answer. Activist engagement on Twitter and Facebook has so far had only a marginal impact on partisan mobilization and policy development. One often has the impression that social-media activities essentially involve passing on information to people who have already made up their mind or are already supporters. In any event, parties cannot ignore social networks, and they plan to use activists to develop an increasingly structured and concerted presence on them.

More targeted political action. Parties must rely on new technologies in their internal operations in order to mobilize their members. They will accordingly build up substantial databases to allow them to reach out to particular categories of voters with more targeted messages. These databases must include information about individuals' socio-economic characteristics and political preferences. Currently, very little use is made of such instruments on the Quebec scene; however, some federal parties, particularly the Conservative Party of Canada, do employ them.

Internal communications instruments have been developed to connect exclusively with members and sympathizers in order to share organizational information and election-campaign tools, such as policy arguments. These instruments also enable parties to conduct targeted fundraising in relation to specific issues that can galvanize segments of the membership. In the Conservative Party of Canada, for example, selected members might receive a request based on their support for a specific policy. Endeavours of this sort imply, of course, that parties use the Web to poll their members and keep their preferences on file in their database.

In elections, the technology makes it possible for parties to target voters, contact particular segments of the population more easily, and design their advertising and electoral commitments accordingly. To do so, parties must do what commercial enterprises do and, again, acquire large databases. In the long run, this practice threatens the traditional role of activists in determining policy.

Parties run the risk, though, of reinforcing a long-standing trend for their conventions to become mere stages from which they broadcast their policies rather than forums for democratic debate. The traditional role of activists in drawing up the party program is thus being transformed. Instead of contributing on different levels to the formulation of policy, activists are becoming "extras" who more likely to be called upon to fill a hall and applaud their leader than to share their ideas.

Redefinition of the concept of the member. The technology makes it possible to open up the candidate-selection process, especially in leadership contests. Indeed, new ways of handling these matters over the Internet or by telephone are spreading in Canada, firstly, because they are less expensive than traditional conventions and, secondly, because in democratic terms, they give the maximum number of people an opportunity to vote for the candidate of their choice. At the same time, however, they are making the very concept of membership more porous.

Traditionally, individuals could join a political party for a minimal fee every year and then exercise a member's privileges in its internal democratic life. They could play a role in selecting the candidate in their constituency, hold office in various party bodies, participate directly or indirectly in electing the leader, and put their own name forward as candidates. Members could also take part in policy conventions to draw up the party program and receive information through internal communications.

However, in Quebec and elsewhere, party membership is in definite decline. As we have seen from the data compiled by Quebec's Chief Electoral Officer, income from membership dues is falling. Some parties have adopted strategies to reverse the trend. In the middle of the last decade, the Parti Québécois sought to renew itself by offering free membership cards to young people. In the Coalition Avenir Québec, membership cards are free and are sent to applicants over the Web for them to print. None of these tactics can compare, though, to the British Conservative Party's ploy of creating a "loyalty program" that entitles members who present their card to discounts in certain stores.

There are two types of strategies that parties may follow in trying to adapt to the decline in membership and maintain their legitimacy. The first aims to make joining more accessible. The second seeks to graft the concept of sympathizer onto the notion of member in order to boost the number of people on its voters' list, for the number is always made public during party leadership races.

In the Liberal Party of Canada, sympathizers who registered online acquired the same right to vote as members have. This development is liable to be imitated by other political parties and would tend to lead to the introduction of open primaries. Whether one is or is not a member thus becomes less and less important for an activity that lies at the very heart of democratic life in a party. At the same time, though, opening up the party in this way allows it to claim greater democratic legitimacy.

The changing role of local organizations. In elections, the advent of robocalls and computerized electoral lists is bringing about significant changes in the organization of election committees. At election time the main duty of party activists used to be identifying supporters; similar tasks can now be executed with increasingly effective automated systems. In addition, the technology makes it possible to establish national databases that parties can use to develop targeted strategies for different electoral clienteles.

The shortage of activists and the advent of reasonably priced technologies provide ample reason to believe that robocalls are here to stay. They are being utilized more and more by local and national party organizations and are having effects in a number of areas.

These effects are being felt in terms of election regulations. As with all new technologies, there is always a risk they will be used improperly, particularly when they first start out. At the federal level in 2011 and the municipal level in Montreal in 2013, a number of candidates consequently landed in hot water. Regulatory authorities have had to adapt in order to manage the expanding use of digital devices for mass telephone calls. Parties now hire specialized companies to handle the work; in the municipal elections in Montreal in 2013, one company worked for two different parties.

In terms of party membership, the new technologies mean that parties have less and less need of activists for their grassroots work. Internally, a new dynamic is emerging. The fall in activist numbers means parties must employ new technologies, and the new technologies mean parties rely less on activists to perform vital duties. This spiraling trend reinforces tendencies to greater internal centralization in parties and to the professionalization of election campaigns.

In policy terms, increased recourse to robocalls makes it possible for parties to build up more databases with more accurate information on issues that concern voters with particular socio-demographic profiles. These databases allow parties to target segments of the electorate in relation to specific policies. The question that now comes to mind is: What use will members then be in organizing elections?

4 Discussion

Is the decline in traditional activism spurring the shift to technological tools? Is activists' lack of interest attributable in part to their being restricted to less essential roles? One thing is certain: political parties are eminently adaptable organizations. Activism and the political roles activists may assume are changing. Will activists now become more involved in social media than in the various bodies of the party? In theoretical terms, the question then is whether tweeting constitutes activism. To find out, one would have to measure whether exchanges on social media have any persuasive power or are limited to party supporters engaged in a dialogue of the deaf. Meanwhile, people seeking to get involved in order to advance their ideas are liable to turn to other organizations, such as interest groups, social movements and the non-established parties. Political activists will be then be left playing walk-on roles at party events or relaying information on behalf of the party.

In Quebec and in Canada as a whole, activists have been crucial to party operations since the middle of the last century. We now have to ask what role they can actually play inside the organization. For example, they used to participate effectively in developing policy in the Parti Québécois, but now they are much less involved. At the same time, there is a general trend under way to open up the leadership-selection process, a trend related, most notably, to the use of social media and the development of technologies that simplify voting procedures.

In terms of party financing, Quebec has chosen to increase state funding while restricting funding by the membership. The decline of activism combined with the advent of new technological methods is liable to reinforce the trend noted earlier towards greater centralization of power in the hands of the leaders. This development too will have an impact on the profile of activists in established parties, who will more likely choose to get involved in a party for reasons other than ideological commitment.

The new technologies also present political parties with a number of opportunities in relation to the electorate. In the face of increasing cynicism and decreasing participation in elections, parties have the ability to understand the socio-demographic profile of their voters more fully and easily. Parties can thus better reach out to them with messages that are adapted to their real-life concerns with the evident hope of rallying their support. In other words, the new technologies allow political parties to target an electorate more effectively and to adapt their campaign, budgets and advertising strategies accordingly. The technology also have the advantage of allowing parties to circumvent the filter of the traditional media and reach voters without incurring high advertising costs.

Still, the new technologies present challenges and even pose the risk of gaffes. They make politics much more impersonal. Direct contact with voters and the experience of campaign offices as places where supporters can meet and talk are fading from political life. The elimination of volunteer engagement and the human dimension from election campaigns undercuts the social interaction that encourages political debate. While social media enable parties to frame debates and share information, they also increase the possibility that mistakes and gaffes will be made because so many more people are involved. For the time being, though, the Twittersphere is more of a closed system that allows already-convinced party supporters to quarrel with each other. The new media are also liable to spur an increase in negative advertising over the Web.

Activists are generally individuals who commit their ideas, their time as volunteers and their financial resources to further a political cause. For a number of years now, their role within parties has been changing. They are ageing, and their numbers are falling. Parties are having difficulty replacing them and attracting younger generations. There is an apparent shift occurring: activists are giving way to supporters. Being a supporter does not entail engaging in any activist work; it primarily involves simply taking a subordinate role and circulating a party's views.

With new technologies and state funding, in future the main political parties operating on the Quebec and Canadian scenes will have less need for committed activists. In return for their voluntary labours, activists could rightfully claim a say in setting policy and selecting local candidates. Parties still need supporters to relay their messages and to secure their leaders' legitimacy, though. If the trend continues, a major structural change will occur in the organization of election campaigns and in internal party democracy. Studying these changes will surely entail a more in-depth, dedicated research program.

References

Bardi, L., Bartolini, S. & Trechsel, A. (2014). Party adaptation and change and the crisis of democracy. *Party Politics, 20*, 151–159.

Carty, K. R. (2004). Parties as franchise systems. *Party politics, 10*, 5–24.

Crête, J. & Blais, A. (2013). Le système électoral et les comportements électoraux. In R. Pelletier & M. Tremblay (Eds.), *Le parlementarisme canadien, 5ème édition revue et mise à jour*. Quebec: PUL.

Diamond, L. & Gunther, R. (Eds.). (2001). *Political parties and democracy*. Baltimore: The John Hopkins University Press.

Cross, W. & Young, L. (2004). The contours of political party membership in Canada. *Party Politics, 10*, 427–444.

Gélineau, F. & Teyssier, R. (2012) Le déclin de la participation électorale au Québec, 1985–2008. *Cahier de recherche électorale et parlementaire*, No. 6.

Giasson, T. et al. (2013). #QC2012: L'utilisation de Twitter par les partis. In F. Bastien, É. Bélanger & F. Gélineau (Eds.), *Les Québécois aux urnes: Les partis, les médias et les citoyens en campagne*. Montreal: PUM.

Howe, P. & Northrup, D. (2002). Strengthening Canadian Democracy: The Views of Canadians. Institute for Research on Public Policy.

Katz, R. & Mair, P. (1995). Changing models of party organization and party democracy: The emergence of the cartel party. *Party Politics, 1*, 5–28.

Montigny, E. (2011). Leadership et militantisme au Parti québécois. Québec: PUL.

Pelletier, R. & Couture, J. (2012). La confiance dans les partis au Canada et au Québec: un Québec distinct? In R. Pelletier (Ed.), Les Partis politiques québécois dans la tourmente: Mieux comprendre et évaluer leur rôle. Québec: PUL.

Quéniart, A. & Jacques, J. (2001) L'engagement politique des jeunes femmes au Québec: de la responsabilité au pouvoir d'agir pour un changement de société. Lien social et Politiques, 46, 45–53.

Russel, M. (2005). Building New Labour: The politics of party organisation. New York: Palgrave McMillan.

van Biezen, I. & Poguntke, T. (2014). The decline of membership-based politics. Party Politics, 20, 205–216

Isabelle Gusse[1]

Party Activists and Partisan Communication in Quebec

Since the 1960s, the combination of television and political marketing has contributed to the emergence of "new" political leaders possessed of on-screen charisma and a "telepresence" separate from that of their party. Political communication has become a space for the production of political personalities and the personalization of politics; the outcome, reflecting the now-dominant norm in entertainment and news programming, may be termed "politics as entertainment." The direct access to voters that leaders now enjoy through television is a corollary of the growing involvement of communications professionals in politics. Political parties have been de-politicized and even de-ideologized, political activism has declined, and the role of the party activist has withered. Today, though, it is widely maintained that the development of social media will allow citizens to communicate and disseminate snapshots of their political moods and so sustain a renaissance in party activism. Given these activists' local (professional, friendship, family, and business) communications relationships, they are able to send messages over the Internet and, it is argued, effectively cut into the politicians' monopoly over the media. Political parties are accordingly deemed to be in a position to rebuild their social and political relationships, for with the Web they can be present both at the centre of political and public space – through the mass media – and on the periphery – through networks of local activists transmitting their own messages.

In light of these developments and contentions, we set out to examine communications activity by Parti Québécois (PQ) and Parti Libéral du Québec (PLQ) activists on the local level (the periphery) and the national[2] level (the centre)[3] in 2013. We had the following questions in mind: Could local party activists of the "new breed" who use the Internet and traditional media be considered producers and transmitters of communications in their own right and thus to be breaking the politicians' long-

---

1 Professor, Department of Political Science, Université du Québec à Montréal.
2 Translator's notes: 1) In keeping with common usage in this context, the term "nation" and its derivatives refer to Quebec institutions and issues. 2) Where possible, the English version of Manin's book on representative government has been used, and the parenthetic references appear as Manin, 1997. Phrases and sentences quoted by the author from the French version that are not in the English publication have been translated here, and the parenthetic references appear as Manin, 1996. 3) Quotations from Albouy, Fillieule & Mayer, Gaxie, Legavre, Manin (1996), Matonti & Poupeau, Subileau, the party websites and the interview subjects are translated from French.
3 In Quebec, only the wealthier parties that can afford the services of political marketing and communications agencies and to hire professionals in the field are able to occupy a communications hub and influence the periphery.

standing monopoly? Or do the messages that activists produce and disseminate merely echo communications strategies developed by the central, national party organizations? We shall begin our discussion, though, with a survey of studies by French researchers on the functions and roles of activists in French political party organizations. We shall refer too to Bernard Manin's study *The Principles of Representative Government* (1997) in which he analyzes the changing, successive forms of representative government in the 19th and 20th centuries. We shall deal more particularly with the forms dubbed "party democracy" and "audience democracy" (Manin, 1997: 193ff.) in which party activists have seen their role and function changed and even eliminated as communications experts have gradually taken their place.

1 Activist engagement in political parties, 1960–1980

From the 1960s to the 1980s, research on activism in French political parties generally centred on the Communist Party, for "communist activists [represent] the ideal standard model in comparison or contrast to which all activists are defined" (Subileau, 1981: 1041). The notion of the activist refers to a range of roles: leader, martyr, militant, fellow traveller, sympathizer, imposter, orator, doctrinaire, ideologue, prophet, virtuoso, convert, registered member, elector or voter, reader of the Communist Party press, and the or future member (Subileau, 1981: 1041–1042). Few of the studies conducted in these decades dealt with activists' actual practices and behaviour. The focus was rather on how activists accumulate duties: engagement in activism is said to intensify activism and lead party members to assume more and more tasks and responsibilities (Subileau, 1981: 1045). This tendency is thought to be particularly deep seated among members of parties of the extreme right and extreme left that demand a total commitment that "erases any distinction between [party] life and private life and relegates professional careers to the sidelines" (Lafont in Fillieule & Mayer, 2001: 22)[4].

Activist political engagement is ascribed to four types of motivation. The first concerns the quest for a political and social identity forged by a sense of solidarity with "an ideological community" (Subileau, 1981: 1043) and shaped by a range of factors: working conditions, participation in political and trade union struggles, confrontations with the police, the subordination of personal life to the life of the

---

4 The compilation by Olivier Fillieule and Nonna Mayer titled "Devenirs militants" published in 2001 by the *Revue française de science politique* is devoted to political engagement. Both authors are members of the Groupe d'étude et de recherche sur les mutations du militantisme of the Association Française de Science Politique.

collectivity, social class, and union membership. The second motivation is the wish to escape a state of alienation and challenge the existing order, in other words "to free oneself from one's condition by participating in the conscious transformation of social relationships" (Subileau, 1981: 1043). The third stems from socialization by the family and through work, for activism is deemed largely to be a "behaviour that is handed down"; that is hereditary, as it were (Subileau, 1981: 1044). The fourth motivation is connected to the possibility of reward and social and political advancement that party membership may bring. In this regard, Gaxie has shown that for activists in western democracies, joining a political party is not essentially a politicized act based on dedication and disinterest (Gaxie, 1977: 127). Nor is it primarily motivated by a wish to defend an idea or an ideology or by support for a political cause. Activists often come from the working class and lack the competencies required to "become conscious of [their] political class interests," Gaxie argues (1977: 127). Only parties that can offer rewards as incentives for political activity, especially in election periods when the aim is to hold onto or gain political power, can rouse and earn activists' "continually sustained commitment" (Gaxie, 1977: 139). The rewards are personal in nature and involve possibilities of social advancement and integration that vary with social class and bring "prestige, power, self-esteem or social status" (Gaxie, 1977: 130).

These rewards stir interest in involvement and stoke the activism that parties, which are highly hierarchical structures, need to operate properly. Positions of responsibility, leadership and employment in a party's internal structures are much sought after and are occupied by activists from the upper classes. The responsibilities that working-class members can assume are more symbolic in nature, perhaps in ceremonial roles (on the board of directors, for example) that a party needs to fill if it claims to represent the workers. In general, only a very few activists can claim these types of rewards. A party therefore has to offer grassroots activists different kinds of incentives: for instance, social activities that foster the members' integration, sense of belonging and attachment to the party as one big supportive family founded on friendship, camaraderie, community, affection, and identification with a political group. Every activist is thus called upon to participate in "the joys of victory, the mutual solace [offered] in [times of] defeat and personal misfortune, the risks and trials confronted together, the meetings where old friends get together and memories are made, the passionate controversies, and long discussions at the café" (Gaxie, 1977: 137).

2 The zenith and the nadir of party activism

From the late 19th century until the 1970s, Manin writes, the stability of electoral behaviour was sustained largely by the sort of "family and local socialization" (Manin, 1996: 267) mentioned earlier: people voted the way their parents or the people they lived among did. They often voted year after year for the same party, not for a personality or a trusted representative. From the time the class conflict engendered by industrialization emerged, "representation [became] ... a reflection of the social structure," and elections came to mirror the cleavage between "social forces ... in conflict with one another" (Manin, 1997: 210). The division in the vote was thus closely associated with "class divisions" (Manin, 1997: 209), especially in social democratic and socialist countries (Austria, Britain, Germany, Sweden) where major parties represented the working class. A sense of belonging to or identifying with a mass party of this sort was more important in reinforcing voters' confidence it than support for the party program was. Indeed, most voters knew little or nothing about the party's policy proposals; strictly speaking, they served to mobilize "the enthusiasm and energy of the activists and party bureaucrats who [did know more about them]" (Manin, 1997: 211).

From the second half of the 19th century to the early 20th century, representative government in western countries depended on three major factors: the delimitation and expansion of the electorate; the gradual introduction of universal suffrage; and the emergence of organized mass and class parties. Seeking to "mobilize the enlarged electorate" (Manin, 1997: 206), these parties acquired networks of -called "grassroots" activists, "ordinary citizens who had reached the top of their parties by dint of militant activity and devotion to a cause" (Manin, 1997: 194). From then on, in election campaigns, parallels were drawn between activists' and candidates' social positions, living conditions and concerns, enshrining the principle of "progress towards greater democratic identity and resemblance between governors and governed" (Manin, 1997: 196). This form of representation, party democracy, was thus an acknowledgment of the ascendancy of both "the activist and the party bureaucrat" (Manin, 1997: 208). Yet, despite their working-class origins, the mass and class parties were actually dominated and led "by [new] 'de-proletarianized' elites," by "party bureaucrats," people who were remote from the base and came from privileged sectors of society that owed their access to power and social status to intelligence, ambition, organizational talents and professional skills that distinguished them from their voters (Manin, 1997: 207).

This trend continued from 1960 to 1980. A number of researchers, notably Daniel Gaxie, pointed out that the leaders of French political parties were not representative of their support base and that certain categories of society were overrepresented at the top of the party hierarchy. In other words, the people "in positions of responsibility ... [were] more often 'bourgeois' than the supporters" were (Subileau, 1981: 1048). In France's leftist political parties (socialists, communists), the top leadership came from the middle class, and it largely centralized power in its own hands (Subileau, 1981: 1047). The activists come mainly from the "salaried middle classes, and the leaders ... from the educated bourgeoisie (bourgeoisie lettrée)" (Subileau, 1981: 1048). The "privileged categories," particularly teachers, were overrepresented, and the "working-class strata" underrepresented. The factors that determined the nature of a person's party membership were related to the practice of "a profession": "being a teacher, having a high level of education [and] having technical skills geared to production" (Subileau, 1981: 1050).

3 From activists to communications experts

The 1970s, Manin writes, saw the advent and entrenchment of "audience democracy." In this form of representative government, which persists to our day, the governed elect their governors on the basis of a personalization of electoral choice and power. In other words, voters are asked to vote for the personality of a candidate, not for a party or for the terms of a party program. Parties, unsurprisingly, have turned into machines for mobilizing support for personalities. Significantly, they mobilize an "already-established organization with [a] relationship and influence network, fundraising capabilities, and volunteer workforce [that] remain decisive assets in the competition for votes" (Manin, 1996: 280).

Meanwhile, "the expression of public opinion" has less and less to do with activists and party bureaucrats working to mobilize their people "to demonstrate or sign petitions." Rather, it is increasingly the responsibility of pollsters and researchers who generally work for organizations that are "independent of political parties" (Manin, 1997: 230–231). In a bid to improve their marketing positioning vis-à-vis their adversaries, candidates make constant, extensive use of public opinion surveys in order to elicit and exploit the differences between them and tailor the choices they offer (the political supply) to the voters' concerns (the demand).

The mass media, which can also shape public opinion, are no longer "structurally linked to parties," as the major party and partisan newspapers were in the age of party democracy. Individuals now form their political opinions based on the same news produced by the same commercial, non-partisan mass media (television, radio) (Manin, 1997: 228–230). The "competing and conflicting images" of personalities circulated by these media amount to little more than "simplified, vague political representations" (Manin, 1996: 291), but they free voters from the onerous task of searching for accurate information about the day's political issues that would enable them to cast an informed vote. The simplified image, Manin explains, provides the public with "alternative shortcuts in the costly search for political information" (Manin, 1997: 228). Moreover, the "new link between the representative and the electors" in audience democracy (Manin, 1996: 291) is intrinsically related to media that offer significant direct visibility to representatives (candidates or elected officials) who have "a better command of the techniques of media communication" (Manin, 1997: 219–220). Among other things, the media allow politicians to make themselves better known to citizens and voters "without the mediation of a party network" (Manin, 1997: 220). In audience democracy, though, elections still involve the selection of individuals who distinguish themselves from others; they "retain the elitist character they have always had,"[5] even as power has shifted to "the *media expert*," the new political and media elite of communications specialists that has supplanted the activists and the party bureaucrats (Manin, 1997: 220).

4 Political marketing communication and activism

From the 1970s on, activists have had to possess skills acquired outside the party, essentially through their education. They are thus products of the middle and upper classes and better educated than their predecessors, They are the ones best equipped to get involved in political party work, for example, by writing leaflets, speaking in public, making notes, taking the minutes of meetings, and compiling files on political and legal issues of varying complexity. The qualities required – essentially communication skills – consequently exclude actors whose education has not afforded them the same level of expertise (Matoni & Poupeau, 2004: 10).

In western societies, the 1980s saw the emergence and development of political marketing, "a set of theories, methods, techniques and social practices inspired by commercial marketing" (Albouy, 1994: 22). The aim is to influence and encourage citizen behaviour and opinions in support, usually, of a politician (a candidate or an elected official) or, more rarely, of a political project, ideology or party. In concrete terms, such support may "take the form ... of a vote, payment of dues or partisan activity" (Albouy, 1994: 24).

Starting in the 1960s in the United States and then gradually in all the western democracies, this new expertise in marketing communication developed as a tool to support political decisions and actions of any stripe. The political marketing that resulted from the combination of television, the archetypal mass medium, political advertising and polling has forced the parties and politicians that were financially best off to do two things. First, they have had to surround themselves with large numbers of professional pollsters and communications technicians who specialize in studying electoral markets in order to make tactical decisions. More often than not, these experts have claimed to possess and to master a complete communications toolbox: They were equipped, they have asserted, to conduct surveys and advertising campaigns, formulate media plans and develop positioning and even packaging strategies which would guarantee their clients political gains and even

---

5 Manin maintains that, despite these changes, representative government has basically remained "what it has been since its foundation, namely a governance of elites distinguished from the bulk of citizens by social standing, way of life and education" (Manin, 1997: 232). Although the rise of a new political and media elite in audience democracy has been accompanied by the decline of the party-bureaucracy elite typical of party democracy, "the persistence, possibly even the aggravation, of the gap between the governed and the governing elite" is more deep seated than ever (Manin, 1997: 233).

electoral victory (Legavre, 1989: 80). Secondly, parties and politicians have had to vastly increase the budgets devoted to their communications and political-marketing activities. (Albouy, 1994: 14).

These expert consultants are products of the public-relations and advertising industries and are equally at home designing and producing a lead slogan, a brand image, political posters, speeches, books, programs, political jokes, commercials, and leaflets. They are also able to carry out fundraising campaigns and conduct simulations or training sessions to teach politicians how to handle the demands of the media and advertising (Albouy, 1994: 125). They are not hired and paid because of their political convictions – indeed, they often claim not to have any – but for their technical competencies and the services they sell. Many of these apolitical actors describe themselves as chameleons, mercenaries who can work for any political organization of any ideology, just as they would for any commercial product. These communicators are primarily recruited in election periods by the richest parties, and they are motivated mainly by money. Moreover, they are often affiliated with organizations that specialize in communications, firms or agencies modelled on the ones that work for industry and commerce (Gaxie, 1977: 124; Albouy, 1994: 115, 123).

It is thus hardly surprising that in audience democracy the personalization of politicians (leaders and candidates) and the emphasis placed on their personal, human qualities (youth, fame, experience, dynamism, generosity, family virtues, honesty) in typical advertising fashion have become the focus of communication campaigns. The party, its program and its political ideas have meanwhile been relegated to the sidelines. To be effective and persuasive, personalization necessarily entails simplification. It thus associates a person, a "star," with a set of superficial ideas that anyone can readily absorb and accept and that convey two or three main themes related to concrete problems and issues elicited by polling and from the social setting. As citizens' political choices are reduced to a choice among political personalities, political marketing transforms "democratic systems into charismatic systems" (Albouy, 1994: 85); the communications professionals produce and manage appealing messages, which, though admittedly attractive, are characterized by a sort of "ideological vacuity" (Albouy, 1994: 19).

Over the decades, this tactical marketing communication has become a fact of life for politicians. They have gradually stopped paying attention to the opinions of "their usual intermediaries" (Legavre, 1989: 80), the activists, association officials, paid staff and paper candidates they encounter in meetings and neighbourhood visits. They have preferred the advice of communications experts from their own political family or outside firms.

According to Albouy, there are two other reasons behind the decline of activism in political parties and the fall in activist numbers; one is ideological, and the other structural. As regards ideology, many activists consider political marketing a major source of the near obliteration of ideologies and programs, which has resulted in clientilistic behaviour and catchall political parties and platforms. As devotees of marketing techniques, competing political parties of both the left and the right "have to a significant degree abandoned any ambition [to provide] mass intellectual training [even to activists] in order to adapt to an electorate that is reputedly increasingly allergic to ideologies and doctrines" (Albouy, 1994: 282). This universal ideological consensus is manifested in two ways.

First, the parties rehash "omnibus values [that are] electorally attractive" (Albouy, 1994: 296) and easy to subscribe to but that mean little and convey negligible information: solidarity, freedom, human rights, full employment, etc. Second – and consequently – they produce messages to popularize these themes. Since the parties of the left and the right now share many economic and social values, Albouy writes, we are witness to the development of a "syncretic ideology." Based on a fusion of doctrines, this ideology is transmitted by the mass media. They disseminate "a woolly and barely intellectualized vision of a desirable society" (Albouy, 1994: 284), a vision with little power to mobilize political participation. Indeed, the issue is no longer to fight for a vision of society or for a cause, but occasionally to take part in a competition, an election, to select those politicians who are best able to sell their talents as good managers or entrepreneurs. The result is simultaneously "high voter abstention" and a decline or deficit in activist numbers (Albouy, 1994: 285).

As regards the structural reasons for the decline of activism, political marketing has a demobilizing effect on local activists who have been gradually deprived of their decision-making power. Decisions are now made by others, by higher-ranking individuals. The local activists are reduced to implementing tasks that afford them little in the way of rewards or power (Albouy, 1994: 258).

The people who run political marketing campaigns operate in a strict hierarchy and perform precise communications and managerial responsibilities. They work in five operational units. The first is the leadership unit, which comprises the politician, campaign manager, treasurer, and principal communications consultants. It sets "the strategic guidelines for the communications campaign" (Albouy, 1994: 118) based on preliminary surveys, draws up the campaign timetable, coordinates the activities of the other four units, and checks progress continually. The second unit is staffed by communications specialists who create and conceive messages for dissemination by various means (posters, leaflets, talking points, political speeches, etc.). The third unit handles public and press relations; it enters into and maintains close relations with journalists with the sole purpose of ensuring that their clients, politicians or parties, get maximum coverage. The fourth unit is responsible for finance and is in charge of raising funds, managing expenses and handling the bookkeeping for the communications campaign. The fifth unit oversees operations in the field, covering a range of tasks that include postering, meetings, door-to-door canvassing, and distribution of promotional materials. It is also in charge of relations with campaign management, the communications specialists and the activist volunteers and provides technical assistance to local organizations (posters, preparing political meetings, organizing shows, etc.) (Albouy, 1994: 118–119).

A political marketing campaign of this sort thus involves a Taylorist division of labour and responsibilities and a clear-cut separation between brain and brawn, between conception and execution. The first two units are the expert thinkers and decision makers, the strategists who guide and conceive campaigns. At the bottom of the hierarchy, activists directed by the field-operations unit are asked to volunteer their time to carry out a variety of communications activities, especially during elections. They go door to door and visit neighbourhoods and public places to hand out flyers designed by political-marketing consultants. The flyers bear a strong resemblance to commercial flyers, and the whole operation is very much akin to the work of door-to-door salesmen (Albouy, 1994: 175).

5 Quebec political parties, communication and activism

Given the elements that this brief survey provides for characterizing the current relationship between political parties, communication and activism, we set out to discover what a party activist in Quebec is nowadays. To explore and try to understand the public representations of activists that two major Quebec political parties, the Parti Québécois (PQ) and the Parti Libéral du Québec (PLQ)[6], construct and project and the way the parties set the parameters for and define activists' communications activities, we proceeded in two stages. We started with an examination of the contents of the parties' respective websites. We then moved to investigate the nature of the local activist networks, how their operations may vary at different times and the local and national communications activities they undertake. We thus sought to see whether there is in fact a division of labour between a central party organization that develops communications strategies and local activists who execute them (that is, disseminate party communications by various means). We accordingly conducted three interviews with representatives of the parties' youth wings from the Montreal and Quebec City regions.

5.1 PQ and PLQ: the activist = youth equation

On the PQ and PLQ websites, the image of the party activist is closely associated with age, specifically young age and the idea of youth. Indeed, the terms "activism"

---

6 The Parti Québécois (PQ, established in 1968) and the Parti Libéral du Québec (PLQ, established 1867) represented approximately equal shares of the voting population after the September 2012 election. The PQ formed a minority government, while the PLQ formed the official opposition.

(*militantisme*) and "activist" (*militant*) are used mainly with reference to the mission, roles and responsibilities of the PQ youth wing, the Comité National des Jeunes du Parti Québécois (CNJPQ)[7], and its Liberal counterpart, the Commission Jeunesse du PLQ (CJPLQ)[8], and their respective members.

For example, the PQ youth-wing website points out that young people historically played a very important role in the party, and it includes numerous references to activism. The CNJPQ's mission is defined as recruiting and training young activists aged 16 to 30 and providing them with the tools to support sovereignty[9], help the PQ succeed and promote "the national youth committee's positions and proposals in their social milieu." The CNJPQ also has several other responsibilities relevant to our discussion: organizing activism within the party; "welcoming every new activist"; providing training about the party's structures and organs; and supporting PQ activists "on every Quebec campus"[10]. The website also makes it clear that active involvement can lead to more responsible positions and even a job. "Many young people play a variety of roles in the Party: constituency presidents, delegates to the National Convention, and even members of the National Assembly"[11]. The CNJPQ website, which is connected by hyperlink to the PQ site, has a tab explicitly titled "Militer" (Being an Activist) under which two links appear. The link "Au quotidien" (Day to Day) includes guidelines for activists who want to support the cause and suggests things they can do: for example, show the PQ colours (the Quebec flag, stickers, buttons); join the PQ; visit PQ and CNJPQ sites to post comments, suggestions and ideas about different issues; sign and forward online petitions; and participate in sovereigntist activities[12]. The link "Je veux militer" (I want to be an activist) leads to an information request form that can be used to organize young activists for future election campaigns and to ensure their support for the sovereigntist cause. Apart from contact (name, email, telephone number) and availability information (day,

---

7 http://cnjpq.org/

8 http://cj.plq.org; According to its website, the Coalition Avenir Québec (CAQ, established in 2012) also has a youth wing, the Commission de la Relève de la Coalition Avenir Québec. Its goal is "to bring together members and activists of the CAQ aged 16 to 25". Young people are, it is said, "the future of Quebec, [and] their voice is therefore important." Youth are "an important factor in the development of the CAQ program." Young activists have to promote their party, innovate and bring new ideas to the table. The website of Québec Solidaire (QS, established in 2006) contains no reference to a youth wing. QS wants activists of all ages to get involved at every level of the organization. However, David Fortin-Côté, who is in charge of the committee on democratic and regional life of the party's political committee, says that a project to establish a youth group has been underway for two years on the initiative of young people involved in QS.

9 Qui sommes-nous. http://cnjpq.org/page/le_cnjpq. Retrieved May 29, 2013.

10 Qui sommes-nous. http://cnjpq.org/page/le_cnjpq. Retrieved May 29, 2013.

11 Fonctionnement. La place des jeunes dans le Parti. http://cnjpq.org/page/fonctionnement. Retrieved May 29, 2013.

12 CNJPQ. Militer: Au quotidien. http://cnjpq.org/page/au_quotidien. Retrieved May 29, 2013.

evening, weekend, full time, etc.), the form asks for the applicant's home constituency and the community college (Collège d'enseignement général et professionnel, CÉGEP) or university he or she attends. Applicants are then asked to select the activities they are interested in performing during the next election. Most are related to communications: for example, going door to door, manning stands in educational establishments, being a Web activist, and canvassing[13].

The Liberal youth organization, the CJPLQ, is for young people aged 16 to 25. According to the website, it holds "thirty-three per cent of the votes in every organ of the [party], making it the most powerful youth wing in a political party in Canada"[14]. Unlike the PQ youth site, the Liberals' specifies the bodies in which young activists can play any of a number of roles. These include the Comité de coordination (CoCo, coordinating committee) which is "responsible for the [CJPLQ's] day-to-day business" and is made up of staff coordinators (PLQ employees) and activists "who have been delegated a specific duty (secretary, communications, new media, educational institutions, English-speaking community, cultural communities, finance, membership)"[15]. Youth members may also take part in the Commission's Conseil des représentants régionaux (CDR, council of regional representatives), "the supreme authority between youth conventions" that decides on policy positions and orientations and acts as "the link between the CJ's national body and the activists in the regions"[16]. Finally, in each of the 25 PLQ regional associations, a minimum of three positions are reserved for young people, whose role is "to represent the interests of young activists ... before the Executive and the CDR"[17].

5.2 PQ and PLQ: Young activists and communication

In light of the use of the French term "militant" (activist) on the Web pages of the PQ and PLQ youth wings, we conducted three telephone interviews with local representatives of the CNJPQ and the CJPLQ. At the outset, we intended to speak with one PQ member and one Liberal in each of three Quebec administrative regions (Montreal, Quebec City, and Estrie), for a total of six interviews. However, many of our repeated telephone calls went unanswered. We had set aside the period from the

---

13 CNJPQ. Militer: Je veux militer. Retrieved May 29, 2013. On the Québec Solidaire site, a link "Agir/Donner du temps" (Taking Action/Giving Time) leads to an almost identical form to help the party find out which communications activities a QS activist could perform: postering, going door to door, distribution, social media, telephoning/canvassing, communications. http://agir.quebecsolidaire.net/donner, Retrieved May 29, 2013.
14 La CJ en bref. http://cj.plq.org, Retrieved May 29, 2013.
15 L'Équipe. http://cj.plq.org, Retrieved May 29, 2013.
16 L'Équipe. http://cj.plq.org, Retrieved May 29, 2013.
17 L'Équipe. http://cj.plq.org, Retrieved May 29, 2013.

beginning of June to July 5, 2013, for this phase of the research, so the season was undoubtedly a factor. Some of those we tried to contact were in fact on vacation. Others, though, simply never replied to our calls or emails. In the end, we had to make do with a small sample of three individuals: one member of the CJPLQ executive committee (PLQ1, interviewed June 23, 2013); one representative of the CJPLQ for the Montréal-Est region (PLQ2, interviewed July 6, 2013,); and one representative of the Quebec City regional committee, the Comité régional des jeunes du PQ, Capitale nationale (PQ1, interviewed July 2, 2013). While the information gathered in these three interviews points to certain trends, it also indicates a need for further, more extensive exploration in a more exhaustive study.

The interviews started with a series of general questions to sketch a portrait of party activists. We found that the young people involved are 18 to 25 years old. They share ideals, a social vision and common values with other members and participate in the activities of their party's local and national bodies, for example, by presenting ideas and drawing up resolutions. They tend to come from the middle (entrepreneurial and business) class and are less likely to have a working-class or disadvantaged background. They have attended community college and university (mainly in an undergraduate program) and have a bachelor's degree in political science, law, political communication, philosophy, or social science more broadly. They generally engage in a party's activities because of its ideology and program and out of a commitment to its values. Seeking reward or gratification, they are eager to take part in a political movement and be a member of the party that forms or may form the government. They want to increase their political knowledge. Doing so gives them "the feeling of being part of something bigger than they are" (PQ1 interview, July 2, 2013). They also want to participate in discussions about public policies, develop political and relationship networks and meet people involved in politics and who exercise political responsibilities.

A second set of questions dealt with general activities and communications tasks (through traditional media, social networks, websites) conducted by young activists for local (regional or constituency) and national party organs during election campaigns and between elections. They revealed that political and communications activities are generally time defined, with the bulk occurring during elections.

5.2.1 The activist communicator between elections

Between elections, the pace of activity is rather slow. "The party doesn't need employees as much [and] our staff is cut" (PLQ2 interview, July 6, 2013). Activists engage principally through the various bodies of the youth wing (political committees, general councils, youth conventions). They debate constituency policy directions and positions that they wish to support and to circulate regionally and nationally within the party and elsewhere. The PLQ regional youth representative from Montréal-Est pointed out that it is the members who supply the party with ideas; it is not the executive council alone "that decides the whole party line without consulting the members. It's actually through ... the conventions ... that people decide, yes or no, whether to agree to a particular party measure or line" (PLQ2 interview, July 6, 2013). According to the PQ youth representative from the Quebec City region, many of the proposals discussed at party conventions and that may make their way onto the election platform "sometimes start from local initiatives" (PQ1 interview, July 6, 2013).

In preparing for and organizing these party activities, young Liberals use digital technologies, such as Twitter and Facebook. They do so at their own initiative, not because the PLQ asked them to.

> [I]t's not strictly speaking official. For example, we don't have someone telling us to organize an event on Facebook or Twitter. It's really left to the discretion of the activists [who] use Twitter, Facebook, and so on because it's just simpler to communicate that way. Apart from that, we have someone at the Commission Jeunesse in charge of communications who in fact is responsible for handling the [Commission's] Facebook account [and] Twitter account... (PLQ2 interview, July 6, 2013).

According to our CNJPQ interviewee, a young PQ member's activities also slow down between elections. However, there is always a nucleus of local activists who, depending on the region, are "present on social media ... to try to promote the party position on a given issue" (PQ1 interview, July 6, 2013).

Still, the communications duties entrusted to activists between elections are relatively slight. They involve circulating information and taking part in activities geared particularly to renewing the membership and recruiting new young members. They hold meetings and debates between young activists and potential new ones, organize information booths and hand out leaflets, flyers and pamphlets in educational institutions (principally universities). "Mainly booths ... that's something I ask people to do a lot because it's relatively simple to organize, and it's fun, it's effective, and for a young person, it's not stressful" (PQ1 interview, July 6, 2013).

5.2.2 The activist communicator during election periods

In contrast, during election periods young activists are highly mobilized, much in demand and active. The main aim for the party is "to go get as many votes as possible" (PLQ2 interview, July 6, 2013).

The communications strategies (positioning, slant of speeches, etc.) of a local candidate, especially one who is not well known or is completely unknown, tend to copy those used to promote the party leader. A candidate's previous level of public recognition, his or her political history as a minister or in handling a particular issue can make a significant difference, though. An incumbent member of the National Assembly or cabinet minister may "enjoy a degree of fame during his term that will have an impact in his riding at election time" (PLQ2 interview, July 6, 2013). An incumbent politician's communications will accordingly lay much more emphasis on his or her own achievements than on the party. The experience of Lise Thériault, Minister of Labour in the Liberal government of Jean Charest, is illustrative. In the September 2012 provincial elections, she held onto her seat in Anjou-Louis-Riel, the riding she had represented since 2002.

> Lise Thériault is extremely well-liked in Anjou-Riel partly because she stood her ground at the parliamentary committee[18] even though she got death threats because of it. And in spite of everything she…how should I put this…without meaning to be crude, had balls and showed it…. In fact, during the election campaign, it was mainly Lise Thériault who was featured rather than the Liberal Party…. It all depends … on the candidate, on the consultant, whether it's a riding where you have a strong chance of winning … or a riding where you're running more of a paper candidate, that is … a riding where you don't much expect to win (PLQ2 interview, July 6, 2013).

Depending on circumstances, young activists get involved and campaign directly for a candidate and/or as part of their youth organization. In some regions "people … are hired for the period of the elections … as computer specialists … in charge of communications" (PLQ2 interview, July 6, 2013). Based on their skills, some young people who are a little more specialized in communications are also asked to do media relations (press reviews, press releases, etc.): "It really depends on each individual's character and skills. There are no predetermined duties. It really depends on each individual's strengths and weaknesses" (PQ1 interview, July 2, 2013). During elections young activists with a little experience can carry out a range of communications activities. Working for free as volunteers and at their own pace and convenience in their local committee or region, they generally circulate and distribute information. They go door to door, put up election posters, and distribute leaflets, flyers, pamphlets and any other kind of election literature. They conduct in-house polls on voting intentions, do telephone canvassing and man booths in educational institutions. They also perform communications duties (media relations, publicity, marketing) using traditional and digital media (email lists, social networks, Facebook, Twitter, Flick, You Tube, Instagram, Ustream). If they have the necessary experience for some of these tasks, young PLQ activists can choose what they want to do, freely and voluntarily: "We try to give them … what they like to do best, whether it's going door to door or canvassing or working on a computer … It's voluntary, so there's no obligation … If they decide one day not to do it anymore, that's perfectly all right" (PLQ2 interview, July 6, 2013).

As for digital technologies, it is young activists who manage partisan social media (Twitter, Facebook). There is a generational technology gap, which the PQ youth

---

18 The October 2011 parliamentary committee hearings on Bill 33 to limit construction-union powers over job placement.

representative from the Quebec City region attributed to the fact that "older activists aren't too familiar with [the technology], and aren't too keen on the idea. Not that they don't think it's useful" (PQ1 interview, July 2, 2013). Again, use of these technologies is due more to the initiative of the individual than of the party. Such activities tend to be performed freely, rather than under party direction:

> [T]here are always … debates on Twitter and Facebook and other [platforms]. But it's not really run by the party. It's mainly activists defending their point of view … The party … doesn't have a squad of young people on Twitter…. It's really up to what the activists want to do … Unless it's on behalf of the PLQ as such on Twitter or wherever, in which case it's managed by the party office, by the people in charge of communications there (PLQ2 interview, July 6, 2013).

Finally, the two parties do not seem to demand that their young activists possess any special skills before they start to carry out traditional or digital communications activities in elections. They learn by doing as they go along: "We don't really ask for any skills … First of all, [it's a matter of] motivation, the person wanting to be there. No one is forced to do anything that doesn't suit them. So it's motivation and, I guess, being open, being willing to meet people" (PLQ1 interview, June 23, 2013). If a young person is a good communicator, "even if he doesn't have a university education yet or is still in CÉGEP" and he has some basic knowledge in public relations, for example, he could be given duties in the area (PLQ2, July 6, 2013). The PQ's regional youth representative considers that a person who is given communications responsibilities should have good judgment: "[T]here's not much supervision, so we've got to have confidence … in people's intelligence, and … that they have … [good] judgment and respect for people … [and] of course, political instinct and a gift of repartee … and … excellent … written French" (PQ1 interview, July 2, 2013). In election periods, the parties do not officially provide their young activists with basic training about communications specifically. Many of the young members already seem to be very comfortable with everything digital (PLQ1 interview, June 23, 2013). Any training they receive is informal. It "is conducted day by day" (PLQ2 interview, July 6, 2013) and makes use of more seasoned activists' previous communications experience, among other things, and, in some cases, of party literature.

6 Conclusion

The engagement of young local activists in Quebec political parties is more of an election-period phenomenon. Their communications activities and responsibilities during campaigns on behalf of their party – through the Internet, social networks and traditional media – derive from communications and positioning strategies developed by the national party organization. Accordingly, the Internet, which both relays and transcends all the so called "traditional" print and broadcast media, should not be seen as helping rehabilitate Quebec's political parties. Rather, it is helping perpetuate and reinforce the use of marketing campaigns that preserve the centre's monopoly over communications in the most powerful and wealthiest political parties and sustain the personalization of politics, especially during elections. Young local activists thus cannot claim to create or conceive the messages they transmit on the Internet, social networks and traditional media or to be breaking the monopoly over communications by the politicians at the centre of the party organization. They are, more accurately, subordinates working to pass on the centre's messages by a variety of means, from door-to-door canvassing, to making telephone calls and handing out flyers.

The information we gleaned, particularly from the CNJPQ website and from the three interviews as well, illustrates a Taylorist division of duties and responsibilities; generally, communications and advertising (particularly in election periods) are devised by national party organs and relayed locally by subordinates in the field, young local activists who invest their time freely.

These two observations thus put the alleged autonomy of local activists networking over the Internet into perspective, but further exploration would be worthwhile. Hypotheses should be tested in a more exhaustive comparative study to elucidate the nature of communications activities by local activists in the PQ and the PLQ; in other parties with elected members in the National Assembly (Coalition Avenir Québec and Québec Solidaire); and in parties that have not yet won seats in general elections (Option Nationale, Parti Vert du Québec, etc.). It would be useful to study and compare communication by activists from all these groups during and between provincial election campaigns. Three hypotheses could be explored specifically regarding the parties with little or no representation in the legislature and which thus have fewer financial resources than the PQ and the PLQ: One may hypothesize, first, that their respective activists are not solely young people but come from all age groups. Second, these activists are perhaps more committed to supporting a "cause" and their party's program and ideology (centre right, social democratic, sovereigntist, environmentalist, etc.) not only in election periods but between elections as well. Third, lacking the financial resources needed to pay for the costly specialized human resources available to the major political parties, the smaller parties' national leaders rely much more on their activist base. Instead of being treated like subordinates, the activists serve as managers, consultants, creators, and developers of messages that are disseminated through traditional and digital media. The small parties can thus be seen as reviving party democracy, albeit in a reinterpreted and updated form, and breaking with two essentially inegalitarian and instrumentalist tendencies that seem to be standard practice for the powerful political leadership of the large parties. As evidenced by their websites, the public and media representations of activists conveyed by the PLQ and the PQ (which the small parties always derisively call the "old parties") reflect a form of ageism and confine activists to the role of subordinates executing decisions on communications that are made at higher levels.

References

Albouy, S. (1994). *Marketing et communication politique*. Paris: L'Harmattan, Collection Logiques sociales.

Fillieule, O. & Mayer, N. (2001) Devenirs militants: Introduction. *Revue française de science politique*, *51*, 19–25.

Gaxie, D. (1977) Économie des partis et rétributions du militantisme. *Revue française de science politique*, *27*, 123–154.

Legavre, J.-B. (189). Du militant à l'expert en communication politique. Le cas de la mairie de Rennes. *Politix*, *2*, (7–8), 80–90.

Manin, B. (1996). *Principes du gouvernement représentatif*. Paris: Flammarion, Collection Champs.

Manin, B. (1997). *The principles of representative government*. Cambridge: Cambridge University Press.

Matonti, F. & Poupeau, F. (2004/5) Le capital militant. Essai et définition. *Actes de la recherche en sciences sociales*, *155*, 4–11.

Subileau, F. (1981) Le militantisme dans les partis politiques sous la Cinquième République: État des travaux de langue française. *Revue française de science politique*, *31*, 1038–1068.

Part III: **The New Role Played by Social Networks**

Ashley Murchison[1]

Changing Communications? Political Parties and Web 2.0 in the 2011 New Zealand General Election

As Internet penetration in New Zealand continues to increase, the potential for online media to alter the dynamic of political communication and campaigning is growing. According to the World Internet Project New Zealand (WIPNZ) survey, 86 % of the population was online prior to the 2011 New Zealand general election[2]. This increased online presence has been coupled with a declining reliance on traditional media, with users rating the Internet ahead of television, newspapers and radio as their most important source of everyday information[3].

Alongside this growth in Internet use among the general populace, New Zealand has experienced an increasing uptake of Web 2.0 tools by political parties. The most recent general election in 2011 saw the potential of social media sites to open up new, unmediated, and more interactive channels of political communication. The growing role of this technology in New Zealand politics raises the question of how parties are using this medium to connect with citizens. This chapter examines this question by analysing the use of Facebook and Twitter by five New Zealand political parties in the 2011 campaign. Of particular interest here is whether these Web 2.0 tools have encouraged parties to forgo traditional approaches to top-down communication and embrace a more interactive dialogue with voters.

1 The Internet and Campaigns: From Web 1.0 to 2.0

Contemporary debate on the health of advanced democracies highlights escalating concerns for representative politics as citizens become increasingly disconnected from political life[4]. New Zealand has not remained immune from these concerns. As the country follows international trends of declining voter turnout[5], political partic-

---

1 Ph.D. Student, Department of Politics, University of Otago, Dunedin, New Zealand.
2 This New Zealand-based survey was conducted as part of the global World Internet Project. Respondents (n = 1255) were surveyed between July-August 2011, just prior to the election on 26 November.
3 Philippa Smith, Andy Gibson, Charles Crothers, Jennie Billot and Allan Bell, *The Internet in New Zealand 2011*.
4 Rachel Gibson, Wainer Lusoli and Stephen Ward, "The Australian Public and Politics On-line [...]"; Stephen Ward, Rachel Gibson and Paul Nixon, "Introduction".
5 Jack Vowles, Down, Down, Down [...].

ipation[6], and party membership[7], political elites face numerous challenges in trying to re-engage a disaffected citizenry. Growing partisan dealignment and electoral volatility increases the significance of communication and campaigning with voters during elections if parties are to maximise their vote-share and achieve electoral success[8]. While much of this campaign communication occurs through mainstream media channels, rising web use among voters has encouraged parties to turn to online channels for electioneering.

Evolution in technology invariably invites speculation about how these new campaign communication channels will alter the political landscape. Those ex-pressing more optimistic views on the impact of the Internet have envisaged it as a democratic panacea[9]. In contrast to the unidirectional and top-down nature of tradi-tional communication channels, online technologies lend themselves more readily to interaction between parties and citizens. It has been suggested that this new-found ability to engage in two-way communication enables voters and political parties to develop stronger connections, unfettered by geographical, temporal or media constraints[10]. Other commentators offer more subdued analyses, contending that political use of online channels replicates offline patterns of communication and engagement. Parties in particular are likely to continue to concentrate their efforts on top-down information provision rather than embrace the web's genuine interactive potential. In this regard, the Internet exists as an extension of offline campaigning, doing little to facilitate new levels of connectedness[11]. This normalisa-tion thesis[12] has been supported by a succession of international studies, which have demonstrated parties' unwillingness to exploit the interactive elements of this tech-nology[13].

Although the initial optimism surrounding the Internet's potential as a vehicle for transforming democratic relationships has been tempered by mixed empirical support, the emergence of more interactive Web 2.0 technologies have renewed expectations. By their very design, "[s]uch sites are not compatible with the top-down, elite-to-mass style of political communication that is traditional of political

---

6 Bronwyn M. Hayward, "Public Participation".

7 Edwards, Bryce, Elections and Campaigns – Voter Participation and Turnout, 2012, Retrieved from http://www.TeAra.govt.nz/en/graph/35157/party-membership-1954-2008.

8 Øyvind Kalnes, "Norwegian Parties and Web 2.0".

9 For example, see Howard Rheingold, *The Virtual Community [...]*.

10 Pippa Norris, *Digital Divide [...]*, p.10.

11 Eva Johanna Schweitzer, "Innovation or Normalization in E-Campaigning? [...]"; Maurice Vergeer, Liesbeth Hermans and Steven Sams, "Online Social Networks and Micro-blogging [...]".

12 Michael Margolis and David Resnick, *Politics as Usual [...]*.

13 Rachel K. Gibson, Michael Margolis, David Resnick and Stephen J. Ward, "Election Campaigning on the WWW [...]"; Nigel Jackson, "MPs and Web Technologies: An Untapped Opportunity?"; Ste-phen Ward and Rachel Gibson, "On-line and on Message? [...]".

parties"[14]. This suggests that Web 2.0 sites, in contrast to their earlier online counterparts, may offer new opportunities for interactivity between parties and voters. The notion of Web 2.0 can best be understood as "[...] a move from an era when web content was dominated by static web pages that individuals passively consumed to a more interactive experience where users could create, exchange and edit content to share within their own networks and with the wider online public"[15]. Examples of Web 2.0 tools include blogs, wikis, social media sites (e.g., Facebook and Twitter), video-sharing sites (e.g., YouTube and Vimeo), and photo-sharing sites (e.g., Instagram and Flickr).

Of particular relevance to this study are the social media sites Facebook and Twitter. Both of these sites demonstrate the Web 2.0 ethos of a socially connected and participatory platform reliant on user-generated, distributed and shared content. Public membership of these sites has grown significantly since their inception in 2004 (Facebook) and 2006 (Twitter). Their global popularity has also permeated New Zealand, with Facebook currently ranking as the number one social media site and the third most popular site overall in New Zealand. Twitter lags behind Facebook in terms of overall popularity, but is still the sixteenth most popular site in New Zealand[16]. In the context of election campaigns, users on these sites can freely post, discuss and share both their own or others' political commentaries, videos, and images. Facebook users can readily connect with political parties, organisations and individuals by 'liking' or 'friending' them, and individuals on Twitter can easily 'follow' political actors of interest.

Despite the initial function of these sites not being geared toward party campaign communication, parties have quickly adapted them for that purpose. These platforms offer numerous advantages. First, they provide a readily accessible and low-cost channel for political exposure. While broadcast media, and to a lesser extent more conventional forms of online communication such as websites, are restricted to those with sufficient resources to produce and disseminate content via these channels, the infrastructure on social media is pre-established. This enables any party, regardless of resources, to easily establish and maintain an online presence[17]. Second, these sites can aid campaigns by allowing parties to mobilise supporters, recruit volunteers, and generate funds[18]. Third, these socially networked channels increase the likelihood of unanticipated exposure to campaign messages. Unlike websites, which require users to actively seek out campaign information, Facebook and Twitter feed through a continuous stream of content from a plurality

---

14 Nigel A. Jackson and Darren G. Lilleker, "Building an Architecture of Participation? [...]", p. 233.
15 Rachel K. Gibson and Ian McAllister, "Normalising or Equalising Party Competition? [...]", p. 4–5.
16 "Top Sites in New Zealand".
17 Stephanie E. Bor, "Using Social Network Sites to Improve Communication [...]", p. 3.
18 Kim Strandberg, "A Social Media Revolution or Just a Case of History Repeating Itself? [...]", p. 1331.

of sources and networks making it easier for users to stumble upon political information[19]. Fourth, the unmediated nature of these channels offers parties a significant degree of choice in and control over the campaign message they disseminate on their profiles. Parties can freely publish, edit, clarify and remove content of their choosing in real-time, and can push out information to viewers that may not have otherwise been received through more traditional media channels[20].

Of course, there are notable challenges associated with using these sites as a campaign tool. Traditional forms of mediated communication do not allow parties the degree of control over the information presented to voters that social media provides. Conversely, social media erodes the ability for parties to completely regulate and manage their message, as any individual can readily post or disseminate content that is unfavourable to the campaign[21]. It is this fear of losing control over the message that is said to underlie numerous campaigners' unwillingness to engage in more interactive forms of online communication[22]. Embracing the more interactive elements of social media places added pressure on already limited resources and time, and creates uncertainty and risk in an environment where carefully crafted and controlled impressions are vital[23].

The often-cited example of Barack Obama's 2008 US presidential campaign highlighted how harnessing the power of social media can reshape the way campaigns connect with voters[24]. But while the Obama campaign demonstrated considerable success in exploiting Web 2.0 platforms to mobilise and engage constituents, it remains uncertain whether parties and candidates in other contexts are yet prepared to fully embrace the genuinely participatory architecture of this media[25].

2 Parties and Online Campaigning in New Zealand

Online campaigning first made its mark in New Zealand through the development of campaign websites in the 1996 election. These early websites, characterised as static, top-down information pages, did not utilise the technology to its full potential, operating as online replications of offline content that aimed to broadcast to rather than

---

19 Sonja Utz, "The (Potential) Benefits of Campaigning via Social Network Sites".
20 Stephanie E. Bor, "Using Social Network Sites to Improve Communication [...]", p. 12–14.
21 Vassia Gueorguieva, "Voters, MySpace, and YouTube [...]", p. 295.
22 Jennifer Stromer-Galley, "On-Line Interaction and Why Candidates Avoid It", p. 122.
23 Jennifer Stromer-Galley, "On-Line Interaction and Why Candidates Avoid It".
24 Cheris A. Carpenter, "The Obamachine: Technopolitics 2.0".
25 Benjamin Lee, "Window Dressing 2.0: Constituency-level Web Campaigns [...]"; Graeme Baxter and Rita Marcella, "Does Scotland 'like' This? [...]"; Nigel A. Jackson and Darren G. Lilleker, "Building an Architecture of Participation? [...]"; Pashchalia-Lia Spyridou and Andreas Veglis, "Political Parties and Web 2.0 Tools [...]".

engage with voters[26]. Analyses of party websites in the 2005 election echoed these sentiments. Although some websites had basic interactive features such as email addresses, opinion polls or feedback forms, these and other more genuine participatory features were used sparingly, if at all[27]. During the 2008 election, several researchers observed an increase in the role of multimedia content and dynamic features on party websites[28]. There were examples of parties utilising interactive functions such as policy calculators, billboard generators[29], online forums, and blogs[30]. However, Gong & Lips' content analysis of party websites notes that these provisions for direct, personal interaction were still relatively limited, with the central focus of campaign websites being information provision and resource generation[31].

Websites remained a key component of the 2008 and 2011 campaigns. There was also, however, an increase in the role of Web 2.0 technologies, particularly blogs and social media. These sites appeared on the New Zealand campaign scene during the 2008 election, marked by a growth in popularity of websites such as Facebook, Bebo, and MySpace. The popularity of the latter two sites has since waned, leaving Facebook as the dominant social platform in New Zealand.

Social media use by New Zealand parties has tended to mirror their use of traditional websites. Research into New Zealand parties' and candidates' use of Facebook in the 2008 election has explored who was on which channels[32], for what strategic purposes[33], and what systemic influences impacted uptake of this new technology[34]. These studies suggest that parties have attempted to make strategic use of social media[35], but have failed to use it to its full potential[36]. Research into Twitter use in New Zealand campaigns is still in its infancy, due in part to Twitter only establishing itself on the political scene during the 2011 campaign (although see Cameron et al 2013 which explores the effects of Facebook and Twitter use on

---

26 Liz Barker, "Party Websites", p. 89.
27 Karina Pedersen, "Electioneering in Cyberspace"; Karina Pederson, "New Zealand Parties in Cyberspace".
28 Peter J. Chen "Online Media"; Edwin de Ronde "Digital Campaigning"; Nicola Kean "2008: The Campaign in Cyberspace".
29 Nicola Kean "2008: The Campaign in Cyberspace", p. 196.
30 Edwin de Ronde "Digital Campaigning", p. 315.
31 Hugo Gong and Miriam Lips, The Use of New Media by Political Parties in the 2008 National Election.
32 Peter J. Chen "Online Media"; Nicola Kean "2008: The Campaign in Cyberspace".
33 Peter J. Chen "Online Media"; Hugo Gong and Miriam Lips, The Use of New Media by Political Parties in the 2008 National Election.
34 Peter Chen, "Adoption and Use of Digital Media in Election Campaigns [...]".
35 Peter Chen, "Adoption and Use of Digital Media in Election Campaigns [...]", p. 136.
36 Nicola Kean "2008: The Campaign in Cyberspace", p. 201.

electoral outcomes)[37]. In terms of New Zealand literature focusing specifically on the interactive potential of Facebook and Twitter, research to date has concentrated on how it has been used by Members of Parliament (MPs) to engage citizens outside of election campaigns[38]. Both studies found that MPs, on average, predominantly relied on these channels for top-down communication, and were either unaware of or unwilling to utilise the truly interactive and participatory features of these sites.

3 The 2011 Election

Some observers anticipated the arrival of the 'e-election' – one increasingly influenced by Web 2.0 – in the lead up to the 2011 campaign[39]. This anticipation of an election conducted via social media was not surprising. Citizens were devoting more of their attention to online media, and numerous parliamentary MPs had adopted Facebook and Twitter prior to the election[40]. During the campaign, 59 % of electorate[41] candidates had a Facebook page or profile, and 28 % were on Twitter[42]. Of the thirteen parties who contested the election, 92 % appeared to have a Facebook presence in some form, and 77 % had a Twitter account[43].

---

37 Michael P. Cameron, Patrick Barrett and Bob Stewardson, *Can Social Media Predict Election Results? [...]*.
38 Steven Barnes, Becoming a Fan [...]; Annastasha Mason, Perceptions of Use: Social Networking Sites [...].
39 Nikki MacDonald, "The E-lection"; Amy Mass, "Election Comments Banned Online".
40 Parliamentary Library, "New Zealand Parliamentarians and Online Social Media".
41 New Zealand political parties are comprised of two types of candidates – electorate and list candidates. These figures are based on a sample consisting of electorate candidates only so there may be some variance in the percentages if list candidates are included to the sample. To the best of my knowledge, no data on the percentage of all candidates using Facebook and Twitter was collated during the campaign.
42 Michael P. Cameron, Patrick Barrett and Bob Stewardson, *Can Social Media Predict Election Results? [...]*.
43 As data regarding the parties' use of social media does not appear to have been collated, I have calculated these figures on the basis of going through parties' existing Facebook and Twitter profiles to determine whether they were active during the election. In the case of Facebook, this is achieved by going to the 2011 time period in their timeline to determine whether the page existed in 2011 and was clearly being used for electioneering purposes. For Twitter, I relied on Topsy.com to determine whether a party's Twitter account was established before the election (determined by looking at the date of their first tweet) and whether they had used this account during the campaign. Where I could not find any record of an account existing, I contacted known party members to verify whether or not such accounts had been used but were since removed. While the majority of parties used Facebook pages during their campaign, the Aotearoa Legalise Cannabis Party appeared to be using a group. United Future was the only party with no record of having run a page during the campaign. In terms of Twitter, only the Conservative, Democrats for Social Credit and United Future parties remained absent from this platform.

There is to some extent a digital divide between the parties establishing an online presence and the actual use of this content by voters. Data from the New Zealand Election Study (NZES) found that only a modest 35 % of voters surveyed reported using the Internet at least once for information about the election[44]. A breakdown of the specific forms of use is presented in Table 1[45].

Table 1: Types of Sites Visited by Voters during the 2011 Election
[Source: NZES 2011 data]

Type of online content	% Respondents accessing content (n=2 475)
News media website	24,8
Party website	12,3
Local MP's website	5,1
Political Blog website	4,8
YouTube or similar website	4,4
Other electorate/list candidate's website	3,4

It is important to note that this survey does not contain any data on the frequency with which voters accessed politicised Facebook and Twitter accounts. Nonetheless, the figures highlighted do provide an important snapshot of how voters are using online media to access political information. For those citizens who do seek out political information on social media we need to look at what information they are likely to receive, and to what extent they can expect two-way engagement from parties. The remainder of this chapter looks at whether connecting with parties on Facebook and Twitter will modify the relationship between parties and the electorate from one based on top-down communication to a more interactive and conversational exchange of ideas.

4 Social Media and Interactivity in the 2011 Election

4.1 Methodology

The findings in this chapter are based on a study conducted by Deos and Murchison, which explored the use of Facebook by five political parties during the 2011 New

---

44 Question wording: During the campaign, did you use the Internet to get news or information? (n=2 475).

45 Question wording: (FOR THOSE WHO USED THE INTERNET) In particular, during the 2011 election and referendum campaigns, did you visit any of the following websites?

Zealand general election[46]. The study assessed the Facebook content of the five largest parties represented in parliament preceding the election – the National, Labour,
Green, Māori and ACT parties. They measured for the type of content posted (e.g.,
plain statements, links to websites, photos and so forth), as well as the level of party
and public interaction on each page (e.g., the number of likes, shares and comments
on each individual wallpost made by either the party itself or a member of the public). The data was drawn from posts made between 26 October and 25 November 2011
across the five parties' pages[47]. They coded a total of 996 posts, which was subsequently narrowed down to 923 following exclusion of posts deemed unrelated to the
campaign. In the original study, the authors relied on manual collection and coding
of the Facebook data, achieved by coding each post as it appeared on the Facebook
page[48]. This study develops capacity for analysis by using an online database that
collected and stored posts made on these parties' Facebook walls[49,50]. This expanded
dataset includes a total of 1 280 posts across all five parties[51].

---

46 Anthony Deos and Ashley Murchison, "What's on Their Mind? [...]".
47 The National Party used their main 'New Zealand National Party' page for campaigning, but also
set up a separate 'Our Brighter Future' page. The latter page was deactivated prior to the authors
undertaking data collection and so is not included in either the original data or this analysis (see
Anthony Deos and Ashley Murchison, "What's on Their Mind? [...]", p. 237).
48 This resulted in an incomplete dataset, primarily in terms of the total number of posts made by
members of the public on the Facebook wall of the Labour Party. The omission of all public
wallposts made on the Labour Party Facebook wall was due in part to a human coding error. In
order to access all posts made by either the party or others, an individual is required to scroll
through the Facebook page's wall (using the 'posts by page' or 'posts by others' options), select the
date of interest, and then manually select that the page display all stories (i.e, posts) made during
that period. Failure to manually select 'show all stories' results in only a sample of posted content
being displayed to the viewer. This is what occurred in Deos and Murchison's original collection and
coding of their data. However, following this protocol does not guarantee that all wallposts will still
be displayed. In my later re-collection and coding of this data, I discovered that Facebook was still
not displaying all public wallposts. For example, my display of Labour's Facebook page did not
show any posts for the days of 1 and 2 November 2011, whereas a colleague's search presented
several posts for this time period (but still fewer posts than the actual number we know were posted). Subsequently, caution should be taken with relying on manual collection of this type of data.
49 This database collects data through the Facebook Graph API. The automated sampling supple-
ments the original manual coding with the aim of creating a more complete dataset. With this in mind
it cannot be guaranteed that the automated sampling still collects all posts. This is possibly because
"[...] manual and automatic data aggregation are both subject to random 'display variations' on Facebook, due to internal algorithms that are not publicly available for analysis" Frank Feinstein, (Director,
Feinstein Doak [Software Engineers & Information Brokers]), personal communication.
50 There will be some fluctuation in the number of total likes, shares and comments across all
posts, particularly where data from the online database has been relied upon. This is because such
interaction, while measurable, is fluid in that it can easily increase or decrease within a relatively
short time frame. For example, a post measured immediately following the election could have five
comments, but this number could change should someone decide to remove their comment or
comment after the post has already been analysed. The online database draws on data retrospec-

I also applied a modified version of Deos and Murchison's Facebook coding scheme to tweets posted by the five parties during the campaign. Using the same 31 day period, I coded each party's campaign-related tweets, measuring for whether they were plain tweets (statements that originated from the party), retweets (tweets sharing content that originated from another user), or replies (tweets replying to another user)[52]. I also coded these tweets for the type of content they contained, including whether they were plain statements, links to party websites, or links to other content.

In this chapter I analyse the level of interaction occurring on parties' pages. For the Facebook analysis I draw on Stromer-Galley's distinction between media and human interactivity[53]. I explore the degree of public interaction with the party via the feedback technology embedded in Facebook pages (i.e., the number of likes and shares received on each post), as well as the degree of human interaction that occurred via Facebook posts and comments. My Twitter analysis focuses on the degree of human interaction occurring between parties and citizens, but I restrict my analysis to the frequency of parties direct replies to users rather than how often users attempt to engage with the parties. My primary interest is in exploring the frequency with which parties engage in a 'responsive dialogue' with the public, that is, directly responding to comments or questions posed by users[54].

4.2 Interaction on Facebook

Deos and Murchison's original study of Facebook pages found that the parties primarily used this site for top-down information provision[55]. In particular, parties relied heavily on their pages to redirect Facebook users to campaign information stored on their main party website[56]. Their analysis also measured the level of publicly visible interaction on these pages, including the total number of comments, likes and shares on posts. Using the new dataset outlined here, I have adjusted the

tively collected during 2014 – approximately three years since the 2011 election when the original data by Deos and Murchison was coded and so some discrepancies are to be expected.
51 Since the original data collection was undertaken, the Māori Party has disabled public posting on their wall. This means that the new dataset could not determine whether any public posts on the Māori Party page were missed during the manual collection. Subsequently, I rely solely on the original data for those public posts.
52 Here I only counted replies where the tweet from the party was clearly in response to another user. Therefore, mentions where the party was simply mentioning or 'tagging' another individual rather than directly responding to a request or engaging in a conversation were excluded.
53 Jennifer Stromer-Galley, "On-Line Interaction and Why Candidates Avoid It".
54 Sonja Utz, "The (Potential) Benefits of Campaigning via Social Network Sites".
55 Anthony Deos and Ashley Murchison, "What's on Their Mind? [...]".
56 While a small selection of additional posts were collected in this chapter's new dataset, the overall patterns in terms of the type of content posted by parties on their pages remains largely unchanged from the original study.

figures for the number of posts, comments, likes and shares for each party. This adjustment mainly incorporates the significant increase in the number of public posts made on the Labour Party's page, as well as some minor amendments to the other parties' datasets. A summary of the core findings is presented in Table 2.

Table 2: Total Wallposts and Interactions on Parties' Facebook Pages

Party	National	Labour	Greens	Māori	ACT
Party posts	180	72	67	140	72
Public posts	108	556	0	26	59
Total posts	288	628	67	166	131
Party comments	6	39	87	31	31
Average party comments per post	0,02	0,06	1,30	0,19	0,24
Public comments	334	2472	798	218	374
Total comments	340	2511	885	249	405
Average comments per post	1,18	4,00	13,21	1,50	3,09
Total likes	1068	4475	3188	760	577
Average likes per post	3,71	7,13	47,58	4,58	4,40
Total shares	69	502	507	38	21
Average shares per post	0,24	0,80	7,57	0,23	0,16

The findings suggest that there were low levels of public interaction with content overall, with the exception of likes across the Facebook pages of the five parties. A core feature of Facebook is the ability for it to facilitate networks whereby users actively participate through the sharing of content[57]. In four of the parties' cases, over 80 % of all posts on a party's wall were not shared. The only exception to this was the content on the Greens' page, where only 30 % of posts remained unshared. However, when posts by the public are excluded to account for the Greens' restrictions on public posting, we see an improvement in Labour's figures, with only 42 % of their party posts remaining unshared. The other three parties also see a slight improvement, but still had between 70 and 80 % of their posts unshared. The relatively low level of sharing of content from parties' pages suggests the potential for Web 2.0 tools to facilitate the 'viral' spread of political communication is yet to be fully realised.

Of particular interest here is the ability for Facebook pages to provide new spaces for vertical and horizontal communication. This communication can occur in two ways. Firstly, the page owner (in this case the party) can share content or updates in

---

57 Darren G. Lilleker and Nigel A. Jackson, "Towards a More Participatory Style of Election Campaigning [...]".

the form of posts. Then, depending on the page's security settings, members of the public can also post content or feedback on that page. Secondly, the page owner and members of the public can also communicate via comments on these posts. It is this second form of communication that is of interest here as this is where public party-to-citizen and citizen-to-citizen dialogue actually unfolds. The Total comments row in Table 2 indicates some variation across parties in terms of the number of total comments received on their Facebook pages. Labour received by far the most comments out of all the parties, followed by the Greens, ACT, National and the Māori Party. It is interesting to note that while Labour received the most comments overall, the Greens had a better spread of comments across posts, with 96 % of all posts on their page being commented on during the election. ACT, the Māori Party and Labour followed with 64, 57 and 55 % respectively. National performed the worst with only 38 % of posts stimulating communication amongst citizens.

The frequency of party comments is also of interest as it provides an indication of whether parties were engaging in dialogue with their constituents, or broadcasting information and leaving citizens to communicate amongst themselves. The findings in Table 2 suggest the latter. Few parties made a concerted effort to engage with Facebook users via the comments function, with the Māori Party and Greens proving the most interactive. Of all comments made on the Māori Party's Facebook page, 31 (12 % of all comments) came directly from the party. The Greens also engaged somewhat regularly with posts on their page, with 87 comments (10 %) coming directly from the party. It is also worth noting that the Greens averaged 1,30 comments per Facebook post, an average comment rate significantly higher than the other parties. The next closest was ACT with 0,24 comments per post. On ACT's page, 31 (8 %) comments were from the party itself. The two major parties, National and Labour, both performed extremely poorly in terms of interaction, with only 6 and 39 comments respectively coming directly from the parties. For both parties this represented less than 2 % of all comments made.

It is worth highlighting that the Greens had disabled public posting on their Facebook wall. This means that the relatively high level of public commentary on their page was attributable to the fact that commenting was the only way to interact with the party. Subsequently, although the Greens were more willing to interact with commenters on their wall, the fact that they blocked people from posting their own content weakens their overall level of interaction. The Māori Party permitted public posts on their wall during the election campaign, but they have since disabled this feature.

4.3 Interaction and Content on Twitter

Looking at Table 3, we can see that @NZNationalParty tweeted 112 times between 26 October and 25 November. Of these, 111 were original tweets made by the party, with only one retweet. In terms of measuring the level of interaction on Twitter, I focused on the number of overall replies the party made to others tweets. National had a total of zero replies to others' tweets. With this information in mind, it is also important to note that @NZNationalParty was not the primary campaign Twitter account for the National Party. National also ran an additional account under the name @natcampaign[58]. The total number of tweets from this account was 163, consisting of 154 original tweets and 9 retweets. Of these, 21 tweets (13 % of all tweets counted) were replies to others.

Table 3: Type of Tweets by Party

Party	@NZNational-Party	@nat-campaign	@nzlabour	@NZGreens	@Maori_Party	@actparty
Original tweets	111	154	299	424	27	41
Retweets	1	9	150	131	0	9
Total tweets	112	163	449	555	27	50
Replies	0	21	15	257	0	5
Replies as % of total tweets	0,0	12,9	3,3	46,3	0,0	10,0

Labour had a total of 449 tweets. Of these, 299 were original tweets compared to 150 retweets. They replied to a total of 15 tweets (3 %) throughout this period. The Greens stood out as the most active user of Twitter, posting 555 tweets in total. Of these tweets, 424 were original tweets, while 131 were retweets. Of their total tweets, 46 % were replies; the most of any of the parties included in this analysis. Compared to the previous three parties discussed, the Māori Party was relatively inactive on Twitter, with only 27 tweets in total, none of which were retweets. Given their infrequent use of Twitter, it is perhaps unsurprising that they had zero replies to followers. The ACT Party had a total of 50 tweets, of which 41 were original tweets compared with 9 retweets. ACT also failed to engage with voters, replying on only five occasions.

Deos and Murchison's original analysis of Facebook posts made by parties included an overview of the type of content posted during the campaign. I have undertaken a similar breakdown here, the results of which are presented in Table 4. The data indicates that National's tweets from the @NZNationalParty account were

---

58 At the time of this analysis @natcampaign had been deleted and data was only available via *Topsy.com*. Having accessed the data from this account, I was unable to verify the exact number of tweets by the party that were retweets. Because the @natcampaign tweets were removed when the account was closed I had to rely on 'RT' indicators and other users retweeting the same tweet.

overwhelmingly link based, with nearly 94 % of their total tweets providing a link to their main party website. Other forms of content barely registered. In terms of information posted by the @natcampaign account, the data indicates somewhat more diversity in content than what was seen from @NZNationalParty. The information tweeted from @natcampaign was still predominantly link based, with links to the main party website totalling just over 58 % of all tweets. However, in contrast to @NZNationalParty where plain tweets and links to other YouTube were negligible, here we see these types of tweets occurring more frequently with 21 % containing plain statements, and 9 % directing followers to YouTube.

Table 4: Type of Content in Tweets Made by Parties

| Party | @NZNationalParty | | @natcampaign | | @nzlabour | | @NZGreens | | @Maori_Party | | @actparty | |
Type of content	n	%	n	%	n	%	n	%	n	%	n	%
Plain tweet statement	3	2,7	34	20,9	196	43,7	264	47,6	15	55,6	11	22,0
Photo	1	0,9	5	3,1	67	14,9	7	1,3	1	3,7	2	4,0
Link to main party website	105	93,8	95	58,3	94	20,9	105	18,9	8	29,6	26	52,0
Link to other party website	0	0,0	3	1,8	30	6,7	26	4,7	0	0,0	0	0,0
Link to leader website	1	0,9	0	0,0	0	0,0	0	0,0	0	0,0	0	0,0
Link to candidate website	0	0,0	0	0,0	0	0,0	0	0,0	0	0,0	0	0,0
Link to media website	0	0,0	1	0,6	36	8,0	58	10,5	3	11,1	5	10,0
Link to other website	0	0,0	4	2,5	9	2,0	62	11,2	0	0,0	2	4,0
Link to YouTube	1	0,9	15	9,2	14	3,1	23	4,1	0	0,0	4	8,0
Link to Facebook	1	0,9	6	3,7	3	0,7	10	1,8	0	0,0	0	0,0
Total tweets by party only	112	100,0	163	100,0	449	100,0	555	100,0	27	100,0	50	100,0

Unlike National, plain tweets were the most prevalent type of information for the Labour Party, totalling almost 44 % of all tweets. Labour also regularly posted links to its party website (21 %) and image-based content (15 %). Less common were tweets containing links to media websites, other party sites such as their *Red Alert* blog, and YouTube. The most prevalent type of content posted by the Greens was plain tweets with nearly 48 % of total tweets falling into this category. The high number of plain tweets by the Greens is in part attributable to their frequent replies to followers. Followed by this were tweets linking to the main party website (19 %), and other miscellaneous websites (11 %).

The majority of Māori Party content was plain tweets, with 56 % of their tweets falling into this category. This was followed by links to their main website (30 %), and links to media websites (11 %). Only one tweet contained an image. The majority of ACT's tweets linked to their party website (52 %). Plain tweets were the second most common type of tweet at 22 %, followed by links to media websites at 10 %.

5 Changing Communications?

In the face of increasing voter disengagement and volatility in New Zealand (as elsewhere), the interactive opportunities afforded by these Web 2.0 platforms raise pertinent questions about their potential to reconnect parties with their electorates. It is evident that online media is playing an increasing role in political communication and campaigning in New Zealand. Political parties are acknowledging that an online presence is a necessary component of today's campaign strategy[59]. However, whether these online channels are facilitating new forms of communication between parties and voters remains uncertain.

My research suggests that they feel more comfortable using online channels for communicating information to citizens rather than engaging with them. For the two largest parties – National and Labour – there was little attempt to converse directly with voters by responding with comments (on Facebook) or replies (on Twitter). National acknowledged that this was a deliberate strategy, while Labour's lack of interaction could be attributed in part to their self-described ad hoc approach to social media during the 2011 campaign[60]. The ACT and Māori parties made modest attempts to interact with voters on Facebook, but their Twitter engagement was either minimal or non-existent. The reasons for this remain unclear, but given the small size of both parties, one explanation could be that they felt it more useful to concentrate their personnel and financial resources elsewhere.

---

59 Stephen Mills, "Use of Social Media in Politics by Young People in Australasia".
60 Stephen Mills, "Use of Social Media in Politics by Young People in Australasia", p. 24–5.

Only the Greens appeared to consistently engage across both platforms. This finding reflects a deliberate strategy to actively connect and interact with their online audience[61]. The caveat in the Greens' case, however, is that this interaction was bounded by top-down restrictions imposed by the party. In preventing people from posting directly to their Facebook wall, they reduced the means by which voters could actively reach out and ask questions of them. Consequently, despite a willingness to engage, the Greens appear to be cognisant of maintaining a degree of control[62]. With these conclusions in mind, I would argue that parties' use of Facebook and Twitter in the 2011 campaign is aligned with what Jackson and Lilleker refer to as Web 1.5[63]. It is evident that parties in New Zealand are establishing a presence on social media, but they remain reticent to fully embrace the participatory ethos underlying Web 2.0.

Research into the effects of Web 2.0 in the New Zealand political environment is still in its infancy. This particular study provides a snapshot of one campaign, and relies on a sample of parties contesting the election. Future studies in this context would benefit from expanding the analysis to include all parties and exploring whether we see shifts in how this technology is used across campaigns. There is also a need to extend this analysis to investigate the use of Facebook and Twitter by candidates during campaigns. While party-specific content provides valuable insight into these organisations' willingness to engage with the electorate, it is possible that we will see greater evidence of interactivity in assessing individual candidates' online campaigns. Finally, this study sought to provide a rudimentary overview of the frequency of interaction occurring between parties and voters online. Investigation into this dialogue in terms of what precisely is being said and by whom will offer a more detailed qualitative insight into this form of political communication.

Looking forward to the 2014 general election, it is anticipated that Facebook and Twitter will maintain their presence as campaign communication tools. The ubiquitous use of social media by parties presently in Parliament, alongside the increasing uptake of these channels by current MPs, suggests that new parties and candidates in the race will have little choice but to be seen as 'keeping up with the Joneses'. Whether they embrace this technology to its full extent, or continue down the path of Web 1.5 seen in 2011, will remain to be seen.

---

61 Stephen Mills, « Use of Social Media in Politics by Young People in Australasia", p. 25.
62 cf. Jennifer Stromer-Galley, "On-Line Interaction and Why Candidates Avoid It".
63 Nigel A. Jackson and Darren G. Lilleker, "Building an Architecture of Participation? [...]".

References

Alexa (2014). *Top Sites in New Zealand*. Retrieved from http://www.alexa.com/topsites/countries/NZ.

Barker, L. (2004). Party Websites. In Hayward, J. & Rudd, C. (Eds.), *Political Communications in New Zealand*. Auckland: Pearson Education New Zealand.

Barnes, S. *Becoming a Fan: New and Social Media as a Tool for Political Communication and Engagement Amongst Canadian and New Zealand MPs*. Retrieved from http://www.scribd.com/doc/78506261/ Barnes-New-and-Social-Media-as-a-Tool-for-Political-Communication-and-Engagement-Amongst-MPs.

Baxter, G. & Marcella, R. (2012). Does Scotland 'like' This? Social Media Use by Political Parties and Candidates in Scotland During the 2010 UK General Election Campaign. *Libri. International Journal of Libraries and Information Services, 62(2)*, 109–124.

Bor, S.E. (2013). Using Social Network Sites to Improve Communication Between Political Campaigns and Citizens in the 2012 Election. *American Behavioral Scientist*, 1–19, doi:10.1177/0002764213490698.

Cameron, M.P., Barrett, P. & Stewardson, B. (2013). *Can Social Media Predict Election Results? Evidence from New Zealan.*, Working Paper in Economics 13/08, Department of Economics, University of Waikato, Hamilton. Retrieved from ftp://mngt.waikato.ac.nz/repec/Wai/econwp/1308.pdf.

Carpenter, C.A. (2010). The Obamachine: Technopolitics 2.0. *Journal of Information Technology & Politics, 7(2–3)*, 216–225.

Chen, P.J. (2009). Online Media. In Rudd, C., Hayward, J. & Craig, G. (Eds.), *Informing Voters? Politics, Media and the New Zealand Election 2008*. North Shore: Pearson.

Chen, P. (2010). Adoption and Use of Digital Media in Election Campaigns: Australia, Canada and New Zealand. *Public Communications Review, 1(1)*, 3–26.

de Ronde, E., (2010). Digital Campaigning. In Miller, R. (Ed.), *New Zealand Government and Politics* (5th ed.). Melbourne: Oxford University Press.

Deos, A. & Murchison, A. (2012). What's on Their Mind? Political Parties and Facebook in the 2011 New Zealand General Election. In Johansson, J. & Levine, S. (Eds.), *Kicking the Tyres: The New Zealand General Election and Electoral Referendum of 2011,* Wellington: Victoria University Press.

Edwards, B. (2012). *Elections and Campaigns – Voter Participation and Turnout*. Retrieved from http://www.TeAra.govt.nz/en/graph/35157/party-membership-1954-2008.

Feinstein, F. (Director, Feinstein Doak [Software Engineers & Information Brokers]), personal communication, March 30, 2014.

Gibson, R.K. & McAllister, I. (2014). Normalising or Equalising Party Competition? Assessing the Impact of the Web on Election Campaigning. *Political Studies*, 1–19, doi/10.1111/1467-9248.12107.

Gibson, R.K., Margolis, M., Resnick, D. & Ward, S.J. (2003). Election Campaigning on the WWW in the USA and UK: A Comparative Analysis. *Party Politics, 9(1)*, 47–75.

Gibson, R., Lusoli, W. & Ward, S. (2008). The Australian Public and Politics On-line: Reinforcing or Reinventing Representation? *Australian Journal of Political Science, 43(1)*, 111–131.

Gong, H. and Lips, M. (2009). *The Use of New Media by Political Parties in the 2008 National Election*, 2009. Retrieved from http://e-government.vuw.ac.nz/research_projects_2009/eCampaigning_NZ_2008.pdf.

Gueorguieva, V. (2008). Voters, MySpace, and YouTube. The Impact of Alternative Communication Channels on the 2006 Election Cycle and Beyond. *Social Science Computer Review, 26(3)*, 288–300.

Hayward, B.M. (2006). Public Participation. In Miller, R. (Ed.), *New Zealand Government and Politics*, (4th ed.). Melbourne: Oxford University Press.

Jackson, N.A. & Lilleker, D.G. (2009). Building an Architecture of Participation? Political Parties and Web 2.0 in Britain. *Journal of Information Technology & Politics, 6*, 232–250.

Jackson, N. (2003). MPs and Web Technologies: An Untapped Opportunity? *Journal of Public Affairs, 3(2)*, 124–137.

Kalnes, Ø. (2009). Norwegian Parties and Web 2.0. *Journal of Information Technology & Politics*, *6(3–4)*, 251–266.

Kean, N. (2010). 2008: The Campaign in Cyberspace. In Levine, S. & Roberts, N.S. (Eds.). *Key to Victory: The New Zealand General Election of 2008*. Wellington: Victoria University Press.

Lee, B. (2014). Window Dressing 2.0: Constituency-level Web Campaigns in the 2010 UK General Election. *Politics, 34(1)*, 45–57.

Lilleker, D.G. & Jackson, N.A. (2010). Towards a More Participatory Style of Election Campaigning: The Impact of Web 2.0 on the UK 2010 General Election. *Policy & Internet, 2(3)*, 69–98.

Maas, A. (2011). *Election Comments Banned Online*. Retrieved from http://www.stuff.co.nz/auckland/local-news/6036253/Election-comments-banned-online.

MacDonald, N. (2011). *The E-lection*. Retrieved from http://www.stuff.co.nz/dominion-post/news/politics/5677268/The-E-lection.

Margolis, M. & Resnick, D. (2000). *Politics as Usual: The Cyberspace Revolution*. Thousand Oaks: Sage Publications.

Mason, A. (2011). *Perceptions of Use: Social Networking Sites, MPs and Citizens*, Master's thesis, University of Otago, Dunedin, New Zealand. Retrieved from http://hdl.handle.net/10523/1891.

Mills, S. (2013). Use of Social Media in Politics by Young People in Australasia. In Carthew, A. & Winkelmann, S. (Eds.), *Social Media and Elections in Asia-Pacific – The Growing Power of the Youth Vote*. Singapore: Konrad-Adenauer-Stiftung.

Norris, P. (2001) *Digital Divide: Civic Engagement, Information Poverty, and the Internet Worldwide*. Cambridge: Cambridge University Press.

Parliamentary Library (2011). *New Zealand Parliamentarians and Online Social Media*. Retrieved from http://www.parliament.nz/en-nz/parl-support/research-papers/00PLSocRP11021/new-zealand-parliamentarians-and-online-social-media.

Pedersen, K. (2007). Electioneering in Cyberspace. In Levine, S. & Roberts, N.S. (Eds.). *The Baubles of Office: The New Zealand General Election of 2005*, Wellington: Victoria University Press.

Pederson, K. (2007). New Zealand Parties in Cyberspace. *Political Science, 57(2)*, 107–116.

Rheingold, H. (1993). *The Virtual Community: Homesteading on the Electronic Frontier*, Reading MA: Addison-Wesley.

Schweitzer, E.J. (2008). Innovation or Normalization in E-Campaigning? : A Longitudinal Content and Structural Analysis of German Party Websites in the 2002 and 2005 National Elections. *European Journal of Communication, 23(4)*, 449–470.

Smith, P., Gibson, A., Crothers, C., Billot, J. & Bell, A. (2011). *The Internet in New Zealand 2011*, Auckland: Institute of Culture, Discourse & Communication, AUT University.

Spyridou, P.-L. & Veglis, A. (2011). Political Parties and Web 2.0 Tools: A Shift in Power or a New Digital Bandwagon? *Int. J. Electronic Governance, 4(1–2)*, 136–155.

Strandberg, K. (2013). A Social Media Revolution or Just a Case of History Repeating Itself? The Use of Social Media in the 2011 Finnish Parliamentary Elections. *New Media Society*, 15(8), 1329–1347.

Stromer-Galley, J. (2000). On-Line Interaction and Why Candidates Avoid It. *Journal of Communication, 50(4)*, 111–132.

Utz, S. (2009). The (Potential) Benefits of Campaigning via Social Network Sites. *Journal of Computer-Mediated Communication, 14(2)*, 221–243.

Vergeer, M., Hermans, L. & Sams, S. (2011). Online Social Networks and Micro-blogging in Political Campaigning: The Exploration of a New Campaign Tool and a New Campaign Style. *Party Politics*, 1–25.

Vowles, J. (2012, November). *Down, Down, Down: Turnout in New Zealand from 1946 to the 2011 Election*, Paper presented at the annual conference of the New Zealand Political Studies Association, New Zealand.

Ward, S. & Gibson, R. (2003). On-line and on Message? Candidate Websites in the 2001 General Election. *British Journal of Politics and International Relations, 5(2)*, 188–205.

Ward, S., Gibson, R. & Nixon, P. (2003). Introduction. In Gibson, R., Nixon, P. & Ward, S. (Eds.), *Political Parties and the Internet: Net Gain?* London: Routledge.

Karine Prémont and Charles-Antoine Millette[1]

Social Media and American Presidential Campaigns: The Dark Side of the Electoral Process

Ever since the very first presidential elections in the 18th century, negative advertising has been central to the American electoral process. This type of advertising refers to a communication strategy where a candidate attacks an opponent by stressing his weaknesses (personality, behaviour, credibility, or competence) in order to make himself look like the better choice. For example, during the 1860 and 1864 campaigns, Abraham Lincoln "was called an Illinois ape [and was accused] of being a tyrant, a dictator, a coward, and a traitor[2]" by his opponents. Such mudslinging became much more prevalent in the early 1950s with the advent of TV election advertising, and in recent decades this medium has been broadcasting more and more negative campaign ads.[3]

In the early 1980s, "a third of televised political messages were negative advertising,"[4] while in 2004 nearly 45 % of all ads paid for by the presidential election candidates were negative.[5] According to Dan Balz, the 2012 presidential election did not escape this trend, as seen in the increased number of attack ads by both candidates and in the tone of their language: "[...] *what was most striking* [...] *in the race was not just the negativity or the sheer volume of attack ads raining down on voters in the swing states. It was the sense that all restraints were gone, the guardrails had disappeared, and there was no incentive for anyone to hold back.*"[6]

Whereas television transformed the way presidential candidates conducted their campaigns in the early 1950s, the advent of social media has changed their electoral strategies even more so, as well as the way potential voters get informed,

1 *Karine Prémont*, Assistant Professor, Department of Political Science, Université de Sherbrooke; *Charles-Antoine Millette*, Ph.D. Student, Department of Political Science, Université du Québec à Montréal.

2 Gilles Vandal (2009). La publicité négative dans les campagnes présidentielles américaines: un phénomène de "dépacification"?, Congrès international de l'Association française de sciences politiques, Grenoble, p. 4.

3 Christopher C. Hull (2007). Has Campaign Finance Reform Provoked Attack Ads? Modeling Candidate and Independent Group Negative Advertising, *Conference Papers – Southern Political Science Association*, p. 4–5.

4 André Gosselin (1997). La publicité électorale, *Les Études de communication publique*, n° 11, p. 11.

5 Ivonne M. Torres, Michael R. Hyman and Jared Hamilton (2012). Candidate-Sponsored TV Ads for the 2004 U.S. Presidential Election: A Content Analysis, *Journal of Political Marketing*, Vol. 11, n° 3, p. 189.

6 Dan Balz (2013). Collision 2012. Obama vs. Romney and the Future of Elections in America, New York, Viking, p. 276.

take part, and make their choices. Through social media, candidates have a means for bypassing mainstream media, and citizens have a platform from which they can be heard by politicians.[7] Nonetheless, use of social media deprives candidates of some control over their message to the benefit of those who search the Internet for the slightest sign of misconduct: *"There is a piece of information… and it begins to bounce around, essentially. It's shared, it's repeated. It reverberates."*[8] Through social media, citizens are exposed to more and more mudslinging by candidates.

The aim of this text is to present the adverse effects of social media on the way election campaigns are conducted in the United States. To be specific, we argue that social media are accentuating the negative side of American presidential campaigns in four ways: by personalizing attacks, by "anecdotizing" campaigns, by decentralizing information, and by micro-targeting voters.

1 Increasingly negative election campaigns. Are social media to blame?

There seems to be a strong consensus that American presidential campaigns are now largely negative, the example of the 2012 campaign being especially striking. The Republican candidate Mitt Romney used 91 % of his advertising budget to produce and disseminate attack ads via all media platforms. This kind of content accounted for 85 % of Barack Obama's advertising budget.[9] In terms of content, 81 % of his TV ads were negative, versus 89 % of Mitt Romney's.[10]

This phenomenon is also very present during the primaries, as seen in 2012 with the Republicans. Group and candidate advertising expenditures were largely for attack ads. Moreover, the ads contain more misleading or simply false information today than in the past, thus making election advertising campaigns even more negative. Some organizations, like FactCheck.org and PolitiFact, rate the truthfulness of

---

7 John Allen Hendricks (2014). The New-Media Campaign of 2012, in Robert E. Denton Jr. (ed.), *The 2012 Presidential Campaign: A Communication Perspective*, Lanham, Rowman & Littlefield, pp. 147 and 149.

8 *Ibid.*, p. 144.

9 Darrell West (2014). Air Wars: TV Advertising and Social Media in Election Campaigns, 1952–2012, 6th edition, London, Sage, p. 70.

10 Elizabeth Wilner (2012). Romney and Republicans Outspent Obama, But Couldn't Out-Advertise Him, *Ad Age*, November 9, [adage.com/article/campaign-trail/romney-outspent-obama-advertise/238241/].

ad content by studying each election ad of candidates and independent groups and then posting their findings on the Internet.[11]

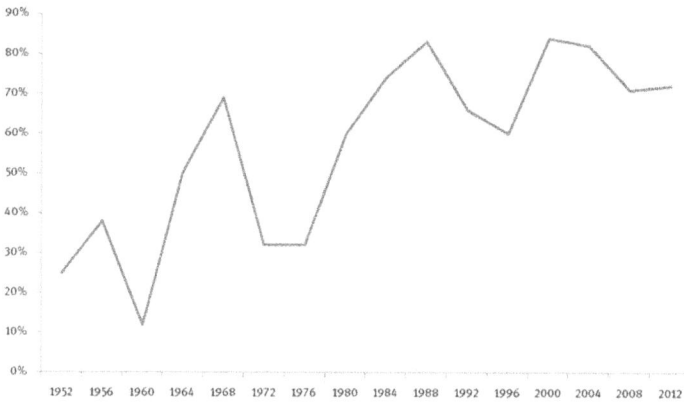

Figure 1: Attack ads as a percentage of all election ads, 1952–2012
[Source: Based on Darrell West (2014). Air Wars: TV Advertising and Social Media in Election Campaigns, 1952–2012, 6th edition, London, Sage, p. 66 and data from the Center Media Analysis Group, http://kantarmedia.com/cmag]

Table 1: Advertising budgets of independent groups and attack ads during the 2012 Republican Primaries
[Source: Based on Darrell West (2014). Air Wars: TV Advertising and Social Media in Election Campaigns, 1952–2012, 6th edition, London, Sage, p. 70]

Candidate or group	Advertising budget ($)	Attack ads (%)
Restore Our Future (pro-Romney)	$27.2 million	91
American Crossroads	$11.8 million	100
Mitt Romney	$7.5 million	54
Americans for Prosperity	$7.2 million	100
Winning Our Future (pro-Gingrich)	$3.8 million	67
Red, White, and Blue Fund (pro-Santorum)	$3.6 million	82
American Future Fund	$3.3 million	100
American Energy Alliance	$2.5 million	100
Ron Paul	$1.6 million	53
Rick Santorum	$1.1 million	65
Newt Gingrich	$909,000	47
Rick Perry	$906,000	33
Make Us Great (pro-Perry)	$869,000	40

---

11 John C. Tedesco and Scott W. Dunn (2014). Political Advertising in the 2012 U.S. Presidential Election, in Robert E. DENTON, Jr., (ed.) *The 2012 Presidential Campaign. A Communication Perspective*, Lanham, Maryland, Rowman & Littlefield, p. 90.

When we examine the behavior of social media more closely, we see they are covering election campaigns even more negatively, especially the candidates, than is the
case with mainstream media. Whereas mainstream media coverage of candidates
was 30 to 40 % negative in 2012, the corresponding figure rose to 50 and even 60 %
for social media.[12]

Table 2: Mainstream media less harsh than social media
[Source: Journalism.org (2012). Winning the Media Campaign 2012,
[http://www.journalism.org/analysis_ report/ winning_media_campaign_2012]

Mainstream News Less Harsh than Social Media
Percent of stories/discussion with tone

	Obama	Romney
Mainstream		
– Positive	19 %	15 %
– Mixed	51 %	47 %
– Negative	30 %	38 %
Twitter		
– Positive	25 %	16 %
– Mixed	31 %	25 %
– Negative	45 %	58 %
Facebook		
– Positive	24 %	23 %
– Mixed	22 %	15 %
– Negative	53 %	62 %
Blogs		
– Positive	19 %	18 %
– Mixed	37 %	36 %
– Negative	44 %	46 %

Date Range: August 27–October 21, 2012
Pew Research Center's Project for Excellence in Journalism

---

12 Despite the negative media coverage of both presidential candidates in 2012, Barack Obama benefit-
ed from a brief respite during the last campaign week. For more details, consult Pew Research Center's
Journalism Project Staff (2012). The Final Days of the Media Campaign 2012, *Pew Research Journalism
Project*, November 19, [www.journalism.org/2012/11/19/final-days-media-campaign-2012/].

There are two reasons. On the one hand, social media are not subject to regulation, as are TV chains, newspapers, and radio broadcasts.[13] For example, advertising spots on YouTube do not need official approval by the candidates, whereas a law requires approval for a TV spot. On the other hand, social media are open to a multitude of often more radical groups and citizens who have neither the opportunity nor the means to spread their message via mainstream channels. Many anti-Clinton Facebook pages appeared during the 2008 Democratic Primaries, having been created by simple citizens.

Lack of social media regulation, together with voluntary, inexpensive, and often anonymous participation by a multitude of civil society actors who can come forward via social media, greatly helps to make election campaigns more negative by amplifying the personalization of attacks, the "anecdotization" of campaigns, the decentralization of information, and the micro-targeting of voters.

---

13 David Mark (2009). *Going Dirty: The Art of Negative Campaigning*, 2nd edition, Lanham, Rowman and Littlefield, pp. 159–162.

Tone of Conversation about Candidates on Twitter
Percent of assertions

Date Range: August 27 – November 5, 2012
PEJ analysis using Crimson Hexagon technology
PEW RESEARCH CENTER'S PROJECT FOR EXCELLENCE IN JOURNALISM

Tone of Conversation about Candidates on Facebook
Percent of assertions

Date Range: August 27 – November 5, 2012
PEJ analysis using Crimson Hexagon technology
PEW RESEARCH CENTER'S PROJECT FOR EXCELLENCE IN JOURNALISM

Tone of Conversation about Candidates in Blogs
Percent of assertions

Date Range: August 27 – November 5, 2012
PEJ analysis using Crimson Hexagon technology
PEW RESEARCH CENTER'S PROJECT FOR EXCELLENCE IN JOURNALISM

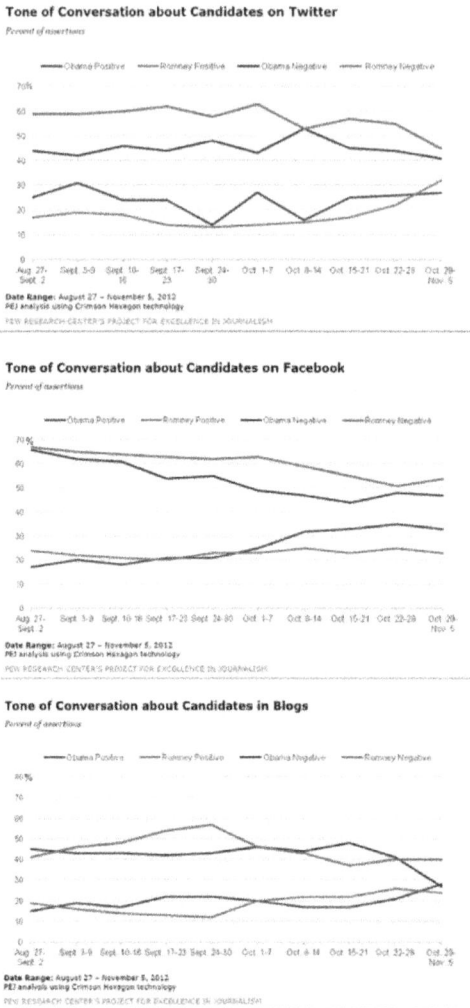

Figure 2: Tone of conversation about candidates on Twitter, Facebook, and blogs (2012)
[Sources: *Twitter*: Pew Research Center's Project for Excellence in Journalism (2012b). The Final Days of the Media Campaign 2012, November 19, [http://www.journalism.org/analysis_ report/final_days_ media_campaign_ 2012], p. 9.; *Facebook*: Pew Research Center's Project for Excellence in Journalism (2012b). The Final Days of the Media Campaign 2012, November 19, [http://www.journalism.org/ analysis_ report/final_days_media_campaign_ 2012], p. 12.; *Blogs*: Pew Research Center's Project for Excellence in Journalism (2012b). The Final Days of the Media Campaign 2012, November 19, [http://www.journalism.org/analysis_report/ final_days_media_campaign_2012], p. 11]

1.1 Personalizing the attacks

Social media often have the effect of playing down political issues while playing up the candidates' personalities – or rather their flaws. Indeed, social media create a star system based on popularity and not on a person's real achievements. This is all the more true for presidential candidates. John McCain, the 2008 Republican candidate, soon grasped this point, as seen in a video titled "Celeb,"[14] which presented the Democrat Obama as a star without substance and therefore as someone without the qualities to become president of the United States. This YouTube ad was viewed nearly 2.5 million times and also had mainstream media coverage. There was also "Barackbook," a Facebook parody that the McCain staff created in 2008 and which showcased Obama's "questionable" friends.[15] In 2008 and 2012, approximately ten YouTube videos ridiculed Romney's changing positions on social issues. The ads came essentially from his more conservative Republican opponents, who reproached him for being a little too close to the Democrats on these issues.

The tone of conversations that may be found on social media about candidates is especially negative, in particular on Twitter and Facebook, which are above all used by ordinary citizens. The gap between positive and negative conversations about candidates is narrower on blogs, which are more often written by specialists or, at the very least, by people who are more interested in politics and the campaign. This trend was clearly observed in 2012, when both candidates, Romney and Obama, were particularly targeted by negative comments rather than positive ones.

1.2 "Anecdotizing" the campaigns

Social media can be used to broadcast photos and videos of the more frivolous or ridiculous sides of candidates. This is how John Edwards' hair and Hillary Clinton's voice had their moments of glory during the 2008 Democratic Primaries as the stars of widely viewed YouTube videos.[16] In the same spirit, the muscles of Romney's 2012 running mate, Paul Ryan, had their own Twitter account (@PaulRyansbicep), which was opened after photos of Ryan exercising appeared in *Time*, on the eve of the October vice-presidential debate.

---

14 Posted July 31, 2008: [http://www.youtube.com/watch?v=oHXYsw_ZDXg].

15 Initially a website (no longer available when these lines were being written), BarackBook was then turned into a YouTube video posted August 5, 2008: [http://www.youtube.com/watch?v=pTC6oLL4oPI]. For more details, see Sarah Lai Stirland (2012). GOP Site 'BarackBook' Mocks Obama's Facebook Support, *Wired*, July 29, [http://www.wired.com/threatlevel/2008/07/obamamania-has/].

16 For the video "I Feel Pretty" starring Edwards and viewed more than a million times: [http://www.youtube.com/results?search_query=i+feel+pretty+edwards&sm=3]. For the video "Off-Key" on Clinton : [http://www.youtube.com/watch?v=tJmPpwfOhJ4].

For voters, the problem is that these messages circulate so fast on social media that political issues may be completely overshadowed and campaigning reduced to a series of anecdotes, which will prevail over the candidates' more substantial messages.[17] The most popular items on social media during the 2012 campaign were the Facebook page BindersFullOfWomen (following a remark by Romney during the second presidential debate in October) and the hashtags #bidenism and #eastwooding on Twitter.[18] The occasional spats on Twitter between David Axelrod, Obama's senior advisor, and Romney's strategists are another clear example. All of these parodies often attracted more attention than did political messages from debates and conventions. In sum, election campaign issues may remain unknown if people rely solely on social media for information.

Finally, social media information is generally less reliable than mainstream media information. This problem is especially visible on blogs, whose authors are regularly lumped in with experts, specialists, and journalists (though not always any of the three). It is made worse when mainstream media journalists pick up anecdotes from social media, thus bringing them into the news cycle and keeping them there.[19]

1.3 Decentralizing information

The emergence and popularity of social media have for all intents ended what is called "top-down spin," i.e., imposition of daily topics by higher-ups (the candidate's election campaign strategists and staff). Although this tactic still exists and although strategists will use social media to spin a message, "bottom-up spin" can now more easily dilute the message with one that comes from citizens or civil society groups and that is often picked up by journalists, who more often consult social media than the candidates' "spin doctors."[20] This decentralization of campaigns sometimes forces candidates to deal with controversial subjects. In 2008, for example, John McCain had to clarify his position on Iran following the posting of a YouTube video showing him singing "Bomb Iran," instead of "Barbara Ann" by the

---

17 Stephen Farnsworth and S. Robert Lichter (2011). *The Nightly News Nightmare: Media Coverage of U.S. Presidential Elections, 1988–2008*, Lanham, Rowman & Littlefield, pp. 181–182.

18 #bidenism referred to the regular verbal gaffes of Joe Biden, Obama's running mate. The hashtag was thus used not only to report gaffes but also to create entirely fictitious ones. As for the hashtag #eastwooding, it referred to actor Clint Eastwood's speech at the August 2012 Republican National Convention, during which he talked to an empty chair that was supposed to incarnate President Obama.

19 Stephen J. Farnsworth (2009). Spinner in Chief: How Presidents Sell Their Policies and Themselves, Boulder, Paradigm Publishers.

20 John Allen Hendricks, *op. cit.*, p. 148.

Beach Boys.[21] When, in 2012, Romney said that 47 % of Americans took more from government in services and benefits than they paid in taxes, his comment was massively reported not only on social media but also on mainstream media, thus swinging the momentum back to Barack Obama at a key point in the campaign.[22] Romney repeatedly had to explain what he meant.

Although this decentralisation is interesting when it forces candidates to confront touchy subjects, it does not always benefit democracy, since it allows social media to be manipulated by anyone: citizens, groups, parties, candidates, strategists, and journalists.[23] For example, you can alter the number of Twitter account users, associate a name with a parody site that will show up on a Google search, or produce fallacious videos and post them on YouTube. This was the case with Hillary Clinton's 2008 video *The Politics of Pile On*, which suggested she was a victim of sexism by the other candidates during the Democratic Primary debates.

1.4 Micro-targeting the voters

With the technological means currently available and with the way social media reach their users, political organizers can now very precisely target the groups they hope to convince.[24] Indeed, "messages are more effectively targeted [...] to rally the faithful, convince the undecided, and frequently inform less attentive and knowledgeable voters [...]."[25] Thanks to applications available on smartphones, candidates can now broadcast attack ads in relation to the geographical location of their supporters and, above all, the type of event they attend: "[...] *people who attended the Minnesota State Fair in 2010 and had a smartphone received targeted ads on their mobile devices from Michelle Bachmann's congressional campaign informing them that her opponent supported food tax increases*."[26] Candidates are thus conversing directly with certain portions of the electorate in order to persuade them on the basis of their location and also the context in which they receive the message.

---

21 Posted April 19, 2007 and viewed over 1.5 million times: [http://www.youtube.com/watch?v=o-zoPgv_nYg].

22 Posted September 18, 2012, this video had few views (less than 300,000) but its wider dissemination by the mainstream media made it a crucial campaign moment: [http://www.youtube.com/watch?v=M2gvY2wqI7M].

23 Panagiotis T. Metaxas, and Eni Mustafaraj (2012). Social Media and Elections, *Science Mag*, vol. 338, October 26, pp. 472–473.

24 Darrell West, *op. cit.*, p. 7–9.

25 Stephen J. Wayne (2007). *Is This Any Way to Run a Democratic Election?*, 3rd edition, Washington, D.C., CQ Press, p. 206.

26 Darrell M. West (2012). M-Campaigning: Mobile Technology and Public Outreach, *Issues in Technology Innovation*, [http://www.insidepolitics.org/brookingsreports/m_campaigning.pdf].

2 Consequences of using social media

The increasingly negative presidential campaigns are affecting not only the electoral process and the way the issues are perceived, as we have seen, but also voter turnout and candidate image. Negative campaigning may be effective for some candidates, as with the incumbent George H. W. Bush during the 1988 presidential election.[27] But this strategy does have several risks, as much for the candidates as for the American political system as a whole. As Kim L. Fridkin and Partick J. Kenney argue: *"people sometimes develop more negative impressions of the candidate airing negative advertisements. [...] In extreme circumstances, negative campaigns may lead voters to stay home on Election Day."*[28] For some authors, including John G. Geer, use of negative strategies nonetheless benefits democracy, mainly by enabling voters to get more information about election issues, as compared to positive communication strategies, which often show only the candidates' good sides.[29]

2.1 Illusory participation?

We should first stress that social media can lead to greater mobilization of the electorate, notably by enabling voters to participate spontaneously and break free from traditional forms of participation. This does not mean that organizers and strategists (or any other group directly involved in an election campaign) are no longer able to impose their ideas and manipulate voters. On the one hand, political actors have adapted to this new reality; on the other, some social media, notably blogs, have gone mainstream and can thus establish ties with these actors.[30]

The other participation problem is that of illusory participation. Sharing a tweet on Twitter or clicking "Like" on a Facebook page does not always translate into votes. The example of Howard Dean, a 2004 Democratic Primary candidate, is instructive on this point. While he was the first to use the Internet to make himself

---

27 By means of some ads, like "Willie Horton" and "Boston Harbor," George H. W. Bush effectively discredited his Democratic opponent Michael Dukakis, who was never able to undo the damage. During the 2004 presidential election, the ad "Sellout," by the independent group Swift Boat Veterans for Truth, also enabled Republicans to undermine the credibility of the Democratic candidate John Kerry, who likewise was never able to reverse its impact.

28 Kim L. Fridkin and Patrick J. Kenney (2012). The Impact of Negative Campaigning on Citizen's Actions and Attitudes, in SEMETKO, Holli A. and Margaret SCAMMELL, (eds.) *The SAGE Handbook of Political Communication*, SAGE Publications.

29 John G. Geer (2010). Negative Campaign Ads Play An Important Role in Political Campaigns, in GERDES, Louise I., (ed.) *Political Campaigns*, Opposing Viewpoints, Greenhaven Press, pp. 102 and 104.

30 Richard Davis (2009). *Typing Politics: The Role of Blogs in American Politics*, New York, Oxford University Press, p. 7.

known, to raise funds (over $50 million in small donations), and to recruit volunteers, this exposure did not translate into popular support or sustained media support.[31] Remember, social media users are constantly solicited and therefore cannot be taken for granted, in particular on a subject as volatile as politics. So it is not easier than before to convince the undecided or anyone who basically does not share similar political convictions with the candidate, all the more so because people still visit sites or take part in social media that share their values and ideologies. This was so with newspapers and television and is still so with the Internet and social media.[32]

2.2 Controlling the candidate's image

The most radical transformation that social media have caused is undoubtedly the loss of control over the image[33] and message of candidates in American presidential elections.[34] Because social media have no central command and because anyone and everyone can contribute to them with very modest means, the ground is fertile for rumours, disinformation campaigns, and parodies of all sorts.[35] It is therefore much harder for organizers to exercise tight control over the image and the message. They must often manage unforeseen events, gaffes, and inadequate statements involving their candidate that are snapped up and posted straightaway on YouTube. This is true during presidential campaigns and truer still at the local level. Governors and congressmen are less protected from situations that spin out of control, and they get less coaching from their campaign staff than do presidential candidates. They are thus more exposed to this type of tactic.[36] Fast reaction time and fast distribution time are increasing the social media's power by making it harder to

---

31 Joseph Graf (2008). New Media: The Cutting Edge of Campaign Communications, in Richard J. Semiatin (ed.), *Campaign on the Cutting Edge*, Washington, D.C., CQ Press, p. 55.

32 Stephen J. Wayne, *op. cit.*, p. 205; Stephen Farnsworth and S. Robert Lichter, *op. cit.*, p. 22.

33 Judith S. Trent, Robert V. Friedenberg, and Robert E. Denton, Jr. (2011). Communication Types and Functions of Televised Political Advertising, in *Political Campaign Communication. Principles & Practices*, 7th edition, Lanham, Maryland, Rowman & Littlefield, p. 71.

34 Melissa M. Smith (2010). Political Campaigns in the Twenty-First Century: Implications of New Media Technology, in John Allen Hendricks and Robert E. Denton Jr. (eds.), *Communicator-in-Chief: How Obama Used the New Media Technology to Win the White House*, Lanham, Lexington, p. 150.

35 Frederic I. Solop (2010). 'RT @BarackObama We just made history': Twitter and the 2008 Presidential Election, in John Allen Hendricks and Robert E. Denton Jr. (eds.), *op. cit.*, p. 39.

36 For more information about the effect of social media during legislative or local campaigns, see Stephen J. Farnsworth, *op. cit.*, p. 117; Richard Davis, *op. cit.*, pp. 4–5; Morley Winograd and Michael D. Hais (2008). *Millennial Makeover: MySpace, YouTube, and the Future of American Politics*, New Brunswick, Rutgers University Press, pp. 133–137 and 175.

offset the negative impacts or even limit the damage caused by an embarrassing situation.

Undeniably, voters have become easier to reach and mobilize through social media. This point has been quickly grasped by politicians. In the U.S. Senate, 9 out of 10 senators have a Facebook page and those who have more "friends" than do their opponents won 81 % of the contested seats during the 2010 midterms.[37] Use of social media does not necessarily give candidates a strategic advantage, even though Obama showed he could win an election by integrating them into his campaign strategy.[38] One must know how to use them prudently, and in direct and consistent relation to more traditional strategies, while always keeping in mind that whatever the strategists do not control may seriously harm their candidate.

Surprisingly, despite the social media's impressive presence in the last American presidential campaign, the candidates did very little to exploit the social angle of such media, i.e., real interaction between people. Only 3 % of Obama's tweets came from citizens or groups outside his campaign, while Romney posted just one message, a tweet from his son Josh.[39] As "loose cannons," social media still frighten candidates, who are now so close in the polls that a single tweet might make the difference between defeat and victory!

3 Conclusion: toward an Americanization of election advertising campaigns?

Social media are now integral to the candidates' communication strategies during American presidential campaigns, though not replacing mainstream media: *"First, candidates still spend vast amounts of money on traditional-media advertising on both television and radio. Second, social media, despite its popularity, is perceived to be less reliable than traditional media."*[40] Nonetheless, the candidates' advertising messages are now designed for social media, i.e., rapidly and with a view to sharing them.[41] According to Balz, the techniques used to persuade voters are less and less appropriate for what elections should be about: *"[...] the techniques [...] are not ones designed ultimately to bring the country or the parties together once the election is*

---

37 Infographics (2012). Social Media's Dramatic Impact on U.S. Elections, *Wired Academy*, November 16, [http://www.wiredacademic.com/2012/11/infographic-social-medias-dramatic-impact-on-us-elections/].

38 Morley Winograd and Michael D. Hais, *op. cit.*, p. 188.

39 Pew Research Center (2012). *Social Media and Political Engagement*, October 19, [http://pewinternet.org/Reports/2012/Political-engagement.aspx].

40 John Allen Hendricks, *op. cit.*, p. 147.

41 *Ibid.*, p. 134.

over. *Slash-and-burn attacks and the demonization of the opposition have made it all the more difficult to overcome genuine philosophical differences.*"[42]

Since the 1960s, we have seen an Americanization of election campaigns around the world. Many techniques developed for American presidential campaigns, including design of election advertising, have been adapted for use in other countries.[43] Attack ads have been integrated into the campaign culture of countries like Indonesia, Japan, Mexico, and Canada. Canadian political parties have been using them since the late 1970s, and especially since the 1988 federal election, whereas Québec political parties have been resorting to this communication strategy since the 1994 provincial election. With young adults getting politically involved almost exclusively via social media, will the effects on election campaigning be the same here as in the United States?

References

Arenyeka, L. (2012). The Impact of Social Media on the US Elections. *Vanguard*, November 6. [http://www.vanguardngr.com/2012/11/the-impact-of-social-media-on-the-us-elections/].

Awareness Inc. (2012). *160 Amazing Social Media Statistics From the 2012 Presidential Race*, November. [http://www.scribd.com/fullscreen/124186759?access_key=key-nlst6ckehd1jeva7lgg&allow_share=true].

Balz, D. (2013). *Collision 2012. Obama vs. Romney and the Future of Elections in America*. New York: Viking.

Baumgartner, J. C. & Francia, P.L. (2010). *Conventional Wisdom and American Elections: Exploding Myths, Exploring Misconceptions* (2nd ed.). Lanham: Rowman & Littlefield.

Burton, M.J. & Shea, D.M. (2010). *Campaign Craft: The Strategies, Tactics, and Art of Political Campaign Management* (4th ed.). Santa Barbara: Praeger.

Davis, R. (2009). *Typing Politics: The Role of Blogs in American Politics*. New York: Oxford University Press.

E.Politics (2013). *Survey Says: Social Media Doesn't Dominate U.S. Elections... Yet*, February 27. [http://www.epolitics.com/2013/02/27/survey-says-social-media-doesnt-dominate-u-s-elections-yet/].

Farnsworth, S.J. (2009). *Spinner in Chief: How Presidents Sell Their Policies and Themselves*. Boulder: Paradigm Publishers.

Farnsworth, S.J. & Lichter, S.R. (2011). *The Nightly News Nightmare: Media Coverage of U.S. Presidential Elections, 1988–2008*. Lanham: Rowman & Littlefield.

Faucheux, R.A. (2003). *Winning Elections: Political Campaign Management, Strategy, and Tactics*. Lanham: M. Evans Co.

Fridkin, K.L. & Kenney, P.J. (2012). The Impact of Negative Campaigning on Citizen's Actions and Attitudes. In Semetko, H.A. & Scammell, M. (Eds.) *The SAGE Handbook of Political Communication*, SAGE Publications.

---

42 Dan Balz, *op. cit.*, p. 353.
43 Fred FLETCHER and Mary Lynn YOUNG. Political Communication in a Changing Media Environment, in SEMETKO, Holli A. and Margaret SCAMMELL, (eds.) The SAGE Handbook of Political Communication, SAGE Publications, 2012.

Gainous, J. B. & Wagner K.M. (2011). *Rebooting American Politics: The Internet Revolution*. Lanham: Rowman & Littlefield.

Geer, J.G. (2010). Negative Campaign Ads Play An Important Role in Political Campaigns. In Gerdes, L.I., (Ed.) *Political Campaigns*. Opposing Viewpoints, Greenhaven Press.

Gosselin, A. (1997). La publicité électorale. *Les Études de communication publique*, n° 11.

Graf, J. (2008). New Media – The Cutting Edge of Campaign Communications. In Semiatin, R.J. (Ed.). *Campaigns on the Cutting Edge*. Washington, D.C.: CQ Press.

Halperin, M. & Harris, J.F. (2006). *The Way to Win: Taking the White House in 2008*. New York: Random House.

Healy, P. (2007). To '08 Hopefuls, Media Technology Can Be Friend of Foe. *New York Times*, January 31, [http://www.nytimes.com/2007/01/31/us/politics/31video.html?pagewanted=print&_r=0].

Heilemann, J. & Halperin M. (2010). *Game Change: Obama and the Clintons, McCain and Palin, and the Race of a Lifetime*. New York: Harper.

Hendricks, J.A. (2014). The New-Media Campaign of 2012. In Denton Jr., R.E. (Ed.). *The 2012 Presidential Campaign: A Communication Perspective*. Lanham: Rowman & Littlefield.

Hendricks, J.A. & Denton Jr., R.E. (Eds.) (2010). *Communicator-in-Chief: How Obama Used the New Media Technology to Win the White House*. Lanham: Lexington.

Hull, C.C. (2007, January). Does Campaign Finance Reform Provoked Attack Ads? Modeling Candidate and Independent Group Negative Advertising. Paper presented at the annual meeting of the Southern Political Science Association, New Orleans, United States.

Infographics (2012). Social Media's Dramatic Impact on U.S. Elections. *Wired Academy* November 16. [http://www.wiredacademic.com/2012/11/infographic-social-medias-dramatic-impact-on-us-elections/].

Journalism.org (2012). *Winning the Media Campaign 2012*. [http://www.journalism.org/analysis_report/winning_media_campaign_2012].

The Living Room Candidate: Presidential Campaign Commercials 1952–2012. [http://www.livingroomcandidate.org/].

Kennedy, K. (2013). Use It or Lose It: Social Media in the 2012 US Election. *Pulitzer Center*, February 22. [http://pulitzercenter.org/reporting/social-media-role-young-voters-increase-future-US-elections-Obama-Facebook-Twitter].

Mark, D. (2009). *Going Dirty: The Art of Negative Campaigning* (2nd ed.). Lanham: Rowman & Littlefield.

McCoy, T. (2012). The Creepiness Factor: How Obama and Romney Are Getting to Know You. *The Atlantic*, April 10. [http://www.theatlantic.com/politics/archive/2012/04/the-creepiness-factor-how-obama-and-romney-are-getting-to-know-you/255499/].

Metaxas, P. T. & Mustafaraj, E. (2012). Social Media and Elections. *Science Mag*, *338*, October 26, 472–473.

PBS, *The 30 Second Candidate*. [http://www.pbs.org/30secondcandidate/].

Pew Research Center's Journalism Project Staff (2012). The Final Days of the Media Campaign 2012. *Pew Research Journalism Project*, November 19. [www.journalism.org/2012/11/19/final-days-media-campaign-2012/].

Pew Research Center, Pew Internet (2012). *Social Media and Political Engagement*, October 19. [http://pewinternet.org/Reports/2012/Political-engagement.aspx].

Pew Research Center for the People and the Press (2008). *Internet's Broader Role in Campaign 2008: Social Networking and Online Videos Take Off*, January 11. [http://www.people-press.org/2008/01/11/internets-broader-role-in-campaign-2008/].

Pew Research Center's Project for Excellence in Journalism (2012a). *How the Presidential Candidates Use the Web and Social Media*, August 15. http://www.journalism.org/analysis_report/how_presidential_candidates_use_web_and_social_media].

Pew Research Center's Project for Excellence in Journalism (2012b). *The Final Days of the Media Campaign 2012*, November 19. [http://www.journalism.org/analysis_report/final_days_media_campaign_2012].

Rutenberg, J. (2012). Secret of the Obama Victory? Rerun Watchers, for One Thing. *New York Times*, November 12. [http://www.nytimes.com/2012/11/13/us/politics/obama-data-system-targeted-tv-viewers-for-support.html?_r=1&].

Rutenberg, J. (2013). Data You Can Believe In. *New York Times*, June 20. http://www.nytimes.com/2013/06/23/magazine/the-obama-campaigns-digital-masterminds-cash-in.html?pagewanted=1&_r=0].

Skewes, E.A. (2007). *Message Control: How News is Made on the Presidential Campaign Trail*. Lanham: Rowman & Littlefield.

Steele, C. (2012). Election 2012: How Social Media Will Convert Followers Into Voters. *PC Mag*, January 20. [http://www.pcmag.com/slideshow/story/293078/election-2012-how-social-media-will-convert-followers-into-v].

Stirland, S.L. (2012). GOP Site 'BarackBook' Mocks Obama's Facebook Support. *Wired*, July 29. [http://www.wired.com/threatlevel/2008/07/obamamania-has/].

Tedesco, J.C. & Dunn, S.W. (2014). Political Advertising in the 2012 U.S. Presidential Election. In Denton Jr., R.E. (Ed.) *The 2012 Presidential Campaign. A Communication Perspective*. Lanham: Rowman & Littlefield.

Torres, I.M., Hyman, M.R. & Hamilton, J. (2012). Candidate-Sponsored TV Ads for the 2004 U.S. Presidential Election: A Content Analysis. *Journal of Politial Marketing*, *11(3)*.

Trent, J. S., Friedenberg, R.V. & Denton, Jr, R.E. (2011). Communication Types and Functions of Televised Political Advertising. In *Political Campaign Communication. Principles & Practices* (7th ed.), Lanham: Rowman & Littlefield.

Twitter (2012). *Political Engagement Map*. [https://election.twitter.com/map/#t243902647571185664].

Vandal, G. (2009, September). La publicité négative dans les campagnes présidentielles américaines : un phénomène de "dépacification" ? Paper presented at the Congrès international de l'Association française de science politique, Grenoble, France.

Warner, B. (2012). The Big Social Media Winners and Losers of the 2012 Elections. *Social Media Influence*, November 7. [http://socialmediainfluence.com/2012/11/07/the-big-social-media-winners-and-losers-of-the-2012-elections/].

Wayne, S.J. (2007). *Is This Any Way to Run a Democratic Election?* (3rd ed.). Washington, D.C.: CQ Press.

West, D. (2012). M-Campaigning: Mobile Technology and Public Outreach. *Issues in Technology Innovation*. [http://www.insidepolitics.org/brookingsreports/m_campaigning.pdf].

West, D. (2014). *Air Wars: Television Advertising and Social Media in Election Campaigns, 1952–2012* (6th ed.). London: Sage.

Wilner, E. (2012). Romney and Republicans Outspent Obama, But Couldn't Out-Advertise Him. *Ad Age*, November 9. [adage.com/article/campaign-trail/romney-outspent-obama-advertise/238241/].

Winograd, M. & Hais, M.D. (2008). *Millennial Makeover: MySpace, YouTube, and the Future of American Politics*. New Brunswick: Rutgers University Press.

Part IV: **The Resilience of the Printed Press
in the United Kingdom**

David Deacon and Dominic Wring[1]

The United Kingdom Independence Party (UKIP) and the British Press: Integration, Immigration and Integrity

This chapter examines the emergence of the UK Independence Party (UKIP), paying particular attention to developments in its campaigning, communication and media strategies. The party was founded in 1993 as a single issue political organisation determined to secure British withdrawal from the European Union. Euro-scepticism remains at the core of the party's identity, but more recently UKIP has extended the range and breadth of its policy portfolio, introducing a distinctive, if not entirely coherent libertarian populism into the British political mainstream. Despite an unpromising start to its electoral career, the party has developed considerable political momentum and now increasingly provokes caution and even fear as opposed to ridicule on the part of its rivals.

Analysis of UKIP's rise raises questions of wider political significance. Its growing influence needs to be seen as a component element in a major shift in party politics in the UK. In the 1964 UK General Election, Labour and the Conservatives accounted for 88 % of the vote; by 2010 this percentage had reduced to 65 % (Denver and Garnett, 2014). Given this factor and a 'first past the post' voting system, margins matter more than ever before and niche parties can no longer be dismissed as being of peripheral significance. This is particularly the case in so-called 'second order' local government and European elections. Allied to this, UKIP continues to confound what was assumed to be a well-established trend of declining rates in party membership because in 2013 its tally rose by 13,000 to 32,000, thereby making it the fourth largest in Britain (BBC, 2013). This is an instructive example of how minority parties can 'expand the ideological boundaries of a political culture and redefine the left-right spectrum providing for a new form of political behaviour, different to that of the main political parties' (Copus et al., 2009: 4).

The rapid development and impact of UKIP has brought to the fore significant tensions within the party as it tries to resolve whether it wishes to remain an 'ideological outsider' or else become more of a 'potential insider', that is within the mainstream (Grant, 1989). To this end, examination of UKIP's treatment by conventional journalism helps identify the tensions and contradictions in relations between the parties and the media. The latter has, like the former, been the subject of

1 *Professor David Deacon*, Professor of Communication and Media Analysis, Loughborough Communication Research Centre, Department of Social Sciences, Loughborough University; *Dr Dominic Wring*, Reader in Political Communication, Loughborough Communication Research Centre, Department of Social Sciences, Loughborough University.

marked changes. Partly because of issues like Europe the authors have previously argued that the partisan orientations of the UK national press have become increasingly 'de-aligned' since the mid-1990s, even if their residual conservativism remains relatively undiminished (Deacon and Wring, 2002). Simultaneously, media disdain for politicians and the conduct of politics has increased. It might be supposed therefore that a strident, media conscious populist party unapologetic in its disdain for supposed 'political correctness' could provide an appealing alternative for some partisan news providers, most obviously those with strong Eurosceptic and anti-immigration propensities. But this cannot be assumed and requires further careful investigation. Before doing so, it is necessary to provide more contextual information concerning the emergence and growth of the UKIP phenomenon.

1 The rise of Euroscepticism in the UK

The emergence of UKIP is fundamentally entwined with the growth of debate over Britain's membership of the European Union during the last three decades. Controversy was never assuaged by the momentous 1975 referendum that confirmed the Westminster parliament's earlier decision to join the then European Economic Community. Britain has long been characterised as the 'awkward partner', the member state in the 'Big Four' most prone to debating its future inside the Union (George, 1998). Although this scepticism was traditionally articulated by rivals from across the political spectrum it began to be increasingly associated with the centre-right Conservatives who formed the government for nearly two decades from 1979 onwards. This was made obvious by the then Prime Minister Margaret Thatcher's Bruges speech in 1988, an address that proved to be a key intervention as her questioning the pace and nature of further European integration encouraged sceptical opinion to mobilize both within her party and beyond.

Given Thatcher's growing concerns over Britain's involvement in Europe, it is ironic that it was her government that had in effect reignited the issue through its then relatively uncontroversial endorsement of the 1986 Single European Act. It was this measure that encouraged federalists inside what was now know as the 'Union' rather than the 'Community' to promote the case for further and more obviously political as well as economic integration. Thatcher's growing antipathy towards EU colleagues proved to be one of the factors that led her own demise. When her former Deputy Prime Minister Geoffrey Howe resigned from government in 1990 and defiantly challenged her judgment on Europe it marked the beginning of the end for her own premiership. Thatcher's subsequent resignation did not, however, stem the bitterness within the Conservative party over EU integration. The issue continued to cause problems for new Prime Minister John Major, notably during the passage of the Maastricht Treaty and a preceding debate that had publicly highlighted the still deep divisions within the governing party over policy.

Although British public opinion was sceptical about further EU integration the matter was not foremost among the issues that most influence voters' decision-making. But the subject continued to feature prominently in media debates, particularly in the centre-right dominated national press. These newspapers' agenda-setting capabilities had collectively helped to reinforce what popularly became known as the Eurosceptic case. Cumulatively this also reflected and reinforced the divisions within the Conservative government over EU policy up to and including the 1997 General Election. John Major's authority over the issue was memorably challenged throughout the campaign by some of his own candidates who became increasingly vocal in stating their hostility to any further integration. Significantly these opinions found sympathy within sceptic inclined media, notably the Rupert Murdoch owned *The Times*, as well as two new electoral challengers who were un-happy what they perceived as the government's integrationist policies. The more prominent of these, the Referendum party led by the flamboyant entrepreneur Sir James Goldsmith, had attracted defectors from the Conservatives including a serving MP who supported his call for a plebiscite over the UK's continuing membership of the European Union. Goldsmith's well-funded intervention in the 1997 election was not decisive but it further contributed to the Conservatives' humiliating loss. It also overshadowed the campaign and electoral performance of the rival sceptic formation, the United Kingdom Independence Party. Things have, however, changed in the intervening years and where once UKIP was a secondary force in Eurosceptic terms, it is now a threat to mainstream rivals.

2 The Gadfly That Won't Die

Nigel Farage, the current UKIP leader, recently asserted that his organisation has 'changed the face of British politics' (Addley, 2013). This follows two decades in which political rivals, if they have commented at all, have largely sought to demean and deny the Eurosceptic party's significance. In 2004 the then leader of the Conservatives, Michael Howard, said the party was 'full of cranks and political gadflies'. Two years later his successor David Cameron dismissed UKIP as a fringe group containing 'fruitcakes, loonies and closet racists'. Since Cameron's installation as Prime Minister, several of his government colleagues have joined the attack. In 2013 the Tory party grandee, Kenneth Clarke, called them 'a collection of clowns'. But the frequency and nature of these and other criticisms indicates the fear that UKIP has instilled in its opponents, particularly on the centre-right from where it has been widely assumed most of its growing base of support and activists has been drawn over the last decade.

The longevity of UKIP and its confounding of elite disdain do not in themselves necessarily support the transformational role that Farage claims for his organisation. The party has made some significant inroads in second order elections over the last decade. For example, in 2004, it came third in the European Parliamentary elections, gaining 16.1 % of the vote and increasing its elected representation quadrupled from 3 to 12. In 2009, it gained a further MEP and edged into second place ahead of Labour, the party then holding national office. This achievement was bettered by UKIP's noteworthy performance in the 2013 local government elections, where it averaged 26 % of the vote in the wards where it stood. This was a 10 % increase on its 2012 local election performance and led to the party gaining 147 seats. This was a marked change from the 7 secured in the equivalent elections a few years back in 2009. What had once been seen as a largely single issue party preoccupied with electing MEPs to a body it was vigorously trying to abolish was now broadening its remit and in turn winning over voters with concerted appeals about domestic matters.

At their 2014 spring conference, Farage announced his belief that UKIP could 'win' the European Parliamentary elections due that year and that this would provide them with huge momentum going into the 2015 UK national campaign. On the same day, Farage informed journalists he would resign if his party failed to gain any parliamentary representation at Westminster. This threat represents more of a gamble than it might at first appear because UKIP has never had a candidate elected to parliament and, even in vote share terms, its performance in national campaigns has been modest. In the 2001 election it attracted 1.48 % of the vote or 2.16 % in contested seats. By 2005 these tallies had risen to 2.2 % and 2.8 % respectively and the equivalents for 2010 were 3.1 % and 3.45 %. This is steady but unspectacular growth. Unlike other minor parties such as the Greens and Nationalists, UKIP's strength has not been sufficiently geographically concentrated to enable the return of an MP for a given constituency.

The reasons for UKIP's limited impact in first order elections, that is those for Westminster, relates to the party's uncertain electoral base. Ford et al. (2012) demonstrate through a detailed analysis of support in the 2009 European Elections that voters tend to fall into two categories. The first are 'strategic defectors' who are typically affluent, middle class and ordinarily Conservatives. These voters have switched to UKIP in second order elections to register opposition to the European Union and dissatisfaction with the performance of the Tory leadership. But they also revert to the Conservatives in General Elections. The other category of UKIP supporters are categorised as 'polite xenophobes'. These are voters who are less affluent citizens, more disaffected with mainstream politics and are attracted by anti-immigration and anti-establishment rhetoric. They are in effect the party's core loyalists and support it across all electoral contexts.

Ford et al. argue that UKIP faces a major dilemma in managing their two distinctive constituencies of support. To retain more support from the 'strategic Eurosceptics' the party needs to cultivate a new, more professional respectability and credibility. But there is an obvious risk because such an approach could in turn alienate the 'polite xenophobes' who value iconoclasm in their politicians. Some argue this creates irreconcilable tensions that mean the party is ultimately 'doomed to fail' as the 'office seeking' ambitions of the leadership come into conflict with the wishes of the membership who want the party to retain its populist, anti-establishment stance (Abedi and Lundberg, 2009). However the most recent successes of UKIP raise questions about this analysis, indicating it is premature in a fast changing political environment where the European Union has sustained and endured major challenges.[2] But the strategic conundrum facing the party remain as can be gleaned from studying the party's electoral and communication strategy.

3 Discipline and Diversification: the Evolving UKIP Strategy

UKIP has been conceptualised as an example of an 'Anti-Political Establishment' (APE) party (ibid.). Such parties have been described as a 'spectre...haunting contemporary party politics' (Schedler, 1996: 291). These insurgent forces' redefinition of 'existing politics as authoritarian' (ibid.) has an inherently right wing affinity that provides a potent populist rallying point for a melange of disaffected floating voters, disgruntled conservatives, overt nationalists and covert racists. Although UKIP undoubtedly shares some of these characteristics, it has not necessarily adopted this mantle in its entirety. There are several explanations why this is the case, notably the fact that the party's anti-establishment stance is not unequivocal and unconditional. Before the 2010 General Election Lord Pearson of Rannoch, a peer of the realm and UKIP's then leader, made an offer to the Conservatives that his party would stand down candidates if a referendum was offered on Britain's membership of the EU. This caused consternation within the party but was a major public confirmation of a more discreet dialogue that had been taking place between politicians on the centre-right fearful of undermining a common cause and benefitting pro-federalist opponents.

A related reason for questioning UKIP's categorisation as an APE force relates to the issue that led to the creation of the party and that continues to define it: British

---

2 Abedi and Lundberg's analysis was written prior to the 2009 European Elections (in which UKIP gained second place) and against the backdrop of a bloody leadership battle within UKIP in 2004, when the controversial ex-broadcaster, Robert Kilroy-Silk, then a recent recruit to the party, sought to depose the party's leader and pursue an ambitious strategy of 'killing off' the Conservative party. Both strategies were rejected by the party's membership and Kilroy-Silk left the party.

membership of the EU. It is evident that the party's adamantly anti-integrationist stance finds resonance in an increasing Eurosceptic UK public. But the significance of this connection should not be overstated: polling consistently demonstrates that European integration is of marginal and declining significance to electors (Abedi and Lundberg, 2009: 85; Clements et al, 2013). Simultaneously the issue has become marginal to the mainstream media agenda. Successive studies undertaken by the Loughborough Communication Research Centre into news media coverage of UK General Elections since 1997 indicate a campaign-by-campaign reduction in the prominence of the European integration theme. This ranges from 15 % of coverage in 1997 to 1 % by 2010 (see Deacon et al., 1998; Deacon and Wring, 2010). In summary, one of the core problems for UKIP in electoral terms, and one of the drawbacks to characterising the party as an exemplar of the APE paradigm, is that its foundational concern is not a populist one. The European Union is unpopular with a not insignificant section of the electorate but it is of marginal concern when compared with other, more salient issues such as health, education and, of course, the economy.

Aside from the political and electoral reasons for challenging UKIP's portrayal as an APE party, there are organisational grounds for doubting this characterisation. Recent changes in the party have been taking place including a discernable push towards professionalism by the leadership. This is most evident in recent attempts to impose discipline on UKIP representatives. There have been numerous occasions over the years where candidates have made eccentric, offensive and even overtly racist comments in public. For a long time these were tolerated internally as 'going with the territory' of the party's libertarian ethos, even formerly regarded as its Unique Selling Point, revealing the 'individualistic DNA' of UKIP in contradistinction to the dragooned and anodyne professionalism of the mainstream parties (Peev, 2013). This kind of intervention now receives censure from the hierarchy. Perhaps most notoriously there is the case of the now ex-MEP Godfrey Bloom which came to a head in September 2013. Bloom had already attracted controversy for various things including his claim UK Foreign Aid was routinely misappropriated by elites in 'Bongo-Bongo land' to 'buy Ray-Ban sunglasses, apartments in Paris, Ferraris and all the rest of it' (London Evening Standard, 7 August 2013). Although he weathered that storm created by his offensive terminology, the party whip was removed the following month after he described a group of women at a fringe meeting as 'sluts' and hit prominent broadcast journalist Michael Crick over the head with the party manifesto after the latter had enquired why the cover of the document had not featured ethnic minority citizens. Leader Nigel Farage had decided there was no longer a place for even prominent spokespeople such as Godfrey Broom because, as he put it, the party needed to now appear 'civilised and grown up'. Further evidence of this harder line came in January 2014, when a UKIP councillor was suspended from membership of the party after he speculated that serious flooding in England constituted a kind of divine retribution from god for the government's decision to approve gay marriage. The party has also recently moved to emphasise its distance from prominent organisations further to the right such as the English Defence League and British National Party, by introducing a unique requirement that all potential candidates sign a form confirming they have 'never engaged in, advocated or condoned racist, violent, criminal or anti-democratic activity... never been a member of or had links with any organisation, group or association which the national executive committee considers is liable to bring the party into disrepute...never been convicted of any offence punishable by a custodial sentence, whether or not a custodial sentence was actually imposed' (Landale, 2014).

Alongside this more disciplined approach, the party has made a concerted attempt to diversify its political portfolio beyond the single issue of European integration. This move to broaden UKIP's remit has resulted in increased scrutiny, particularly from those mainstream media hardly well disposed towards the organisation and its philosophy. For instance on the eve of the 2013 local government elections, several national newspapers reported leaked internal UKIP emails that indicated internal disarray and the possibility that the party would consider buying policies 'off the shelf' from right wing think tanks. This was in itself evidence of UKIP struggling to build a credible manifesto that was made difficult through its 'attempts to please its politically divergent support' (Boffey, 2013). This also led to a retrospective analysis by *The Times* that concluded the party's 2010 manifesto was deeply flawed, to the scale of £120 billion funding shortfall (Sherman, 2013).

This diversification strategy, a key component in the professionalisation process, has also created internal divisions. For example, In December 2012, Will Gilpin was appointed as Chief Executive with the task of making the party more professional by developing training for staff and candidates and introducing structures and procedures for developing policies. He resigned in frustration eight months later, and in an interview with the *Daily Telegraph* criticised Farage's dominance of the party and complained UKIP remained 'a bunch of enthusiastic amateurs having a good time rather than the professional fighting team they could be' (Kirkup and Laurence, 2013). In noting the ongoing difficulties the party is experiencing in developing a credible and diverse portfolio, it is important to not underestimate the scale of the transitions that have already occurred.

In the 2010 General Election Farage promised the 'edgiest campaign in history' and this quality manifested in two distinct changes of direction in the focus of the campaign. First, the party sought to accentuate its 'anti-establishment' credentials through seeking to connect with growing public disillusionment with mainstream politicians over the MPs' expenses scandal of 2009. This theme was most stridently articulated in a poster depicting the three main party leaders under the headline slogan 'Sod The Lot'. At UKIP's manifesto launch, Farage declared: '(F)rankly, the campaign so far has been a piddling irrelevancy and it's becoming increasingly clear that the choice the British public are being offered here is not for a change of government but for a change of management' ('Ukip's short, sharp message: Sod the lot', *Northern Echo*, 14 April 2010). This populist impulse was reinforced by the second key focus of the campaign, specifically on immigration policy and the party's manifesto commitment to introduce a five year freeze on immigration and thereby ensure 'that any future immigration does not exceed 50,000 people per annum'. Taken together the centre-staging of *integrity* and *immigration* provided UKIP with a far more populist platform than *integration* alone. Furthermore, they offered ways of popularising the party's Eurosceptic agenda, on the one hand by denouncing the EU as an exemplar of non-accountability, political corruption and bureaucratic inefficiency; and on the other as the institution most responsible for the alleged 'flooding' of the country by migrant, particularly from newer member state countries.

At first sight, it might seem that the discipline and diversification strategies are creating greater paradoxes for the party; as in presentational and organisational terms, UKIP seems to be cultivating its mainstream respectability, whereas in policy terms, it is promoting and asserting its anti-establishment and populist credentials. But these tensions may not be as irreconcilable as they first appear, when we consider how the parameters of political discussion in the UK have altered recently regarding the three cornerstones of UKIP's core campaign agenda: integration, immigration and integrity[3]. To take the issue of European integration first, where once discussion was devoted to arguing for reforms of the terms for UK membership, it is now more likely to countenance the prospect of the country leaving the Union. David Cameron's recent announcement that Britain would hold an in/out referendum by 2017 on withdrawing from the EU in the event of his being re-elected Prime Minister underlines UKIP's success in re-engineering the essentials in this debate. With respect to integrity, research shows public trust in politicians and government have reduced significantly in the wake of political scandals, such as the controversy about politicians' abuse of personal expense allowances that broke in 2009. In the keynote findings of the 2013 British Social Attitudes survey it was noted that 'While a degree of scepticism towards politicians might be thought healthy, those who govern Britain today have an uphill struggle to persuade the public that their hearts are in the right place' (Clery et al., 2013). Regarding immigration, UKIP's reiteration of its opposition to what it regards as excessive levels has connected with the preoccupations of many right wing news organisations on this issue and their belief that liberal orthodoxy has stifled and curtailed proper debate (Deacon and Wring, 2010). This has started to resonate more widely across the media mainstream, for example, being the subject of a recent prime time documentary authored by the BBC political editor Nick Robinson (Robinson, 2014). At the same time, politicians, notably those belonging to the interior ministry headed by Home Secretary Theresa May, have launched initiatives that can be seen as part of governmental attempts to be doing something to tackle the 'crisis'. The most high profile of these has been a mobile

---

3 Our thanks to Sam Marston for contributing to our analysis on this point (see Marston, 2014).

advertising campaign featuring the slogan 'Go Home'. If the blunt message proved controversial then so did the deployment of the vehicles displaying it to areas traditionally home to non-white immigrant communities. Ironically, this particular policy was dismissed as a nasty and unhelpful stunt by Farage who also acknowledged the initiative owed something to his party's growing ability to influence and shape public perceptions and the wider agenda:

> 'What the billboards should say is please don't vote UKIP, we're doing something. That's what it's all about, of course it is. I think the actual tone of the billboards is nasty, unpleasant, Big Brother. It'll make no difference. I don't think using messages like this will make any difference, what will make a difference is enforcing our borders properly' (Groves, 2013).

In noting how conducive the terms of much contemporary political discourse is for UKIP's agenda, we are not suggesting that the party is responsible for creating this new climate of debate. Indeed, in our view, it is more probable that UKIP is a dependent rather than independent factor, benefiting from wider political trends rather than initiating them. But this is not to deny how the party's political opportunism has served to accelerate and accentuate public and media discussion of these matters.

The perceived potency of UKIP both as an electoral and agenda-setting force devoted to transforming the British political landscape has understandably attracted considerable and growing interest. Determining whether the party is successfully moving 'towards the mainstream' (Hayton, 2010) and thereby 'coming of age as a permanent force in UK politics' (BBC, 2014) or is else likely 'doomed to failure' (Adebi and Lundberg, 2009) may be determined by its performance in the 2015 General Election. Nigel Farage has, as has already been noted, announced he will resign his leadership if UKIP fails to make inroads through winning parliamentary representation in this first order election. This is evidence of his determination to convince commentators, particularly in the mainstream media, that his is a serious potential power broker with ambitions to rapidly move from the periphery to the centre of debate. Farage will be acutely aware that the more Eurosceptic minded newspapers in Britain could be pivotal to this strategy.

This UK wide national press has long enjoyed an influential opinion-forming role in British politics. Many of the major titles have made their partisanship a distinctive aspect of their identity if not necessarily their appeal. Elections provide an obvious and important opportunity to consider this factor because they offer the arena in which the fullest and widest exposition of editorial discourses are mobilised. Furthermore these printed titles have long exerted influence in 'formatting' public debate on a range of topics (Seaton, 1995: 134). Of particular significance here is the degree of connection between UKIP and the more populist newspapers: while these media are inclined to share some of the defining concerns of the party, their approval cannot be presupposed. This is because, as Krämer argues, media populism and populism *per se* are not necessarily the same thing and there is a need to be

sensitive to the varying occasions when the former acts as 'a substitute or competi-
tor to populism in the political landscape...when do they contribute to its contain-
ment and in what cases is there a symbiosis or positive feedback between them?'
(2014: 57). Although newspapers may be well habituated in expressing their discon-
tent with many aspects of existing political culture, their accompanying role as
'legitimating tools of the social and political order' cannot be disregarded
(Mazzoleni, 2003: 10).

The remainder of this chapter will focus on the media and review the major
trends and changes in national press reporting of UKIP in the 2001 and 2010 UK
General Election campaigns. This commentary is based on content analysis of the
major daily and weekly national newspapers published in the 28 days up to polling
day in both years, namely: *The Times, Sunday Times, Guardian, Observer, Independent, Independent on Sunday, Daily Telegraph, Sunday Telegraph, Daily Mail, Mail on
Sunday, Daily Express, Sunday Express, Daily Mirror, Sunday Mirror, Daily Star, Star
on Sunday* and *Sun* although not its *News of the World* sister (see note[4]).

4 UK National Press General Election coverage of the UK Independence Party: Enthusiasm, Indifference or Indignation?

The most obvious issue to address in assessing the reporting of any given party is to
establish the extent to which it has established and developed its news presence in the
hyper-competitive arena of a General Election. Table 1 quantifies the number of items
that contained any editorial reference to UKIP in the 2001 and 2010 UK campaigns,
differentiating between those items that had the party as a main or prominent focus in
an item and those that referred to it in an incidental way. The results show that aggregate coverage of the party more than doubled, although this was starting from a relatively low base of 123 items in 2001 to 256 items by 2010. The number of prominent
references to UKIP also increased from 42 to 77 but not proportionally. In 2001 the
ratio of main to incidental references was 1 to 1.9; in 2010 it was 1 to 2.3.

---

4 Relevant items were identified by using the keywords 'UKIP' and/or 'UK Independence Party' to
search the Nexis newspaper database. The resulting content was then vetted following the principles set out in Deacon, 2007 (i.e. all false positives and duplicated content were removed and tests
were conducted to ensure that there were no general gaps in the coverage of the data base that
might produce 'false negatives' [this was found to be the case with *News of the World* content]). To
ensure comparability, we excluded all material that was only published on titles' web only content
(for example, the *Telegraph* and *Sunday Telegraph* included blogs in 2010). We also ignored items
that solely logged UKIPs candidacy in particular constituencies.

Table 1: Prominence of UKIP in General Elections: Items by Newspaper and Campaign

	2001		2010	
	Principal focus	Incidental reference	Principal focus	Incidental reference
Dailies				
Guardian	5	14	15	57
Times	7	11	8	24
Daily Telegraph	14	12	7	20
Independent	5	18	5	16
Daily Express	4	3	14	9
Daily Mail	3	3	4	13
Sun	1	3	2	4
Daily Mirror	1	5	–	3
Daily Star	–	–	4	2
Sundays				
Observer	–	2	3	4
Sunday Times	–	5	6	7
Independent on Sunday	–	1	1	6
Sunday Telegraph	1	2	2	5
Mail on Sunday	1	1	2	2
The People	–	–	–	2
Sunday Express	–	1	4	5
Total	42	81	77	179

The detailed title-by-title comparison in Table 1 reveals some surprising results. The first is that this purportedly populist party attracted negligible coverage in the most popular titles. Across both elections, the *Sun*, *Mirror*, *Star* and *People* only ran 21 items that made any reference to UKIP, and only four of which had it as a main or significant point of focus. The *Sunday Mirror* made no reference to the party at all in its coverage of both campaigns. These results may in part be explained by the general lack of sustained engagement of the popular so-called 'redtop' titles with the formal conduct of recent General Elections (for more on this see Deacon et al, 2001: 668; Deacon et al., 2006). That said, UKIP's lack of traction with even the most popular titles is striking, particularly in 2010 following the recent changes in its campaigning focus. In terms of the mid-market or 'blacktop' titles, there was some apparent difference between the *Mail/Mail on Sunday* and *Daily Express/Sunday Express*. While neither pair has increased its coverage dramatically, it is noticeable that the *Express* titles were carrying more items with UKIP as their main or sole focus by 2010.

Possible explanations for the growing *Express* coverage of UKIP will be discussed after further consideration of the supposed 'quality' newspapers. Here the
amount of reporting of UKIP did not correlate with a given title's editorial stance
on the integration question. The traditionally more Eurosceptic print media such
as the *Daily Telegraph*, *Sunday Telegraph*, *The Times* and *Sunday Times* did not
devote appreciably greater coverage than those of their rivals who were inclined
to take a more detached approach to reporting EU related matters. Indeed, the
main outlier in 2010 and exemplar of the latter tendency was the *Guardian*, whose
coverage of UKIP far exceeded that of its competitors among the elite opinion-
forming titles.

Table 2: Coverage of UKIP in General Elections: type of item published

	2001		2010	
	Principle focus	**Incidental reference**	**Principle focus**	**Incidental reference**
News	21	32	27	36
Feature	2	22	14	48
Comment	9	22	25	82
Editorial	–	–	2	3
Letter	10	5	7	8
Other	–	–	2	2
Total	42	81	77	179

Table 2 disaggregates the figures for coverage according to item type and thereby
adds a further perspective on the increased national press presence of UKIP by 2010.
This was mainly due to increases in the number of references made to the party in
feature items and commentaries. By comparison 'hard' news coverage, providing
factual reporting about the actions and activities of UKIP, increased but only negli-
gibly. The party also received scant mention in editorials, which is significant because these pieces are often important indicators of a given newspaper's political
concerns and orientations (Deacon and Wring, 2002: 200). The two editorials that
gave prominence to UKIP both appeared in 2010 and were published in titles that
have long harboured Eurosceptic tendencies. For its part *The Times* was exercised
by Nigel Farage's decision to stand as a candidate in the constituency of the current
Speaker of the House of Commons, John Bercow, thereby flouting a longstanding
convention that the holder of the post is able to stand unopposed by rival parties in
order to ensure they can continue to fulfil their constitutional duties from a position
of partisan independence. The editorial item in question delivered a withering as-

sessment of Farage, who had temporarily stepped down from the party leadership to devote his energies to campaigning as parliamentary candidate for Buckingham:

> 'The fact that the person seeking to unseat [Bercow] – UKIP's publicity-craving, perma-blazered Nigel Farage – is the sort of man to whom people take an instant dislike, because it saves time; a man so lacking in charisma that he manages to give cravats an even worse name than they already have...Mr Farage accuses Mr Bercow of representing "all that is wrong with British politics today". Really? We had Mr Farage down for that' (*The Times*, 2010).

The editorial in the *Daily Express*, published on the eve of polling day, was appreciably more sympathetic in its comments about UKIP and its erstwhile leader. Pointedly it even encouraged those who could to vote for Farage over Bercow. But the editorial also cautioned readers about the danger of undermining support for the Conservatives through the splitting of the centre-right vote:

> Following the parliamentary expenses scandal of last year, many readers may still be considering a vote for one of the smaller parties. We hope that nobody will back the poisonous BNP, whose attempt to create a hierarchy of British subjects based upon racial background is fundamentally un-British. No such disqualification applies to UKIP. Under Lord Pearson it has set out attractive policies on everything from relations with the EU to education, taxation and law and order. But UKIP cannot win this election and in many constituencies a vote for it is likely to increase the risk of a pro-EU socialist being returned rather than a sensible Conservative.
>
> There are exceptions, such as in Buckingham, where this newspaper would love to see Nigel Farage unseat the Commons Speaker John Bercow – nominally still a Tory but the sort of Tory who has climbed the greasy pole by agreeing with most items of Labour policy. But in general, a UKIP vote tomorrow will risk keeping Brown in Downing Street by depriving Conservatives of vital extra seats and that would be a tragedy (*Daily Express*, 2010).

The rare acknowledgement and expression of sympathy for UKIP by a mainstream newspaper at such a momentous time in the electoral cycle points to a growing rapprochement between the party and at least one major proprietor. Consequently it will be instructive to further consider and monitor the developing editorial responses of *Express* group titles (*Daily Express, Sunday Express, Star* and *Star on Sunday*) towards UKIP. It has already been noted that cumulatively these titles were giving more prominence to the party than rival publications by 2010. On one particular occasion this translated into a more fulsome endorsement in which the *Sunday Express* ran an 871 word piece by a former MP entitled: 'voting is the best form of protest'. The piece lamented what it perceived to be the travails of the country and the failings of the main parties. Towards the end it concluded:

> None of the major parties tells the truth about the scale of the task that lies ahead... For heaven's sake, don't waste your vote by abstaining. Of the three main parties, the Tories with all their deficiencies are unquestionably the best choice. If you can't face them, make a positive protest. Kidderminster has twice elected independent Dr Richard Taylor. UKIP got 16 % in the Euro elections and advocates the straight talking the country needs.

Rather than abstain, vote to throw the rascals out. Nothing would do more to send a shockwave through our moribund political system than a strong showing by a respectable alternative like UKIP or an independent like Esther Rantzen in Luton (*Daily Express*, 2010).

The analysis contained in the *Express* piece conveyed a key message of the UKIP campaign, specifically that by endorsing it voters were not wasting their ballots. This was a major theme that the party attempted to get across in order to establish its credentials in future first order elections. Perhaps unsurprisingly the author of the *Express* commentary, former Conservative government minister Neil Hamilton, became a member of UKIP in 2002 and was appointed as Deputy Chair in late 2013. In early 2014, Hamilton was joined by another, more prolific *Express* contributor Patrick O'Flynn who resigned as Chief Political Commentator of the newspaper group to become the party's Director of Communications and also a candidate who is set to be elected to the European Parliament in the forthcoming poll.

The most significant change in the national press representation of UKIP between 2001 and 2010 was in the issues it was associated with. Whereas in 2001 items about the singular European integration issue dominated coverage of the party, by 2010 immigration and integrity had emerged to complement and diversify this reporting (see Figure 1). Table 3 shows what other topics were linked to UKIP in coverage. At first sight, the results for 2010 suggest that there was an increased diversification in the topics with which UKIP was associated, but the really significant point to note is the infrequency with which coverage linked UKIP to issues beyond immigration, integrity or integrity. In media terms, UKIP moved from being a one-trick pony to a three-trick pony, but beyond these expanding core concerns the party contributed very little to the wider terms of national press electoral debate.

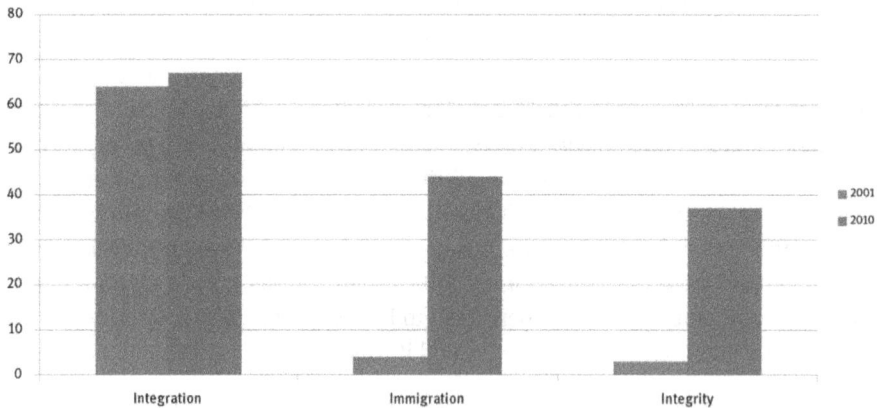

Figure 1: General Election Reporting of UKIP: the growth and diversification in the party's coverage [Notes: The three categories are separate (i.e. individual items could mention some, all or none of these three topics)]

Table 3: UKIP General Election Coverage: other topics

	Election	
	2001	2010
Business	3	2
Constitutional Issues	2	4
Crime/Law and Order	10	2
Defence/Diplomacy	–	1
Economy	3	1
Education	–	2
Environment	–	3
Farming/Agriculture	–	1
Health	–	3
Public Services	–	1
Social Security	–	1
Taxation	–	1
Transport	3	3
Other	1	3
Totals	22	34

5 Summary and conclusion

In this discussion we have examined the rise and sustained political presence of the UK Independence Party. The vagaries of the British electoral system were once said to be anathema to a smaller party making significant headway and gaining representation. The last few decades have undermined this assumption with the emergence of challengers such as the Nationalists, Greens and single-issue candidates who have been able to channel local grievances and regularly win seats at Westminster. Similarly, the Liberal Democrats have demonstrated the efficacy of targeting resources on certain winnable constituencies. By contrast, and more than a little ironically, UKIP has greatly benefitted from the system of proportional representation adopted for the European Union elections in 1999, giving it enormous scope to develop as a party. Its sizeable, now established group of representatives at Brussels and Strasbourg provide resources and a vital political platform for reiterating its core proposition: withdrawal.

The first part of this chapter has charted how UKIP has developed its campaigning, partly out of recognition that its anti-integration message is an insufficient means for exerting wider political influence. Alongside political diversification, it has attempted to introduce more discipline to its political organisation and activities, although this remains a work in progress. The second part of the discussion examined mainstream newspaper responses to the party and its changing strategies in 'first order' election contests, the domains where UKIP needs to establish a significant presence if they are to gain any parliamentary presence. The findings reveal that UKIP made modest gains between 2001 and 2010: achieving more media exposure from a low base and a more diverse policy presence. Overall, the results find scant evidence of any 'mediatic legitimization' (Mazzoleni, 2003: 7) for its activities from these quarters, in these contexts. With the qualified exception of the *Express*, even the more Eurosceptic newspapers either ignored or raised doubts about the party. The popular press hardly reported on the party in either election and UKIP's increased presence in 'quality press' coverage was mainly explained by an increase in reportage (commentaries and features) rather than reporting (hard news). In 2010, UKIP added to the colour rather than the content of the campaign, with many of the comment pieces variously focusing on the eccentricities, inconsistencies, intemperance and amateurishness of its representatives (which can hardly be construed as 'on message' with the party's strategy to professionalise). UKIP's failure to achieve greater prominence in news coverage in 2010 is even more significant when one considers that immigration and integrity were very much on the election news agenda at the time (see Deacon and Wring, 2010). It is evident that UKIP has so far failed to establish itself in the eyes of the national press as a significant 'political leadership arena' (Seymoure-Ure, 1987) in General Election contexts, even on the hot button issues it campaigns upon.

The key question is whether this is likely to change in the 2015 General Election? Recent developments in the lead up to the 2014 European elections raise some suggestive indications that this could lead to a breakthrough. There is growing evidence that anxiety about UKIP has started to mobilise a 'get Farage' campaign within the Conservative supporting media (Jones, 2014), the most recent manifestation of which was a series of exposes in the *Daily Mail* and *Sun* newspaper about Nigel Farage's private life. Although this is not the kind of coverage any politician ordinarily covets, Farage has prided himself on his maverick status and is therefore perhaps better placed to face down such criticisms of this kind than his mainstream rivals. But it should also be noted that while allegations concerning his supposed marital infidelity might not be so damaging, claims that he employed his alleged lover as a personal aide using the funds available to him as an MEP could prove more problematic and undermine his party's previous campaigning over the MPs' expense scandal. That said, such exposure might ultimately be regarded as a kind of marker of success and how far UKIP has come. It is difficult to imagine the Green's Natalie Bennett, leader of the other countrywide formation with elected representation at various levels of government, achieving anything like this kind of name recognition on the front-pages of the two best-selling daily newspapers. On the surface the recent expose has been about a so-called 'human interest' story, but its prominence underlines the now established fear that UKIP has become increasingly able to set the 'hard news' reporting agenda and this at a crucial period in the electoral cycle.

At the same time, it is evident that UKIP is exerting greater presence and influence in other national media contexts. On 31 March 2014, Channel 4 ran an hour long documentary 'Nigel Farage – Who Are You?' by Martin Durkin, which was based on 6 month's access to the UKIP leader. It was a largely sympathetic portrayal by a film maker who declared himself in the film as 'a wicked, middle aged, libertarian' and which in the view of the *Daily Telegraph*'s TV critic produced a portrait that 'was so cloying even UKIP fans would find it sickly' (Midgley, 2014). In the same month, OFCOM ruled that UKIP should be deemed by broadcasters as a major party for the 2014 European election, which means it will be entitled to equivalent amounts of Party Election Broadcasts and election coverage as the main political parties (with exemptions made for Scotland, where UKIP commands little public support). This raises the possibility that it could be similarly defined in the 2015 General Election, thereby strengthening Nigel Farage's insistence that he participate in any televised leaders' debates. This would have an exponential impact on the party's exposure across all media sectors throughout the campaign.

Also in March 2014, Nigel Farage and Deputy Prime Minister and LibDem leader Nick Clegg began a series of live broadcast debates for the 2014 European Election that replicated the kind that dominated the 2010 General Election agenda. The joint move is perhaps mutual recognition that both politicians might exploit this increased media exposure to take votes off the major parties, if not each other. Significantly, unlike Clegg, Farage's stridently anti-federalist message finds resonance in more populist UK print titles such as the *Sun* and *Mail*, and just days after reporting allegations about the UKIP leader's personal conduct, these papers gave considerable prominence to opinion poll data that suggested Farage had 'won' the first debate. It is difficult not to see the apparent inconsistencies and contradictions in these editorial responses as emblematic of wider uncertainties among journalists and politicians about UKIP's future role and influence in the British political firmament.

References

Abedi, A. & Lundberg, T. (2009). Doomed to Failure: UKIP and the Organisational Challenges Facing Right-Wing Populist Anti-Political Establishment Parties. *Parliamentary Affairs, 62 (1)*, 72–87

Addley, R. (2013). UKIP Conference: It's Easy to Mock, But They Like It. *The Guardian*, 20 September.

BBC (2013). UKIP has signed up 13,000 new members since 2013. *BBC News* online, 31 December.

BBC (2014). *Politics Show*, Broadcast BBC1, 2nd March.

Boffey, D. (2013). Ukip in Chaos Over Policy on Eve of Key Poll, Emails Reveal. *The Observer*, 27 April, p. 1.

Clements, B., Lynch, P. & Whitaker, R. (2013). The low salience of European integration for British voters means that UKIP will have to expand their platform to gain more support. *LSE European Politics and Policy (EUROPP) Blog Entry*, 8th March.

Clery, L., Park, A., Phillips, M., Lee, L. Taylor, E., Finnegan, J. & Cullinane, C. (2013). *British Social Attitudes Survey, 30*, London: Natcen. Retrieved on 1 April 2014, from http://bsa-30.natcen.ac.uk/read-the-report/key-findings/trust,-politics-and-institutions.aspx.

Copus, C., Clark, A., Herwig, R & Kristof, S. (2009). Minor Party and Independent Politics beyond the Mainstream: Fluctuating Fortunes but a Permanent Presence. *Parliamentary Affairs, 62(1)*, 4–18.

Deacon, D. Golding, P. & Billig, M. (1998). Between Fear and Loathing: National Press Coverage of the 1997 General Election. In Denver, D., Fisher, J., Cowley, P. & Pattie, C. (Eds), *British Elections and Parties Review, 8*.

Deacon, D., Golding, P. & Billig, M. (2001). Press and Broadcasting: 'Real Issues' and Real Coverage. *Parliamentary Affairs, 54(4)*, 666–678.

Deacon, D., Wring, D. & Golding, P. (2006). Same Campaign, Differing Agendas. *British Politics, 1*, 222–256.

Deacon, D. (2007). Yesterday's Papers and Today's Technology: Digital Newspaper Archives and "Push Button" Content Analysis. *European Journal of Communication, 22(1)*, 5–25.

Deacon, D. & Wring, D. (2002). Partisan Dealignment and the British Press. In Bartle, J., Mortimore, R. and Atkinson, S. (Eds.), *Political Communications: the British General Election of 2001*. London: Frank Cass.

Deacon, D. & Wring, D. (2010). Reporting the 2010 General Election: Old Media, New Media – Old Politics, New Politics. In Wring, D., Mortimore, R. & Atkinson, S. (Eds) *Political Communication in Britain: The Leader's Debates, the Campaign and the Media in the 2010 General Election*. Basingstoke: Palgrave Macmillan.

Denver, D. & Garnett, M. (2014). *British General Elections since 1964*. Hampshire: Palgrave Macmillan.

Ford, R., Goodwin, M. & Cutts, D. (2012). Strategic Eurosceptics and Polite Xenophobes: Support for the United Kingdom Independence Party in the 2009 European Party Elections. *European Journal of Political Research, 51*, 204–234.

George, S. (1998). *An Awkward Partner: Britain in the European Community*. Oxford: Oxford University Press.

Grant, W. (1989). *Pressure Groups, Politics and Democracy in Britain*. London: Philip Allen.

Groves, J. (2013). Tory posters telling illegal immigrants to 'Go Home' branded 'nasty' by UKIP's Farage as Lib Dems demand they be 'shredded now'. *Daily Mail*, 25 July.

Jones, O. (2014). Operation Get Nigel Farage is politics of the lowest form. *The Guardian*, 13 March.

Kirkup, J. & Laurence, J. (2013). Nigel Farage Wants UKIP to Remain "A Bunch of Amateurs". *Daily Telegraph*, 20 August.

Krämer, B. (2014). Media Populism: A Conceptual Clarification and Some Theses on its Effects. *Communication Theory, 24(1)*, 42–60.

Landale, J. (2014). UKIP: 'No skeletons in my cupboard'. BBC News, 28 February. Retrieved on 26 March, 2014, from http://www.bbc.co.uk/news/uk-politics-26385178.

Marston, S. (2014). A completed "life-cycle": UKIP's transition from an anti-political-establishment party into the mainstream? (Undergraduate dissertation submitted to the Department of Politics, History and Industrial Relations, Loughborough University).

Mazzoleni, G. (2003). The Media and the Growth of Neo-Populism in Contemporary Democracies. In Mazzoleni, G., Stewart, J. & Horsfield, B. (Eds). *The Media and Neo-Populism: A Contemporary Comparative Analysis*, Westport: Praeger.

Midgley, N. (2014). Nigel Farage: Who Are You?, Channel 4, review. *Daily Telegraph*, 1 April.

Peev, G. (2013). UKIP chief walks out after only eight months after struggling to adapt to 'individualistic DNA' of the party. *Daily Mail*, 21 August.

Robinson, N. (2014). The Truth About Immigration. *Broadcast BBC2*, 7th January. Retrieved from http://www.bbc.co.uk/mediacentre/proginfo/2014/01/nick-robinson-immigration.html.

Schedler, A. (1996). Anti-Political-Establishment Parties. Party Politics, *2(3)*, 291–312

Seaton, J. (2005). *Carnage & the Media: The Making & Breaking of News About Violence*, London: Penguin.

Seymoure-Ure, C. (1987). Leaders. In Pimlott, B. & Seaton, J. (Eds). *The Media in British Politics*. Aldershot: Avebury.

Sherman, J. (2013). UKIP dream for a better Britain Vanishes into a '£120bn Black Hole. *The Times*, 29 April, p. 9.

Part V: **New Technologies and Leadership Evolution**

Guy Lachapelle[1]

Political parties and the Internet: changes in society, changing politics – the case of the Parti Québécois

The advent of the Internet as a source of political information has resulted in an increasingly fragmented public space. Today, political parties seek to mobilize "netizens" both during and outside election-campaign periods to make their platforms known and, as far as possible, spark public debate. The Internet expands the arsenal of tools available to professional communicators. Initially, some observers thought the "Internet revolution" would be as socially significant as the discovery of the contraceptive pill in the early 1960s. The enthusiasm that researchers first evinced for the "democratic" values of the Internet – on the assumption that all citizens have or would eventually have access it – quickly gave way to a more sober view. Political scientists have asked and continue to ask what the actual properties of this new "participatory democracy" in this new "public space" are. Does the Internet really allow for greater citizen mobilization, new forms of cultural interaction and the emergence of "new citizens" who are markedly better informed about public policy? The true impact of the Internet on political decisions, voter participation and election outcomes also remain core concerns for researchers in the discipline.

In this paper, we shall discuss the concept of "public space" with specific reference to leadership contests in political parties and more particularly in the Parti Québécois (PQ). The PQ first appointed an Internet communications officer in 2001 and a director of IT in 2008; it now also has a project manager for Web publishing. We shall outline our theory of public communication, which we have called "Screening Theory," in accordance with which the development of the Internet and the new communications technologies (NCT) simply provides us with an additional source of information and in no way constitutes a challenge to the basic principles of political communication.

The fact is that the development of the Internet has not suddenly made people more interested in political matters or led to an increase in their political knowledge. Rather, the Internet allows citizens to select the information they want to be exposed to, thus confirming the hypotheses of "selective exposure" theory: people seek to avoid cognitive dissonance by reading and listening to information that agrees with their existing attitudes. Moreover, we do not believe that the Internet has, or indeed will, become the principal source of political communication for

1 Professor, Department of Political Science, Concordia University.

the public. It is more properly considered one more medium used in addition to other, already available media. It does not significantly change the way political decisions are made. We should also bear in mind that not everyone necessarily aspires to become a "global citizen." As in the past, some social groups are quicker than others to look for new sources of information.

Howard Dean's campaign for the Democratic presidential nomination in 2004, which ultimately proved to be a flash in the pan, provides a good illustration of the limitations of e-campaigning. Thanks to the Internet, Dean was able to reach and attract the support of large numbers of people who helped him over the course of the primaries. In addition, the Democratic Party was able to collect considerable sums of money to conduct its presidential campaign and engage the Republicans on an equal footing. The emergence of the Internet also led many people to jettison conventional media as their main sources of information about elections. While such media services as *C-Span* noted an increase in the numbers of people using their browsers to look for information on political subjects, some of the regular networks lost a great deal of ground on this score.

In countries in the process of democratization, the emergence of the Internet may, on the face of it, pose a threat to their political integrity. The issue of the control of "public communication" is hardly a new one: state authorities have always feared challenges to their legitimacy from media outlets or from individuals ready to use new techniques to get their messages out. Could the Internet provide a safe haven for "subversive" opinions and become an enormous big-character poster, as it were? Will it spark "social revolutions" fueled by long-simmering citizen demands?

To date, political science has offered only partial answers to these questions. We shall try to answer some through a closer examination of the 2005 Parti Québécois leadership campaign.

1 The 2004 American election campaign: "public space" and social communication

Screening Theory, the analytic model of political behaviour which we have put forward elsewhere, is based on the hypothesis that *the cognitive process by which elites and citizens reach their opinions rests on a continual evaluation of the forces at play, an evaluation that takes into account both structural and situational factors.* In accordance with this perspective – which includes consideration of the Internet, NCT and the public-communication process as a whole – social context and personal influence play as important a role during major political crises and election periods as the mobilization campaigns conducted by civil organizations and social movements (Lachapelle, 2003a, 2003b, 1998).

Citizens are not amorphous creatures; they speculate, draw comparisons, discuss and go out to demonstrate on the basis of a whole range of factors that lead them to decide whether to endorse or reject a particular cause. In our view, political and social elites play a part both in defining social issues and in facilitating the formation of social coalitions. Indeed, one of the essential features of Screening Theory is the notion that there are in every political community individuals who act as channels of communication and influence vis-à-vis citizens. In other words, social communication in the public space is a dynamic process in which citizens and the political classes are in constant listening mode, and, though consensus is sometimes hard to reach[2], the tendency is to produce a convergence of opinion between governors and governed.

In a climate of persistent uncertainty and sharp polarization, such as that which prevailed throughout the tight presidential race between John F. Kerry and George W. Bush in 2004, situational factors (in this case, the war in Iraq and the struggle against terrorism) can play a major role in determining outcomes. This in no way means that structural factors, which, after all, provide the underpinnings of stability in western democracies, are no longer important. Social cleavages – based, for example on religious observance, left-right ideologies, individual and collectivist values – may well act to define or redefine the positions held in popular opinion; so too may elements of "collective memory," including primal events in a nation's political history, such as the attacks of September 11, 2001.

In circumstances such as those of the 2004 presidential race, how is one to judge whether the Internet is more influential than traditional media like *Fox News* and *ABC News* or local religious and political elites? The 24-hour news channels like *Fox News*, which emerged at almost simultaneously with the Internet, are arguably all part of the same unremitting stream of communication.

For the past ten years or so, the dominant paradigm in political communication research has attributed greater influence to local elites, newspapers publishers and notables than to the ordinary citizen. In this light, the process would be more in line with elitist theory (top down) than democratic theory (bottom up). In our view, though, the social-communication process and the use of social media operate in a markedly more complex fashion. In the public space, citizens evaluate the positions taken by elites and by members of their community on an ongoing basis. They continually observe, discuss and weigh the merits of the arguments before taking a position in – or refraining from – a debate. In the 2004 US presidential elections, the three televised debates thus had a direct impact. They gave the public an opportunity to assess the candidates' positions unfiltered by the media, and John Kerry's performances reignited the Democratic campaign. In other words, the television de-

---

2 In the 2014 debate over the *Charte des valeurs québécoises*, the PQ government wanted to hear from the public to see whether there was a consensus over its plans. When the discussion indicated that unanimity was unlikely, the government had to reconsider some of its proposals.

bates did more than all the media and NCT to relaunch the public dialogue and bring the issues of the campaign back into the public space.

2 The impact of the Internet on political parties

The Internet is thought to affect political parties, election campaigns and political life in many ways. We shall consider just a few of these. First, the Internet is regarded to have a strong potential for social mobilization both locally and globally. Second, it is deemed to facilitate the development of large numbers of social groups and political action committees. Third, it is supposed to make it possible to recruit large numbers of volunteers, a task political parties find it increasingly difficult to accomplish. Fourth, it is held to be an excellent means of quickly conducting opinion polls and facilitating marketing campaigns among representative voters. Lastly, it is considered to simplify campaign financing by allowing parties to connect with voters. We shall now examine these points in greater detail.

In terms of voter mobilization, we can start by looking at how the Internet was able to raise the awareness of American voters and international opinion about certain issues during the 2004 US election. Given all the talk about citizen civic engagement, the efforts by groups and organizations to mobilize support around specific campaign issues (e.g., same-sex marriage, abortion, gun control) attracted a great deal of attention. The Internet was used as an instrument for mobilization and lobbying, but it did not replace more traditional marketing tools, such as television advertising. It would be rash to claim that the rise in voter participation in 2004 was in some measure due to the Internet. With the Iraq war dominating the campaign and everyone in the world feeling concerned, the election was in some ways unique.

The second and more measurable effect ascribed to the Internet relates to the creation and development of political organizations. *MoveOn*, apparently the first Web-based political organization, was founded in 1998 by Joan Blades and Wes Boyd of the University of California at Berkeley. In 2000, MoveOn encouraged Americans to donate money to help defeat candidates who had supported the impeachment of Bill Clinton. With funding from *MoveOn*, the campaign was able to defeat 13 of the 30 targeted candidates (Cornfield, 2004: 73–74).

The first candidate or political organization to realize the full potential of the Internet was surely John McCain in 2000. In his run in the Republican primaries, he attracted the attention of interest groups and the media in part because of his crusade for election-spending limits. It resulted in an amendment to the Revenue Act, section 527, under which partisan organizations may take financial contributions without having to pay tax on them as long as the money is used for political purposes.

In 2004, Howard Dean's online performance also drew wide attention. As well, numerous groups emerged which were active in the campaign but had a relatively low profile. These "527 organizations" are not considered "political committees" under the Federal Election Campaign Act. A political organization may, like a political committee, have its own Internet site and promote or criticize a particular candidate or issue. In 2004, most memorably, Vietnam War veterans engaged in a negative television and Internet campaign against John Kerry. Under the 2001 electoral reforms (Bipartisan Campaign Reform Act) candidates and members of political parties are prohibited from raising money for these committees. For their part, the committees are forbidden to use money from unions or businesses to pay for radio or television advertisements that mention a federal candidate during the 30 days before a primary or convention or the 60 days before an election in which that person is running. Still, the mobilization around John Kerry's Vietnam record, the constant questioning of his bravery and decisions during the war, had a major impact, especially among servicemen, who were generally very sympathetic to George W. Bush.

The third way in which the Internet is said to have an impact on election campaigns is as a means of facilitating volunteer recruitment. In the 2004 US primaries, Howard Dean used the Internet to organize local "meetups", or political meetings, in cities in the United States and even in Quebec and Canada. At the start of his campaign, in the summer of 2003, his organization succeeded in reaching out to an impressive number of people who then worked to arrange meetings in support of his candidacy. By early October 2003, 123,331 individuals had attended such meetings, and the Dean organization had connected with 466,884 supporters through the Internet. On the day of a primary, this army of activists was tasked with getting out the vote, but at this stage its shortcomings became apparent, and it was revealed as little more than a virtual organization revolving around such websites as *DeanforAmerica*. Dean's adversaries, particularly John Kerry and John Edwards, meanwhile had the support of the Democratic Party establishment and organizers working more closely in the field.

The fourth impact ascribed to the Internet, facilitating targeted marketing campaigns by making it possible to quickly reach large numbers of electronically connected voters, has attracted the widest attention. The Internet allows a political organization to draw up a database of email addresses in very short order. However, the fact one has ready access to telephone numbers and email addresses of large numbers of voters does not necessarily mean that they can be convinced to support a candidate. In our opinion, the persuasive effects of the Internet on voters are a myth, though a persistent one. Nor do "straw votes" on the Internet have any scientific value; the population they reach is undoubtedly unrepresentative because it is more educated and more likely to use the Internet than average citizens. Representativeness is an issue in all polling, especially in the United States; respondents who intend to vote must be distinguished from those who are likely to stay home, but the factors that motivate voters to go out and cast their ballot vary widely.

Last but not least, the Internet allows an organization to raise large sums of money quickly. In 2000, *MoveOn* reportedly collected more than $14.4 million from approximately 750,000 citizens to defeat candidates who had supported the impeachment of Bill Clinton (Cornfield, 2004: 73–74). That same year, John McCain is said to have raised 27 % of his $6.4 million in funding through the Internet. From July to September 2003, Howard Dean apparently raised $14.8 million online, nearly 60 % of the total contributions of $25.3 million made to his campaign. (Cornfield, 2004). Yet, in the end, neither McCain nor Dean was on his party's ticket. It is also noteworthy that in the 2004 presidential campaign the Democratic Party raised as much if not more money than the Republicans.

3 The 2005 Parti Québécois leadership race and the election of André Boisclair

Soon after Bernard Landry's surprise announcement that he was resigning the leadership of the Parti Québécois, the process to elect a new leader was set in motion. While Bloc Québécois leader Gilles Duceppe dithered over whether to run, other possible candidates also held back. In political contests of this sort, though, an early announcement often gives a contender a good head start, and Richard Legendre rushed in to take up the campaign when, to everyone's surprise, François Legault dropped out for family reasons. Legendre was thus the first to open hostilities but was quickly joined by Louis Bernard, Pauline Marois, André Boisclair, and others.

Howard Dean's experience had clearly impressed many political organizers, who wondered whether the enthusiasm his campaign had generated could be reproduced elsewhere. In Quebec, the 2005 Parti Québécois leadership campaign drew inspiration from the American model; for the first time in Quebec party history, not only would all members in good standing be allowed to vote for the leader, but candidates would also be permitted to recruit new members. The journalist Bruno Guglielminetti commented further: "The American model and the recent race for the leadership of the Democratic Party doubtless led many to think about the importance of the Web and especially of establishing an online presence" (Guglielminetti, 2005, October 21) [Translated from French]. This was not the first time the Parti Québécois acted as a trailblazer in internal democracy; in 1985, it was the first party in Canada to adopt universal suffrage of the members in a leadership race, leading to the election of Pierre-Marc Johnson.

Because the PQ voluntarily chose to open itself up to the public and because it used Internet instruments consistently to connect with voters, many observers viewed the 2005 Parti Québécois race as clearly the most democratic ever. Bruno Guglielminetti lauded the party and singled out the website that it set up for the campaign, Course2005.pq.org, for special praise.

It is a fine example illustrating the usefulness of the Web as an educational tool for a new voting system. The site has the virtue of being clear and instructive about the preferential voting
system that PQ members [would] use to choose their next leader. The PQ also had the good idea
to webcast the debates with the nine candidates and to archive them on the leadership-race
site (Guglielminetti, 2005, October 21) [Translated from French].

The PQ leadership campaign was a long one, lasting more than five months. At the
starting line, nine candidates filed nomination papers. Party organizers had to find
a formula that would give the contenders time to explain their respective positions
and give the members an opportunity to ask them questions.

The organizers suggested a series of debates on specific topics (health, education, culture and communication, sustainable development and globalization, fiscal
imbalance, etc.) to be held in conjunction with a tour of the regions of Quebec. All
the candidates agreed. Some observers might find it surprising that the language
issue did not from the outset feature in the contenders' declared priorities, given
that the different teams' strategists sought quite legitimately to highlight their candidate's strengths. However, although the language debate in Quebec will never
really be resolved, the members of the party today understand that the issue is, in a
way, a common denominator – and a necessarily crucial aspect – of a range of other
concerns.

All the teams also agreed on the debate ground rules formulated by the convention chair, Lyne Marcoux, and the party executive. Each debate would be divided
into four segments: an opening speech, three-sided debates, questions chosen at
random for each of the candidates, and a closing address. A small six-to-eight-
member panel (*panel des tribunes)* was tasked with preparing the questions for every debate over the course of the campaign, and I was appointed to it as an academic
researcher. In each region, a local party member was added to the panel. Questions
could also be submitted by the general public through the PQ website. Once a week,
usually on the Monday evening before a debate, the panel met to prepare the questions. At the very start, we agreed on the principle that the questions should be of
equal value and relatively similar difficulty. While the questions were more or less
equal, clearly not all the contenders were equally experienced or competent. Thus,
the panel did not set out to test the candidates' knowledge or ask them about people
or events in the news but to give them an opportunity to lay out their vision of Québec (not a full-blown election platform). The point was, first and foremost, to elect
the best leader. The panel's weekly discussions were fascinating, for the members
all had their particular view of things based on their professional experience, party
activism and age. The brainstorming sessions for each debate yielded about twenty
questions that we considered most important.

Many analysts were puzzled by the leadership campaign. Robert Dutrisac and
Antoine Robitaille wrote:

There is an air of unreality rising from the first week of the Parti Québécois leadership campaign. According to a survey, André Boisclair's half-hearted admission that he used cocaine
has won him the spontaneous support of a large majority of Quebecers and, more especially,
roused conspicuous enthusiasm among young people to whom the 39-year-old candidate has
delivered three well-attended CÉGEP and university addresses (Dutrisac & Robitaille, 2005,
September 23) [Translated from French].

Indeed, the population soon came to view Boisclair's campaign and his peccadilloes
in terms of a generational conflict. Many voters saw expressions of concern about
his homosexuality and cocaine use as tactics deployed by his adversaries and the
party establishment to block a controversial candidacy. Reporters and bloggers who
determinedly and incessantly raked over his behaviour – there was even an anti-
Boisclair website – also stirred up public sympathy for him. The only woman in the
race, Pauline Marois, was by far the most experienced candidate of the lot. However,
she never succeeded in demonstrating how competent she was or exciting the voters, probably because she seemed too much like a civil-service mandarin in the style
of previous PQ leaders.

The Parti Québécois's prime objective in opening up the selection process to
new voters was obviously to expand its support base and foster membership growth.
When the campaign began in May 2005, the PQ had 57,605 members. By September 12, 2005, renewals of expired memberships brought the number to 83,084. According to party president Monique Richard, at that point 59 % of the members were
aged 50 or older; those aged 18 to 30 accounted for barely 15 %; those 31 to 40, 9 %;
and those 41 to 50, 17 % (Lévesque, 2005, October 19). In the end, at 5 P.M. on November 15, 2005, 137,238 individuals were members with the right to vote. It was
relatively easy to join; all one had to do was visit the PQ website and pay the $5 fee.
Barack Obama followed the same game plan. Meanwhile, rumours abounded to the
effect that members of other political groups, particularly the Quebec Liberal Party,
had joined the PQ deliberately to back the candidate they thought would do the
least damage to their party's chances of re-election.

The Parti Québécois also opted to use a preferential voting system. Every voter
had to choose four different candidates for his or her ballot to be valid. Voting was
conducted by telephone. Voters had to dial 1-877-333-2222, enter their membership
card number and access code and vote for four of the nine contenders in order of
preference. In alphabetical order, the candidates were 1. Louis Bernard; 2. André
Boisclair; 3. Pierre Dubuc; 4. Ghislain Lebel; 5. Richard Legendre; 6. Pauline Marois;
7. Jean Ouimet; 8. Gilbert Paquette; and 9. Jean-Claude St-André. Telephone voting
took place over 57 hours from 8 A.M., November 13 to 5 P.M., November 15.

Under the rules, the election was to be determined by an absolute majority
(50 % + 1) of the votes. After the first count, if no candidate had won a majority of
first-choice votes, those who had garnered fewer than 15 % would be dropped and
their supporters' subsequent choices counted on second and further ballots until

one of the nine emerged with a majority. Each voter would thus have one vote counted at every stage of the process.

Many observers were surprised by the outcome; Boisclair won on the first count with 53.68 % of the votes, followed by Marois with 30.56 %. None of the other candidates obtained more than 7.5 % of the votes; and three of them, Jean-Claude St-André, Ghislain Lebel and Jean Ouimet, had less than 1 %. Boisclair's win may be attributed to his ability to galvanize young people and recruit more than 32,000 members, who thus accounted for more than 23 % of all the eligible voters (Lévesque, 2005, October 19). He owed much of his success to the Internet and to his ability throughout the campaign to generate excitement around his candidacy, just as Dean had done in the United States. Marois's support came mainly from "older" party members, among whom, given her 42,000 votes, she seems to have been on an equal footing with Boisclair.

4 Where we stand today: the relationship between digital citizens and political parties

Our colleagues Thierry Giasson and Mélanie Verville (2013) have conducted a meticulous examination of the websites and Facebook and Twitter accounts of Quebec's five main political parties and concluded that "the political parties and members [of the National Assembly] are not using the potential of Web 2.0 to the full and tend to prefer a marketing option." In time, they hoped, they would acquire "the competencies and openness they need to incorporate a real architecture of participation." [Translated from French]

One cannot help wondering why our political parties are not more actively trying to galvanize their supporters and send us polarizing messages. Throughout the 2008 US campaign, the Obama teams were unremitting in using the Web to mobilize their troops. They peppered them constantly with reminders of how damaging the Bush years had been for Americans and of the need to contribute to electing Obama this time. At the Democratic Party convention in Denver, we were able to gauge the power and capabilities of the new technologies as a tool for voter participation. The message hit home so strongly that people from around the world wanted to invest in the campaign.

In Quebec another question that comes to mind is why the Parti Québécois does not use the Internet to better advantage in an all-out campaign to promote sovereignty; for example, with weekly messages about the vagaries of the Harper Government and the PQ's adversaries in the National Assembly (Cloutier, 2007, February 20). Effective use of information technologies would help parties recruit more supporters and generate more resources to fight elections. Social networks, which are used mainly by people under 30, would be an excellent campaign tool.

Governments and political parties and candidates in leadership races or conventions obviously try to connect with citizens. However, not everyone is equal when it comes to information technologies. Simply putting information online does not necessarily make it accessible or persuasive; for the vast majority of people, television, the press and radio are still the principal sources of political information. To truly involve citizens in public debates, governments and political parties must realize the potential of the new technologies in the public space but be aware of their limitations. They must also avoid creating new social cleavages between groups of citizens based on whether or not they use Web 2.0.

5 Conclusion

Over the past twenty years or so, the Internet has revolutionized the way we live. Some observers thought it would be an extraordinary tool to democratize our societies by making information more accessible and increasing participation in the political process; we are still far from realizing these objectives. The Government of Quebec and our political parties should surely be asking questions about the development and uses of Web tools rather than investing public funds without clearly defining their goals. Every time a new technology has emerged (radio, television, fax, etc.), parties have had to adapt the way they operate to connect with voters. However, communication between parties and the electorate is only one component of the relationship of trust that the political class can develop with the citizenry. It is illusory to think that the Internet can make up for every democratic deficit.

According to Screening Theory, political elites and citizens go through a series of steps in choosing their leaders. They start by observing the candidates and move on to engaging in the public discussion and then to deciding to support one of the contenders.

Governments and parties must make more room in both public space and virtual space for citizens to take part in decision-making processes. Up to now, the Internet has figured most prominently in election campaigns in wealthier societies. There is no doubt that just as television has become an essential tool in election campaigns, so too will the Web. We remain cautious, though, as to the direct impact this new technology will have on democratic life. In our opinion, the debate around the Internet is rather utopian insofar as it posits that a communications system that is egalitarian, pluralistic and interactive will lay the foundations for a truly participatory democracy. It remains to be seen whether this vision will come to pass.

References

Bastien, F. & Greffet, F. (2009). Les campagnes électorales à l'âge d'Internet: une comparaison des sites partisans en France et au Québec. *Hermès, 54*, 209–217.

Bastien, F. & Greffet, F. (2008, June). Plus ça change, plus c'est pareil? Le Web et les partis politiques au Québec et en France. Paper presented at the annual conference of the Canadian Political Science Association, Victoria, Canada.

Beange, P. & Roebuck, N. (2013, June). The 2011 Canadian federal election: Have the Canadian parties finally made the jump to social media? Paper presented at the annual conference of the Canadian Political Science Association, Victoria, Canada.

Bergeron, L. C. (2005, September 22). C'est ma génération que vous attaquez. *Le Devoir*, p. A-7.

Bernier, M.-F. (2005, September 21). Quand l'intérêt public se frotte à la méfiance du public. *Le Devoir*, p. A–7.

Bilodeau, É. (2012, July 19). Propos sur Twitter: Legault sème de nouveau la controverse. *La Presse*, p. A13.

Breindl, Y. & Francq, P. (2008). Can Web 2.0 applications save e-democracy? A study of how new internet applications may enhance citizen participation in the political process online. *International Journal of Electronic Democracy, 1(1)*, 14–31.

Cauchy, C. (2005, October 15–16). Le mystère de l'image – La course à la direction du Parti québécois déconcerte les experts. *Le Devoir*, pp. B1–B3.

Cauchy, C. (2005, October 13). Boisclair pris à partie pour avoir aboli les COFI. *Le Devoir*, p. A-3.

Cauchy, C. (2005, November 11). Paquette se retire et appuie Marois. *Le Devoir*, pp. A-1 & A-10.

Chen, P. J. (2010). Adoption and use of digital media in election campaigns: Australia, Canada and New Zealand. *Public Communication Review, 1(1)*, 3–26.

Cloutier, P. (2007, February 20). Le PQ ne comprend pas le peuple Internet. Lettres, *Le Devoir*.

Collard, N. (2012, August 25). Une campagne 2.0? Vraiment? *La Presse*, p. A18.

Cornfield, M. (2004). *Politics moves online – campaigning and the Internet*. New York: The Century Foundation Press.

Descôteaux, B. (2005, September). Écarts de jeunesse. *Le Devoir*, p. A-6.

Desrosiers, É. (2005, October 11). Pauline Marois reçoit l'appui d'une centaine de femmes d'influence. *Le Devoir*, p. A-3.

Dutrisac, R. (2005, October 2). Richard Legendre a commandé un sondage auprès des membres du PQ. *Le Devoir*, p. A-5.

Dutrisac, R. & Robitaille, A. (2005, September 25). La semaine du pardon. *Le Devoir*, p. B-1.

Farries, G. (2005). What voters want, what campaigns provide: examining Internet based campaigns in Canadian federal elections. (Master's thesis, University of Lethbridge).

Ferretti, A. (2005, November 11). Pauline Marois nous conduira à l'indépendance. *Le Devoir*, p. A-9.

Francoli, M. (2009). The digital MP or how I learned to stop worrying and love MP. *Journal of Media Practice, 10(23)*, 215–225.

Giasson, T., Le Bars G., Bastien F. & Verville M. (2013, June). *L'usage du web social par les partis politiques au Québec. Le cas de #Qc2012*. Paper presented at the annual conference of the Canadian Political Science Association, Victoria, Canada.

Giasson, T., Raynauld, V. & Darisse. C. (2011). Hypercitizens from a distinct society: characterizing Quebec's political bloggers online and offline political involvement. *International Journal of Interactive Communication Systems and Technologies, 1(2)*, 29–45.

Gibson, R. & Ward, S. J. (2009). Parties in the digital age – a review article. *Representation, 45(1)*, 87–100.

Giguère, J. (2005, September 28). Pardonner n'est pas oublier. *Le Devoir*, p. B4.

Gingras, A.-M. (2006). *Médias et démocratie : le grand malentendu*. Québec: Presses de l'Université du Québec.

Goupil, S. (2004, May). Médiatisation de l'espace public et nouvelles technologies de l'information et de la communication : vers le citoyen virtuel ? Paper presented at the annual conference of the Société québécoise de science politique, Montreal, Canada.

Guglielminetti, B. (2005, October 31). Surprises péquistes sur le Web – André Boisclair déçoit, Pauline Marois surprend. *Le Devoir*, p. B-6.

Jackson, N. A. & Lilleker, D. G. (2004). Just public relations or an attempt at interaction? British MPs in the press, on the Web and 'in your face'. *European Journal of Communication, 19(4)*, 507–533.

Lachapelle, G. (2003a). Pourquoi le gouvernement canadien a refusé de participer à la guerre en Irak? *Revue française de science politique, 53*, 911–927.

Lachapelle, G. (2003b). Political communication and personal influence. In P. J. Maarek & G. Wolfsfeld (Eds.), *Political communication into the third millenium*, (pp. 82–92). London: Routledge.

Lachapelle, G. (1998). Le comportement politique des Québécoises lors de la campagne référendaire de 1995: une application de la théorie du dépistage. *Politique et Sociétés, 17(1–2)*, 91–120.

Lacroix Couture, F. (2012, August 18). Une campagne électorale 2.0. *Le Nouvelliste*, p. 35.

Lalancette, M. (2013, June). Almost a Biopic. Les web-mises en scène des candidats aux élections québécoises de 2012. Paper presented at the Annual Conference of the Canadian Political Science Association, Victoria, Canada.

Leclerc, J.-C. (2005, September 26). Le PQ et la cocaïne – Une question qui ne s'adresse pas au seul candidat Boisclair. *Le Devoir*, p. B-5.

Lessard, D. (2012a, July 30). Une campagne 2.0 qui s'annonce palpitante. *La Presse*, p. A5.

Lessard, D. (2012b, August 18). Entrevue exclusive avec Jean Charest: Sa famille a souhaité qu'il quitte la politique. *La Presse*, p. A2.

Lévesque, K. (2005, October 19). Campagne à la direction : le PQ a doublé le nombre de ses membres. *Le Devoir*, p. A-4.

Lévesque, L. (2005, October 12). 111 femmes pour Marois : plus que de la solidarité. *Le Devoir*, p. A-3.

Lévesque, K. (2013, October 12). Quatre candidats de la gauche, c'est trop, juge Gilbert Paquette. *Le Devoir*, p. A-3.

Lévesque, K. (2005, September 30). Lebel concède la victoire à Boisclair. *Le Devoir*, p. A-3.

Lévesque, K. (2005, September 23). Boisclair veut rajeunir le Parti québécois – Le candidat attire 1400 étudiants lors d'une conférence à l'Université de Montréal. *Le Devoir*, p. A-3.

Lévesque, K. (2005, September 23). Le PQ doit s'allier aux syndicats. *Le Devoir*, p. A-3.

Lévesque, K. (2005, September 22). Les plus de 50 ans éliront le chef péquiste. *Le Devoir*, pp. A-1 & A-8.

Lilleker, D. G. (2006). *Key concepts in political communication*. London: Sage.

Marissal, V. (2012, June 29). La première vraie campagne 2.0. *La Presse*, p. A12.

Mayfield, A. (2007). What is social media? Retrieved January 6, 2013, from http://www.icrossing.co.uk/fileadmin/uploads/eBooks/What_is_Social_Media_iCrossing_ebook.pdf.

Parmalee, J. & Bichard, S. (2012). *Politics and the Twitter revolution. How tweets influence the relationship between political leaders and the public*. Lanham, MD: Lexington Books.

Proulx, S., Millerand, F. & Rueff, J. (2010). *Web social: mutation de la communication*. Québec: Presses de l'Université du Québec.

Raynauld, V., Giasson, T. & Darisse, C. (2011). Citizen-driven political blogs as Web-based research samples: opportunities and challenges. *Graduate Journal of Social Science, 8(1)*, 65–92.

Richer, J. (2005, October 15–16). Marois entend maintenir le cap. *Le Devoir*, p. A-3.

Robitaille, A. (2005, September 26). PQ : un programme introuvable. *Le Devoir*, p. A-2.

Robitaille, A. & Lévesque, K. (2005, September 20). Cocaïne : Boisclair avoue. *Le Devoir*, pp. A-1 & A-8.

Römmele, A. (2003), Political parties, party communication and new information and communication technologies. *Party Politics, 9(1)*, 7–20.

Small, T. A. (2012, June). The not-so social network: the use of Twitter by Canada's party leaders. Paper presented at the annual conference of the Canadian Political Science Association, Edmonton, Canada.

Small, T. A. (2010). Canadian politics in 140 characters: Party politics in the twitterverse. *Canadian Parliamentary Review, 33(3)*, 41–48.

Small, T. A. (2008a). The Facebook effect? Online campaigning in the 2008 Canadian and US elections. *Policy Options, 14(1)*, 51–70.

Small, T. A. (2008b). Equal access, unequal success – major and minor Canadian parties on the Net. *Party Politics, 14(1)*, 51–70.

Small, T. A. (2006). elections.ca: Canadian political parties and candidates on the Net. A case study of the 2004 cyber campaign (Doctoral dissertation, Queen's University).

Small, T. A. (2001). CyberCampaign 2000: The function of the Internet in Canadian electoral politics (Master's thesis, University of Calgary).

Smith, P. & Chen, P. J. (2009, May). A Canadian election 2008? Online media and political competition. Paper presented at the Annual Conference of the Canadian Political Science Association, Ottawa, Canada.

St-André, J.-C. (2005, September 26) Les plans de MM. Bernard et Turp ne mènent pas à un pays. *Le Devoir*, p. A-6.

St-Pierre, G. (2012, August 13). La campagne électorale se vit aussi sur Twitter et Facebook. *Le Droit*, p. 5.

Tardy, É. (2005, September 30). Ah! si elle était un homme... *Le Devoir*, p. A-9.

Tessier, M. (2012a, July 6). Twitter: Duel entre François Legault et Martine Desjardins. *La Presse*, p. A10.

Twitter Blog (2011). One hundred million voices. Available online at http://blog.twitter.com/2011/09/onehundredmillionvoices.html

Twitter (2013). À propos de Twitter. Available online at https://twitter.com/about#about

Verville, M. (2012). Usages politiques des médias sociaux et du Web 2.0. Le cas des partis politiques provinciaux québécois. (Master's thesis, Département d'information et de communication, Université Laval).

Philippe J. Maarek[1]

Political communication, electronic media and social networks in France

Since Nicolas Sarkozy's successful bid for the presidency in the 2007 election, political communication in France has changed radically and reached a major watershed. First, he personalized campaigning to a degree hitherto undreamt of in France and previously attained only by American politicians. Second, Presidential and thus State political communication has changed as well since Nicolas Sarkozy began to engage with the media to an extent that was quite exceptional for a French head of state. As a matter of fact, quite differently, Jacques Pilhan, who handled communications for Nicolas Sarkozy's two predecessors, François Mitterrand and Jacques Chirac, had kept their media appearances deliberately infrequent (Bazin, 2011).

Nicolas Sarkozy's greater engagement with the media was reflected in a number of ways: *The President was omnipresent* in the traditional media and on social networks on the Internet. *Power was highly personalized* as the President's private life was given public exposure and used in his communications. *The President personally engaged with the media very frequently,* overshadowing his Prime Minister, François Fillon, and reducing him to the role of mere executor of presidential decisions. These changes were initially thought to be due solely to Nicolas Sarkozy and his personality, and he was variously dubbed the "Hyperpresident" (Maigret, 2008) and the "Telepresident" (Jost & Muzet, 2011). He was even compared to the extroverted Silvio Berlusconi, the then Prime Minister of Italy (Musso, 2011).

The first two years of the presidency of Nicolas Sarkozy's successor, François Hollande, have shown that these changes in political communication both during elections and while in office were not ephemeral as once thought. They emerged when they did because of circumstances at the time, but they were also a corollary of developments in political marketing and of the sudden rise of electronic media and social networks.

In this paper we shall begin by showing how these changes were clearly aided by institutional changes that occurred at the turn of the 21st century when the President's term of office was shortened and elections to the National Assembly became dependent on the election of the President. The powers of the head of state were consequently substantially, albeit indirectly, reinforced at the expense of the Prime Minister's.

---

1 Philippe J. Maarek, Professor, Université Paris Est – UPEC; Director of the Center for Comparative Studies in Political and Public Communication (CECCOPOP).

1 Institutional and situational factors favouring extensive personalization of political communication

1.1 The institutional "presidentialization" of France since the turn of the 21st century and developments in political communication

Since the 19th century, the long term of office of France's presidents automatically placed them above the day-to-day wrangling of the country's politicians. The constitution of the Fifth Republic endowed presidents with considerable powers, but their seven-year term meant that they could abstract themselves from the constraints that the shorter five-year term imposed on deputies to the National Assembly. They could consequently treat the whims of the electorate with greater detachment.

The constitutional reform of the year 2000 which cut their term to five years and the decision to hold legislative elections just after the presidential ones changed matters, leading almost inevitably to an increase in the power of the office. The shorter term essentially obliges the President to take much greater direct responsibility for the affairs of state simply because he has less time to do anything. He can no longer be as removed from matters as the longer term allowed him to be.

Also, holding elections to the lower chamber just after the presidential ballot implicitly gives the President a degree of authority over the Assembly that he did not necessarily have before. Under the new system, voters are highly unlikely to disavow a President they elected barely a few weeks earlier by giving the opposition a majority in parliament. The deputies, who are elected for the same term as the President, are thus, as it were, indebted to him for their seat for the duration of their term and are symbolically subordinate to him, at least at first. Barring major surprises (which are always possible), there seems little likelihood a President will have to cohabit with a chamber and a Prime Minister from another political party.

Many politicians and constitutional lawyers were quick to point out that shortening the president's term raised a serious risk of transforming the Fifth Republic into a presidential regime. Jacques Delors gave full expression to these concerns in an interview with *L'Express* magazine in 2000:

> Does the five-year term imply a shift to a presidential regime?One of the risks of the five-year term is that it may one day lead to the abolition of the right to dissolve [the National Assembly] and the weakening of the prime minister"[2].

---

2 *L'Express*, May 18, 2000.

Didier Maus, the president of France's association of constitutional lawyers made a similar argument:

> [I]f, as is logically likely, the five-year term helps re-establish the primacy of the President, there is less and less chance of asserting the parliamentary interpretation of the constitution, which favours the Prime Minister. Holding the presidential election and parliamentary elections at the same time, something President Georges Pompidou opposed in 1973, should give political precedence to the presidential election and diminish interest in the legislative elections and [reduce] the already very limited autonomy of deputies from the governing party.[3]

Presidential involvement in day-to-day politics was furthered too by the fact that the constitutional reform also imposed a limit of two consecutive terms on the office. A politician elected to a first term is thus almost bound to consider the idea and the prospect of running again, like in the United States. In that country, after Franklin D. Roosevelt's four victories and a similar constitutional amendment in 1947, the eight-year "double term" became the norm, barring the occasional election mishap in an incumbent's "midway" bid to be returned to office[4]. Though barely elected, presidents must consequently deal with the prospect – and the handicap – of having to prepare for potential re-election, with the logical outcome that they are much more interventionist. The shorter term and the tendency for the first term to be burdened by a concern for re-election very clearly encouraged post-reform presidents to keep a tighter grip on the reins of power than their predecessors had done.

It is thus logical that the shorter presidential term consigned to oblivion the much-vaunted "duality" of executive authority initially established under the constitution of the Fifth Republic. The Prime Minister is subordinated to the President even more than before. Consequently and paradoxically, the President can no longer use the Prime Minister as a scapegoat, as he could when he intervened (at least publicly) only in the most important affairs of state. The loss of prime-ministerial authority is clearly demonstrated by the fact that throughout his term, Nicolas Sarkozy never felt the need to replace François Fillon, a man reduced (in the President's own words) to the role of an "associate (*collaborateur*)"[5]. Similarly, despite the notorious problems of Jean-Marc Ayrault's Government, François Hollande kept him in office much longer than, for example, François Mitterrand kept Edith Cresson

---

3 Dossiers d'Actualité, Le quinquennat : référendum du 24 septembre 2000. La Documentation Française, September 2000
4 Seven of the ten sitting American presidents who ran for re-election after the 1947 constitutional amendment were returned: Eisenhower, Johnson, Nixon, Reagan, Clinton, Bush Junior, and Obama. Only Ford, Carter and Bush Senior failed in their bid – and Ford's case is exceptional since he had succeeded to the office after Nixon's resignation and had never been elected president or vice-president.
5 "The Prime Minister is an associate (*collaborateur*). I am the boss." Nicolas Sarkozy to the journalist Bruno Dive as reported in the daily newspaper *Sud-Ouest*, August 22, 2007.

when she was quickly discredited in the political media. Admittedly, she was much less resilient, but she can hardly be blamed given the way the press harassed her.

French political institutions have thus clearly entered a new era, one unlikely to have been foreseen by Jacques Chirac and his then Prime Minister in a government of cohabitation, Lionel Jospin, who initiated the amendments in a rare moment of agreement. Nicolas Sarkozy was thus the first President of France elected to a first term under the new constitutional prescription and to truly experiment the new system: Chirac had already served a first seven-year term when he was re-elected under the new system and had no concern about being elected again.

In practice, the 2000 reform of the constitution has resulted in greater personalization of communication by the major actor in French politics, the President of the Republic. As we shall see, the trend to personalization was reinforced as developments in electoral political marketing made it even more necessary to professionalize his communications.

1.2 The impact of political marketing: personalization and depoliticization of political communication

The rise of political marketing in France can be precisely dated to the 1965 presidential election when Jean Lecanuet's unexpectedly good showing in the first round of balloting forced the incumbent, General de Gaulle, into a run-off. At least some of the credit for Lecanuet's breakthrough has gone to Michel Bongrand, a French political-communications specialist and a discerning observer of John F. Kennedy's 1960 campaign in the United States. Since 1965, French politicians have constantly sought to retain the services of political marketers, preferably of "successful" consultants who played or claimed to have played a manifestly important part in the election campaign of a top-ranking politician. After performing so effectively for Lecanuet, Bongrand was even poached by the Gaullists! Another archetypal "successful" communications specialist, Jacques Séguéla, boasted that he had been instrumental in the election of François Mitterrand in 1981 with the slogan "*La force tranquille*" (Quiet strength), which was doubtless adopted after meticulous field research. Thereafter, Séguéla has been for many years the de facto political-communication guru of the Socialist Party and its elected officials[6].

One of the main measures deployed in political marketing is the targeting of voters on the basis of their political affinities. The electorate is accordingly divided into five categories, as the following chart illustrates:

---

6 For the history of the breakthrough of political marketing in France, see Maarek (2014).

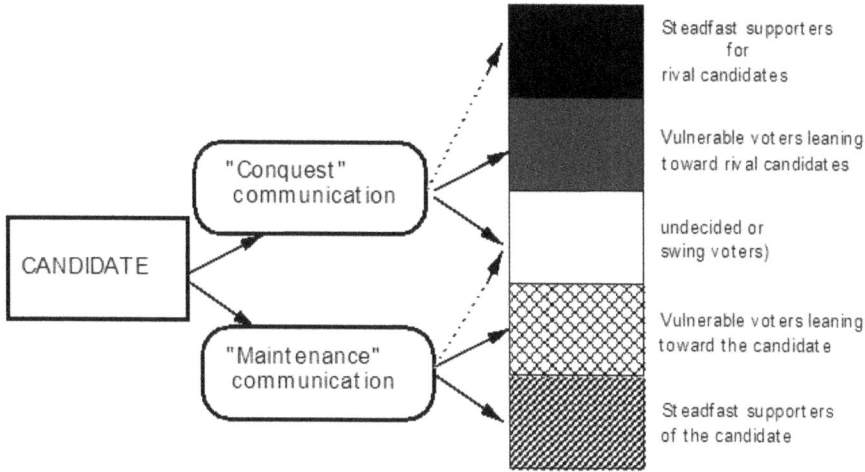

As the chart[7] shows, targeting involves two main choices. Marketers may decide to settle for "maintenance" communications; for example, in order to hold on to an incumbent's strong lead in the polls, as they did in the deliberately low-key campaign that returned Angela Merkel to power in Germany in 2009. Alternatively, they may decide to opt for "conquest" communication; efforts would then focus on an adversary's softer supporters but would evidently involve choosing campaign themes at some remove from the politician's original ideas. Such a shift could result in his neglecting his base constituency and even, as the case of Lionel Jospin in 2002 demonstrates, bring about his defeat.

In any event, there is one category of the electorate that is clearly and consistently targeted by political communications: undecided voters and non-voters, the "swing voters" in North American political-marketing parlance, whose vote – or decision not to vote – can swing the outcome one way or the other.

Political-marketing consultants almost always advise politicians to dedicate a major part of their campaign efforts to undecided voters and non-voters. The trend to this focus has intensified over the years as the gap between the main governing parties has narrowed. Indeed, voters in France and other democracies are having an increasingly hard time deciding between parties whose proposed solutions to globalization issues and frequent economic crises are often very similar and consequently confusing to the electorate.

The problem is how to get through to target populations that have little or no evident interest in politics and cannot be reached by the "traditional" means of political communication. They do not read the political pages of the newspapers; they seldom watch programs about politics on television; and they are even less likely to

---

7 Chart from Maarek (2011).

attend political meetings. As a result, political marketing has led politicians to "professionalize" their campaigns vis-à-vis this category of targets and adopt two approaches that paradoxically imply that they depoliticize their communications: personalization and entertainment.

1.2.1 Personalization of political communication

At the urging of the consultants, politicians have made their personal life and changes in their family situation integral aspects of their communications so that the potential voters who are least interested in political argumentation may see them as people they can easily relate to.

Since the targeted populations are hardly likely to be swayed by political arguments, politicians find themselves driven to present themselves as individuals and even to push their family into the limelight. The aim is to encourage people to vote for the personal qualities they claim or are presumed to have. Bringing a politician's family into the public eye is deemed to highlight these qualities by creating a sense that the candidates are people just like the voters. This approach was first adopted in France by Jean Lecanuet in 1965. He introduced himself on television not as "a mythical hero, but a man like other men." In explicit contrast to General de Gaulle and in a marked departure from previous practice, Lecanuet was shown smiling on his posters. The personalization of political communication has intensified over the years and culminated most recently in the deliberate revelations by Nicolas Sarkozy and François Hollande of their private life.

Nicolas Sarkozy put his family life on public display, highlighting it in his communications and personalizing his campaign in a way that was quite new. At the meeting to launch his bid on January 14, 2007, he said, "I have changed because life's hardships have changed me." He thus likened the vicissitudes of his private life to those of his fellow citizens, nearly half of whose marriages end in separation.

His successor, François Hollande, also played on the interpenetration of the public and private spheres. After having been out of the news for a time since leaving the leadership of the Socialist Party, he laid the groundwork for his future candidacy by publicly closing the books on his life together with Ségolène Royal. He used the celebrity magazine *Gala* to announce that the "woman of (his) life" was now Valérie Trierweiler, illustrating the point with numerous photographs. During the 2012 election campaign, François Hollande personalized his political communication just as his predecessor had. He proclaimed a self-styled "normality," implicitly differentiating himself from his adversary's commonly held "bling-bling" image. Nor did he shrink from revealing other aspects of his private life; for example, his efforts to lose weight suggested that he was prepared to make personal sacrifices to dedicate himself to the service of the people of France and that he thus displayed a determination worthy of a head of state.

Such an approach evidently runs the risk of turning politicians into celebrities, so-called "peopolization" transforming them into playthings for popular magazines and television programs (Dahklia, 2008 and 2010, Maarek, 2008 and 2010). François Hollande's romantic travails and his relationship with a film actress would not have had as much of an impact or piqued the curiosity of the paparazzi as much if he had not injected his "normal" private life into his campaign. Magazines such as *Voici*, *VSD*, *Closer*, and *Point de vue* were pushing on a door that had already been opened.

1.2.2 Political communication through entertainment

Further impetus to the politicians' move from the political pages of daily newspapers to the covers of entertainment magazines came from changes in the channels selected to communicate with undecided voters, again on the advice of the political marketers.

Undecided voters and non-voters – the core target audience – are not very interested in political broadcasts. To reach them, politicians have been encouraged to appear on entertainment shows, provide large-circulation celebrity magazines with entertaining copy, and participate similarly in other entertainment-news media. At first, a degree of decorum was observed in such appearances. For example, in the Eighties, the TF1 channel carried a program, *Questions à domicile*, on which politicians were interviewed in their home; they would introduce their family (as it were, in passing) and talk about some of their personal tastes in food, music, and the like. With time, society changed, and the television appearances has become rowdier. On today's talk shows, hosted by the likes of Laurent Ruquier and Thierry Ardisson, guests have no real guarantee as to how they will be treated. They are asked sly questions, and their answers or non-answers can generally be counted out to prompt jeers from a complicit studio audience and, by extension, from the viewers at home. France certainly does not have a monopoly on such performances: even a US President, Barack Obama, became the butt of jokes when he made a risky appearance on Jon Stewart's show on the Comedy Central cable channel.

Contemporary election campaigns thus have a paradoxical result. At the urging of their political-marketing consultants and in order to run campaigns as professionally as possible, politicians depoliticize their communications. Political arguments are considered unwieldy; they are thought to harm efforts to get through to the usual targets of political marketing, the population of undecided voters and potential non-voters.

2 The introduction of electronic media and social networks into political communication in France: an asset and a liability

We shall see here that electronic media and social networks have come quickly into play in France as political communication has been personalized and stripped of political content; in fact, though, these media can just as easily hurt as help the politicians' communications.

2.1 A useful new element in French political communication

The electronic media began to figure prominently, albeit unexpectedly, in political communication in France during the 2005 referendum campaign for the European constitution. To be sure, some politicians and parties had used telematics and Minitel Videotext services to enhance their communication programs as early as the 1980s, and a fair number had gone online with their own website before 2005. However, these endeavors seem to have had little influence on the voters, let alone the vote. In 2005, though, while almost every political party and everyone in the media encouraged people to vote "yes", the "no" side won. Opponents to the constitution were only dominant on the Internet, particularly in the blogosphere, where they were beyond the direct control of the established parties. As the table below shows, there were twice as many hyperlinks leading to political blog sites advocating a "no" vote as to sites supporting the "yes" side.

Linked pages	"Yes" sites	"No" sites	Independent	Institutions	Medias	Total (out)
"Yes" sites	231	74	36	52	47	440
"No" sites	60	643	33	41	72	849
Independent	18	22	6	10	14	70
Institutions	13	10	3	21	25	78
Medias	10	10	4	8	17	49
Total (in)	332	759	82	138	175	1486

[Source: Thieulin et al. in Maarek (2005)]

Even more striking, as the following figure shows, is the fact that the main communication nodes opposed to the constitution were largely blogs written by unknowns using a more didactic approach simply in order to make their personal views known. It is particularly notable that a blog by an unknown high-school teacher named Etienne Chouard, who attacked the project as the "European anti-constitution," stands at the centre of the diagram. The citizen Web was born.

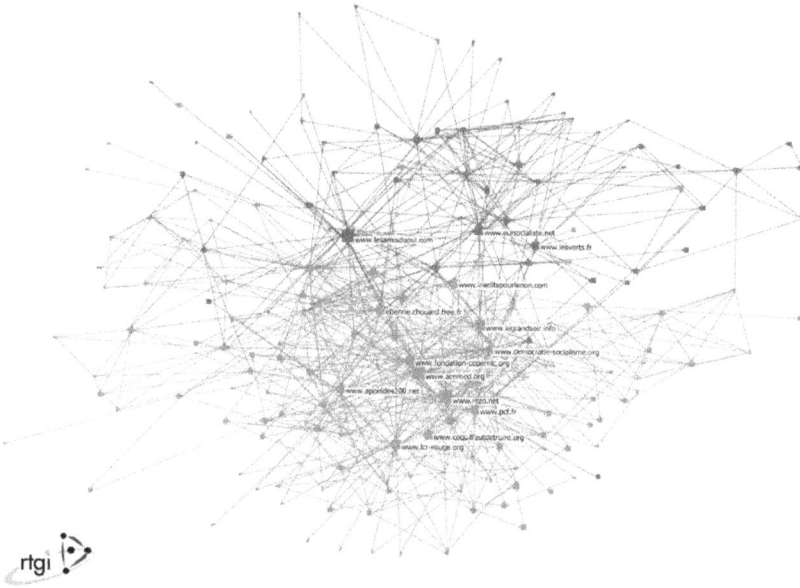

[Source: http://www.observatoire-presidentielle.fr/]

French politicians were quick to seize on this development and to understand that, instead of following the old career paths mapped out inside political parties, they could use the Internet even more than they had used television to bolster their personal ambitions.

In the 1960s, television burst through to change the standard political career path in France and elsewhere. Apparatchiks trying to work their way up through the hierarchy to the top of the party pyramid were increasingly bypassed by politicians who had "audiovisual charisma" and became household names because they were telegenic and therefore appeared often on television. This is still going on. For instance former Minister Rachida Dati was is still often invited to take part in debates on major national issues on television despite having now relatively minor responsibilities: journalists and talk-show hosts consider her a good "customer" who will boost their ratings by enlivening political debates that are otherwise often characterized by cant.

Today, some politicians have further realized that the Internet can help them get ahead even without favors from the party apparatus, and a few have understood that they can circumvent the party machine entirely. They can use the Internet practically for free without having to depend on the good graces of political parties or media gatekeepers. They can bypass the hurdles set up by the journalists and talk-show hosts who control access to the print and audiovisual media that were formerly the only way to reach the public quickly. Sometimes, a politician can do without a connection to an existing party altogether, as Beppe Grillo demonstrated in Italy with his largely virtual Cinque Stelle (Five Stars) movement.

To date, the best-known French example of this individualistic approach is surely provided by Ségolène Royal, who surprised her party's bosses by carrying the Socialist primaries for the 2007 presidential election. Her success was in large measure due to her clever use of the blogosphere and her main blog site Désirs d'avenir developed by Benoit Thieulin[8].

The Internet has thus become a major sounding board for politicians' communications and an indispensible instrument for building a personal reputation. Moreover, politicians can even benefit effectively from the Internet and social media without having to engage directly. Also Journalists from the print and audiovisual media are well aware of what is occurring on the Internet and concur to that phenomenon: nearly all of them monitor it for information and use their own channels to relay the slightest whisper on the electronic media to their public.

In addition, the interactivity of the electronic media makes it easy to break away from a traditional top-down approach. It opens up possibilities of horizontal and bottom-up political communication. Sympathizers and activists can help the politicians they support by relaying their political messages over social media either on their own initiative or at the request (overt or confidential) of their candidates' campaign teams. Activity of this sort, as Jean-Luc Mélenchon's clever presidential campaign in 2012 demonstrates, is especially effective because it seems to be or actually is spontaneous. A highly professional and atypical approach was devised for Mélenchon under the leadership of campaign manager François Delapierre, who later became national secretary of the Parti de Gauche. The key to the campaign's success was the masterful combination of very didactic television commercials broadcast over the "official" media (Maarek, 2013) with more entertaining presentations for the Internet, including a Web series. The best-known episode was modeled on the sexy, humorous American video that was viewed online time and time again in 2008, *Obama Girl, I have a crush on Obama* (it featured a young woman of Latino appearance sensually and humorously declaring her love for the candidate).

In France and the United States, websites, which are already considered "traditional" media, still play a significant role as forums for providing information and disseminating propaganda to activists and sympathizers as well as to journalists seeking material for their reports. Additionally, French politicians and parties use more and more social networks – they now markedly prefer Twitter over Facebook – to reach broader target publics, as many candidates demonstrated during the 2014 municipal elections. YouTube and Dailymotion were used even by politicians in

---

8 He would later go on to found La Netscouade, a well-known communications agency specializing in the social Web.

small communities to broadcast often rudimentary and variably successful campaign commercials.

The Internet has thus become the Swiss Army Knife of political communication and has unquestionably furthered the trend to the personalization of politics in France. In their use of the Web, French politicians and political-communication specialists have caught up almost completely with their American counterparts, who were the first off the mark, Internet use becoming very important there as soon as in 2004[9].

The Internet could be further exploited in political marketing by drawing more extensively on the masses of computerized personal data ("big data") that can be more or less discreetly compiled through it, as Barack Obama showed in his successful bid for re-election in 2012[10]. In France, for the time being, strict controls over the utilization of personal electronic data and the computer files containing them and rigorous supervision by the responsible authority, the Commission Nationale Informatique et Libertés (CNIL), prevent the application of such advanced methods. Still, in the 2012 presidential election campaign, a group of Socialist activists, dubbed "the Bostonians," nonetheless succeeded in deploying a few aspects of this novel approach which made it possible to conduct targeted door-to-door canvassing with unprecedented precision and on a scale never before seen in France (Liégey & al., 2013).

In some cases, shrewd observation of the Internet may provide parties and politicians with an ability to understand developments in their electoral base in a way never before thought possible. The mapping (below) of the political blogosphere in France in late 2012 shows an emerging rift among supporters of the rightist party then in power between those inclined to draw closer to voters on the extreme right and those leaning towards the center. The graph interestingly displays the then governing right apparently splitting into two. One group is moving towards the left of the graph where the extreme-right blogosphere is located. In the lower right, the other group abuts on the blogosphere of the center. The situation of the greens, located between the center and the socialists, is also significant, as is the scattered distribution of the extreme left.

---

9 This surge of Internet was due to Howard Dean, a little-known former governor of Vermont, one of the smallest states in the Union. He pioneered the approach when he made a shrewd investment in the potentialities of Web 2.0 to enter the Democratic primaries for the 2004 presidential nomination. Dean was, in fact, one of the first to combine the use of a website, Deanforamerica.com, with a blog, Blogforamerica.com, to create a leveraging effect for his e-campaign, and he collected large donations and a record number of petitions to support his candidacy – but he then failed in the Primaries.

10 Large quantities of computerized data, or "big data," were gathered through the use of cookies, invisible spyware mini-apps downloaded onto a computer whenever someone visited any of the sites or blogs associated with the Obama campaign. The cookies then "followed" the visitor without his knowledge and collected information about his behaviour on the Web, on other sites he visited and on the purchases he made online and transmitted it to the campaign organization. After the data were processed using specialized software, very detailed instructions could be sent to activists responsible for door-to-door canvassing with stupefyingly precise data about the voters they were contacting.

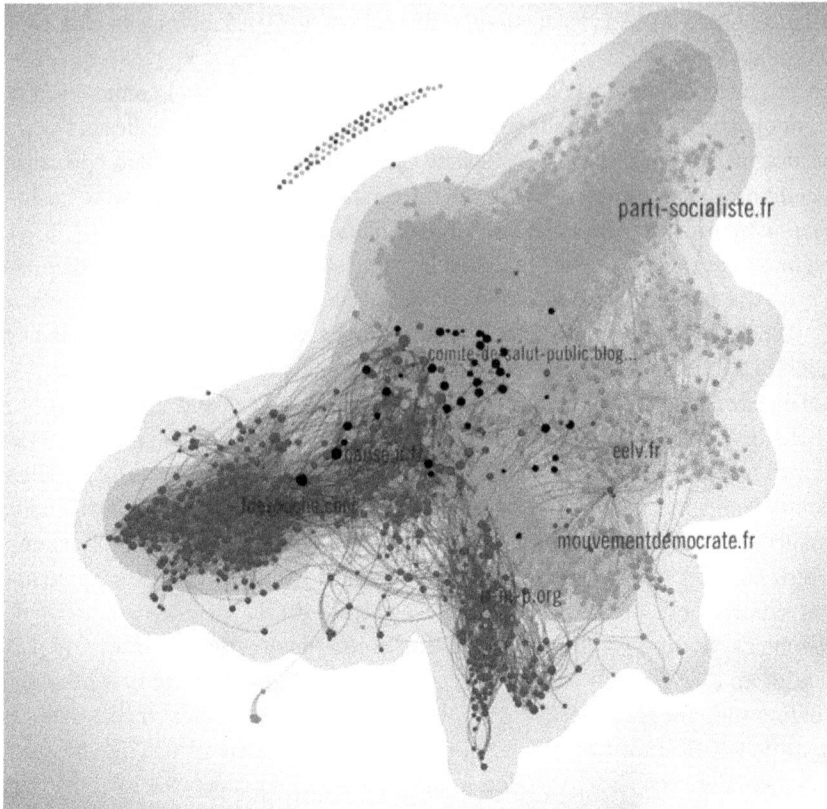

2.2 New media, novel problems

2.2.1 Problems in using the Internet and social media

The Internet, though apparently easy to use, is actually very difficult to control. The medium's accessibility and rapidity of use are illusory. In reality, a high level of professionalism is required, for the smallest mistake can be magnified as it is relayed mercilessly over social media. Even Ségolène Royal, who largely owed her breakthrough in the 2006 Socialist Party primaries to her skillful use of the Internet, had to make urgent changes to the new website she put online in 2009, Désirs d'Avenir. The home page, which awkwardly recalled one of the worse versions of Microsoft Windows, was greeted with sarcasm and parodies, as illustrated by the second image below.

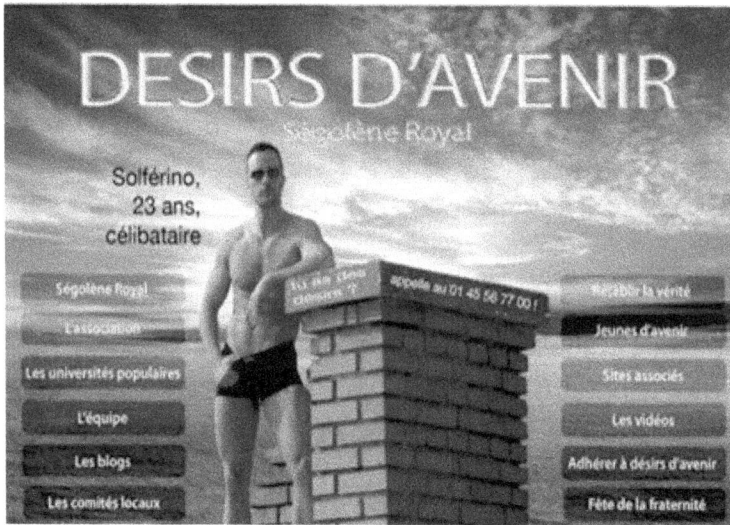

In France, Valérie Trierweiler, François Hollande's then partner, caused a huge scandal shortly after he was elected in 2012. Despite being a journalist wise in the ways of the world, she saw fit to post a hasty, sharp tweet in support of a candidate in the legislative elections who was running against Ségolène Royal, who happened to be François Hollande's previous partner[11].

Posting videos to YouTube and Dailymotion is also more difficult than it seems and creates more opportunities to look like a fool than one would think. Because of

---

11 The tweet ("Good luck to Olivier Falorni who has proved himself worthy, who has fought alongside the people of La Rochelle for so many years with selfless commitment,") created a particularly big stir because Ségolène Royal lost to Falorni and was thus ejected from the National Assembly.

their very accessibility, these sites can often ensnare poorly advised politicians. The naiveté of many of the candidates in the French municipal elections in 2014 is edifying in this respect, for it resulted in a plethora of clumsy efforts that actually undermined some politicians and caused considerable harm to their image. Their videos provide a seemingly inexhaustible catalogue of ways to mishandle social media. For example, one candidate felt he had to show that, like many of his fellow citizens, he knew how to skate, looking even sillier when he could not make himself heard over the noise in the rink; another candidate used horribly dated disco music as his soundtrack; yet another, an older politician, appeared in a head-and-shoulders shot, completely immobile, expressionless, listening impassively while a bland voice-over recited his virtues; a ridiculous parody of the television series *Game of Thrones* was used somewhere else; etc.

The Internet and social media are thus not as easy to handle as they appear. While they seem to be a simple-to-use tool for politicians, especially the ones who cannot take advantage of other media, they can be as hard to use properly as they are easy to access.

2.2.2 Almost constant danger

The other – major – problem posed by social networks and electronic media, especially given the accelerating pace of media convergence, is the almost constant danger they pose to politicians during election campaigns and when communicating about actions taken by their government once in power.

Because of media convergence, anyone with a Smartphone can record a politician's slightest moment of weakness and smallest mistake and share it instantly with thousands, if not millions, of people linked to a social network, such as Instagram for photos and YouTube and Dailymotion for videos.

Many French political figures have suffered after running the gauntlet of the social media. During the 2007 campaign, Ségolène Royal was surprised by a video indiscreetly recorded by mobile telephone and posted on Dailymotion; it showed her taking issue with teachers for not staying at school outside their class hours. While President, Nicolas Sarkozy's image was battered when he let slip a coarse insult at a farm show after someone refused to shake his hand. Later, numerous Internet posts recorded François Hollande's first tentative steps as president, showing him unsure what to do when he had to pay his respects to the flags on his first official visit to Germany, while his new glasses were mocked all around social media for being Danish made, not French. Even as experienced a politician as Nathalie Kosciusko-Morizet was attacked on social media during the 2014 municipal campaign for wearing a pair of expensive boots from a luxury brand.

Formerly, politicians and elected officials had to be wary about what they said or did only on "official" occasions, during election campaigns and political activities. Today, because of the Internet and social media, they must be constantly on guard. Even day to day appearances are minutely scrutinized. For instance, François Hollande's tendency to wear his tie askew was the subject of many disdainful blogs; the most exhaustive one provided a list – illustrated by about a thousand photographs – of practically every single public appearance by the President with a crooked tie (which usually veered to the right)[12].

Social media and the Internet are also constantly used to challenge communication by political figures about their actions when they come to power. A government's ability to act may well be handicapped as a result. Early in his term, François Hollande thus had to hastily cancel a planned tax increase on small businesses under intense pressure from an Internet campaign. Using a pigeon as their logo (playing on the slang term "pigeonner," meaning "to get ripped off"), campaign organizers put humorous posts about their activities on the website of every local branch of the French employer's federation, the MEDEF, which supported them. Social media have also been used to convey often-very-aggressive calls for François Hollande's resignation that have become widespread to a degree that would have been highly unusual for such protests before the advent of the Internet. Later, the strong protests all around France against his leftist family policy decisions were united under the banner "La manif' pour tous" by a spontaneous upsurge in Internet social media without any kind of traditional political initiative or control.

3 Conclusion

The simultaneous appearance in France of two phenomena – the growing personalization of political communication and the rise of the electronic media and social networks – is rather remarkable and has had a significant impact on the way political communication has evolved there.

The changes were much more abrupt in France than in countries like the United States where relatively stable institutions were in position to manage the electronic media when they came into play. In France, by a chance of timing, the rapid increase in the power of the Internet and social media coincided with an institutional shift to a more presidential system and the simultaneous personalization of political communication. Political figures in France immediately took to these vehicles. Though they have admittedly had some success, they have not mastered them completely. The national political leaders have become constant preys to anyone with an online connection while the lower-level political actors are still unschooled in the intricacies of the electronic media.

---

12 See the site http://www.francois-tacravate.fr; the exact figures are 458 "crooked" ties and 940 public appearances as of March 24, 2014.

The electronic media and social networks have thus without any doubt facilitated if not intensified the personalization of political communication in France. With the addition of the change of the French Institutional system due to the 2000 Constitutional reform, this has clearly destabilized French politics, notably at the Presidential level.

References

Bazin, F. (2011). Jacques Pilhan, le sorcier de l'Elysée. Paris: Librairie Académique Perrin.

Dahklia, J. (2008). Politique People. Rosny-sous-Bois: Bréal.

Dakhlia, J. (2010). Mythologie de la Peopolisation. Paris: Le Cavalier Bleu.

Jost, F. & Muzet, D. (2011). Le Téléprésident – Essai sur un pouvoir médiatique. La Tour-d'Aigues: Editions de l'Aube.

Liégey, G., Muller A. & Pons V. (2013). Porte à porte: Reconquérir la démocratie sur le terrain. Paris: Calman-Lévy.

Maarek, P.J. (Ed.). (2005). Chronique d'un "non" annoncé : la communication politique et l'Europe (juin 2004-mai 2005). Paris: L'Harmattan, Coll. Communication et civilisation.

Maarek, P.J. (2008). La Comunicacion Politica : Una perspectiva internacional. Telos, 74, 92–97.

Maarek, P.J. (2010). La communication politique en France sous la V° République : professionnalisation, personnalisation ou 'peopolisation ? In D. Campus, G. Pasquino & S. Ventura (Eds.), Una splendida cinquantenne : la Quinta Repubblica Francese. Milan: Il Mulino.

Maarek, P.J. (2011) Campaign Communication and Political Marketing, Wiley-Blackwell, Boston

Maarek, P.J. (2014).Communication et marketing de l'homme politique (4th ed.). Paris: LexisNexis.

Maigret, E. (2008). L'hyperprésident. Paris: Armand Colin.

Musso. P. (2011). Sarkoberlusconisme, la crise finale ? La Tour-d'Aigues: Editions de l'Aube.

Index of Proper Nouns